HOLLOWS, PEEPERS, AND HIGHLANDERS

HOLLOWS, PEEPERS,
AND
HIGHLANDERS
AN APPALACHIAN MOUNTAIN ECOLOGY

by

George Constantz

Second Edition

West Virginia University Press
Morgantown 2004

© 2004 by West Virginia University Press

14 13 12 11 10 09 08   2 3 4 5 6 7 8

ISBN (paperback) 0-937058-86-6 (alk. paper)

Library of Congress Cataloguing-in-Publication Data

Constantz, George. 1947 –
    Hollows, peepers, and highlanders : an Appalachian Mountain
    ecology / by George Constantz
    Second edition.
       p. cm. —
       Includes illustrations and index
       ISBN 0-937058-86-6

    1. Natural history— Appalachian Region. 2. Forest
animals— Adaptation — Appalachian Region. 3. Forest
plants— Adaptation — Appalachian Region. 4. Forest
ecology— Appalachian Region. 5. Appalachian Region.
I. Title. II. Constantz, George.

IN PROCESS

Library of Congress Control Number: 2003116400

Design by Lisa Bridges Design
Printed in U.S.A.

Contents

Thanks vii
1. Prologue 1

Stage and Theater

2. Origins 7
3. Forest Design 17
4. Creating Diversity 25
5. Catastrophe and the Appalachian Quilt 33
6. Balds 41
7. The Asian Connection 45

The Players

8. The Improbable Lady's-slipper 51
9. Sexual Decisions of Jack-in-the-Pulpit 59
10. Nuptial Gift of the Hangingfly 67
11. Femmes Fatales of Twilight 73
12. Small Fishes in Shallow Headwaters 81
13. Darter Daddies 89
14. To the Brook Trout, with Esteem 95
15. A Lungless Salamander Trilogy: Primer 101
16. A Lungless Salamander Trilogy: Coexistence 109
17. A Lungless Salamander Trilogy: Mimicry............ 115
18. Love Among the Frogs 119
19. Box Turtle's Independence............................. 127
20. Copperhead's Year 133
21. Oaks and Squirrels 143
22. Highlanders 151

Seasonal Acts

23. Autumn Leaves 165
24. Window on Bird Politics 171

25. Thwarting Swords of Ice 179
26. Spring Tensions 189
27. Dawn Chorus 195
28. Trees and Caterpillars................................. 205

Epilogue

29. The Remnant Archipelago 217
30. Abuse, Resurrection, Hope 229
Actors 242
Jargon 252
Sources 279
Index 343
Author 361

Thanks

I owe a great deal to many generous people. John Ailes, Maurice Donohue, Marshall Sprague, and David Vis encouraged me to make the commitment. The following highlanders provided literature: Jerry Atkins, Russell LaFollette, Gerald Lewis, Harold Parsons, Andy Rogers, Bob Smith, Gary Strawn, Charlie Streisel, Roger Thomas, Dr. Randy Thornhill, Ro Wauer, and Dr. Peter White. Dr. Quinn Constantz and Gary Wilson helped with the field work. For word processing help, I thank Tammy Barnes, Mary Kay Clem, Carol Fultz, Beth and Betty Loy, Jo Ann Shepherd, Jane Small, Bill and Dan Snyder, and Robby Pyles. Several chapters were critically reviewed by Dr. George Bunting, Mike Clark, Rick Eades, Phil Gallery, Bob Groves, Mode Johnson, Jim Matheson, Philip Nixon, Ron Preston, Jim Rawson, Gian Rocco, Tom Stump, Dave Trimmier, and Paula Worden. The following people read and criticized the entire manuscript: Sylvia Donohue, Dr. Ed Flaccus, Dr. Bronson Griscom, Eric Patterson, Dr. Gary Evans, Kat Ort, Danny Williams, and several classes of biology students. Although their contributions do not fit neatly into a single category, I appreciate the help of the following mountaineers: Rodney Bartgis, Fred Carter, Grey Cassell, Dr. Patrick Conner, Kathy Emerson, Bob Faulkner, Ashley Judd, Dr. Ross Kiester, Gary Morfoot, Shirley Parsons, Arlene Saville, Charlie See, Phyllis Starkey, Harold Smallwood, John Rimel, and Linda Ullery. Two anonymous reviewers provided good ideas for this second edition.

My wife, Nancy Ailes, helped me every step of the way.

Thanks to all.

George Constantz
May 1, 2004

1

Prologue

I am an unabashed partisan of the Appalachian Mountains. It is not that there are rocky, majestic peaks here; quite the contrary: Eons of erosion have delivered rounded highlands that are approachable and gentle on the eye. But beneath Appalachia's soft exterior run myriad short-lived scenes, each being played out by an individual organism competing for its part in the evolutionary play. No play runs in a vacuum, though. As G. Evelyn Hutchinson, the intellectual grandfather of many contemporary ecologists, put it, the long-term evolutionary drama can only be appreciated within the context of its environmental theater.

The play is complex, showcasing a tremendous diversity of actors. Appalachia hosts more species of deciduous trees, salamanders, darters, and shrews than any other region of North America. Mosses, ferns, sedges, and heaths also abound. This huge variety of living things is due in large part to the highlands' antiquity and convoluted topography. Appalachia's beauty is dynamic, though, and every walk unique. Autumn colors, wing prints in snow, spring wildflowers, and a stream of tiger swallowtails punctuate my year. If you are open to it, every day will reveal a new sight, sound, or smell. Even in the dead of winter I can detect change in the tufted titmouse's call, a shifting to the serious song of spring.

I have written this book for three reasons. First, I want to share my excitement for viewing Appalachian plants and animals from an evolutionary perspective. Contemplating a leaf or laughing at a squirrel, friends often ask me, "What good is it?" or "Why does it

1

do that?" Such prodding questions provide this book's thread: *Most* traits of a living thing exist because they have contributed to the reproductive success of that individual's ancestors; therefore, the ultimate function of most traits we see in contemporary organisms is to promote the reproduction of the individual. According to this view, survival of the species is merely an incidental, statistical by-product of the behavior of many individuals, each selfishly pursuing its own reproduction. The essay "Autumn Leaves" registers my caveat on why "most" is underlined.

I interpret the existence of an organism's traits in terms of "why" questions in addition to "what" or how" questions. That is, I try to maintain an explicit distinction between what historical, evolutionary causes may account for the traits of an organism compared to how that trait develops and functions in an individual. The foundation for many of the following chapters, then, is the critical application of the theory of natural selection. This theory embraces some of the most basic concepts of evolutionary biology, such as adaptation, tradeoffs, and sexual selection.

Grappling with such questions is called "selection thinking," a type of logic introduced by Charles Darwin and reinforced more recently by George C. Williams, a contemporary synthesizer of evolutionary biology. Over the last twenty years, I have been applying the theory of natural selection to interpret the lives of organisms in my local environment. Viewed through this neo-Darwinian paradigm, I see individuals as life-long reproductive competitors and thereby have come to appreciate the role of conflict in shaping the daily routines of plants and animals. One of my priorities is to expose the conflicts that underlie the beauty and mystery of Appalachian life: violence among fireflies, sexual parasitism within frog choruses, deception by flowers. The bottom line is that natural selection has led to traits that best contribute to individual reproductive success, not necessarily to characteristics we would judge as generous or ethical.

The second reason for writing this book stems from my experience as a teacher: I want to see people do more "backyard biology." Even though the processes of photosynthesis and meiosis are crucial to living systems, we cannot readily experience these concepts firsthand. We can, however, peer out a frosted window, identify a northern junco, and based on its size and color, predict whether it will drive off another flock-mate to steal its food or whether it is subordinate and will be displaced.

Most of Appalachia's living wealth is within a day's drive of half the people in North America, an association that brings both advantages and disadvantages. On the positive side, our hills are close to long-standing centers of scientific research, so we have been able to learn a great deal of their natural history. However, on the negative side, growing demands for minerals and timber, fish and game, and open space have led to major environmental changes. Thus, my third motive is to stimulate conservation through appreciation.

This is not a broad survey of Appalachian natural history — other books, such as Maurice Brooks' *The Appalachians*, do that very well. Instead, I paint specific vignettes that residents, summer campers, and lost travelers can reflect on as they bump into Appalachian organisms. As you might intuit, some stories (e.g., chps. 6, 15, 22) grow in relevance as you move southward along the range; others (e.g., chps. 14, 24, 25) are increasingly useful northward. Although a few of the chapters deal with topics I have personally researched, most are stories that have piqued my curiosity via the labors of other biologists. For most of the essays, I gathered the data from research journals and recast the stories in friendlier prose.

I will lead you through the following drama. "Stage and Theater" traces the geological origins of the Appalachian Mountains, sketches the processes by which many species evolved in isolated hollows and mountaintops, and presents several views of the structure and functions of today's forest. "The Players" is a series of essays on the unique, even quirky, adaptations of selected species. We explore why Jack-in-the-pulpits undergo sex change and how box turtles seem to live in the past. The third section, "Seasonal Acts," takes us through the Appalachian year, examining topics such as how an animal's body shape affects its chances of coping with winter and what, if any, are the reasons for fall colors. In a reflective "Epilogue," I register my views on Appalachia's most pressing environmental problems.

Because I love living in a little hollow in the Ridge and Valley province of central Appalachia and because my writing teachers have exhorted me to write about what I know, many of my examples may strike you as parochial. I assure you, though, that the concepts engage not only the full range of Appalachia but the entire eastern deciduous forest, which covers half of the United States.

A note about jargon. I have tried to avoid technical words wherever possible, but I have also not been afraid to jump right in where precision, efficiency, and color may reward a curious reader. I have settled on the following compromise: In each chapter, I define the technical words on first use; thereafter, I hold you to remembering the definition or using the glossary.

This second edition reflects ten years worth of new research findings, the criticisms of thoughtful readers, and my continuing growth as a writer. *Hollows, Peepers, and Highlanders*, then, is a collection of narratives and essays about some of my favorite natural events in Appalachia and their evolutionary interpretations. In setting the tone for this trip, I'd like to borrow the ideas from two earlier travelers. In *Life on a Little-Known Planet* entomologist Howard Ensign Evans felt awe when he discovered another new detail about the life of a little insect. In *Pilgrim at Tinker Creek*, essayist Annie Dillard stressed the importance of practice in sensing the moods of nature. As you move through this book, consider a blend: We have the power to see wonder in the commonplace, but only with a little practice.

Stage and Theater

2
Origins

On the surface, defining this mountain range appears a straight-forward proposition. Most authorities agree that the Appalachian Mountains are a loose group of peaks and ridges that form the sinuous axis of eastern North America, that they roughly parallel the Atlantic coast, and that they stretch about eleven hundred miles as the raven flies. We also agree that the chain's southern limit extends into northern Georgia and Alabama, where the highlands abruptly give way to coastal plain.

Here, however, the consensus ends. For example, we disagree about Appalachia's northern limit. Some stretch the Appalachians northward onto the Gaspe Peninsula of Quebec; others draw the line at the Hudson River in eastern New York. The southern limit of the last glacial advance, running through northern Pennsylvania, yields a neat and, as we shall see, biologically relevant southern border for northern Appalachia. But here again, we disagree on how to divide the remainder. For our purposes, let us consider central Appalachia as gradually merging into a southern section centered in the Great Smoky Mountains. Central Appalachia consists of low ridges of four thousand feet, while the other two sections top six thousand feet.

The eastern half of North America consists of several geographic regions, called physiographic provinces, each featuring a distinct topography. Although again lacking a professional consensus, I consider the core of Appalachia as, from east to west, the Blue Ridge, Ridge and Valley, and Appalachian Plateau physiographic provinces. The two flanking provinces — the Piedmont to the east and the

7

Interior Plateau to the west — lack a mountain flavor and, more importantly, have presented organisms with some evolutionary pressures different from those enforced by the mountains.

The Blue Ridge, the easternmost zone of Appalachia, runs from Carlisle, Pennsylvania, southward into Georgia as a single ridge averaging three thousand feet in elevation. This narrow belt, fourteen miles wide in the north and seventy miles wide in the south, includes the Great Smoky Mountains in Tennessee and North Carolina. For a while the Blue Ridge escarpment penned European colonists along the east coast.

Between the Blue Ridge and the Ridge and Valley provinces lies the Great Valley, which some geographers place within the Ridge and Valley. Varying in width from two to fifty miles, this giant trough stretches almost the entire length of the Appalachians. As the Great Valley extends southward, its name changes from Cumberland Valley to Shenandoah Valley, and then to Tennessee Valley. Overflowing from Pennsylvania, settlers finally colonized areas west of the Blue Ridge by streaming southward through the Great Valley.

West of the Great Valley lies the Ridge and Valley province, also called the Folded Appalachians because of their corrugated topography. Here, even-crested, roughly parallel mountain ridges alternate with valleys. The Ridge and Valley stretches the entire length of the Appalachians and varies in width from fourteen to eighty miles. Where I live, this zone cuts a forty-six-mile-wide swath from Winchester, Virginia, to Keyser, West Virginia. Throughout the Ridge and Valley, erosion-prone rocks such as limestone underlie the valleys and erosion-resistant strata such as sandstone and conglomerate form the ridges. Amazingly, even though the province narrows by half as it stretches southward, the number of ridges and valleys remains constant. This squeeze is accommodated by steeper strata and deeper fractures in the narrow parts than in the wide zones.

I will never forget my first view of the Ridge and Valley — from an airplane in early spring. The skinny, brown, forested ridges alternated with valleys of bright green cover crops. It seemed so uniform, so perfect. For a moment I was incredulous — the scene could have

been a painting. It's no wonder that some geographers have called our Ridge and Valley the most elegant folded mountain belt on earth.

To the west of the Ridge and Valley lies the Appalachian Plateau province — mildly folded strata and plateaulike mountains dissected by deep valleys. In general, the Plateau was uplifted less and the strata remain less deformed than the Ridge and Valley. The Plateau's dissected surface causes streams to branch at almost any angle, a condition called dendritic drainage. On a topographic map, dendritic streams contrast strikingly to the parallel, or trellised, drainage typical of the Ridge and Valley. The highest Appalachian province, the Plateau gradually loses altitude westward.

The highlands and their green blanket have undergone a long and complex evolution. In fact, scientists are still coaxing the stories out of the rocks and trees — today's theories may be superseded tomorrow. In Appalachia, older strata overlie younger layers, pieces of Africa cling to North America, and geologic forces have shoved surface layers many miles westward. A series of collisions of drifting continental plates folded, faulted, and metamorphosed the geologic terrain, eventually uniting North America with Africa and raising the Appalachians during Paleozoic time, 570 to 248 million years ago. A period of nearly complete erosion followed each episode of mountain building. The degree of deformation of strata decreases away from the front of tectonic collision: greatest corrugation in the Piedmont, moderate in the Ridge and Valley, and least in the Appalachian Plateau. The Andes and Alps display a similar pattern relative to their zones of geologic upheaval.

The early Appalachians, then, rose as the first primitive fishes appeared over 500 million years ago. Here's a telling comparison: Appalachia existed for 200 million years before terrestrial organisms evolved to occupy it. Today, the seaward portion of the Appalachian belt includes large and small blocks of distinctive rocks, called terranes. These terranes were welded onto North America. The suture of the two megacontinents that collided to raise our Appalachians forms today's Brevard zone, a long fault trending northeast-southwest through Brevard, North Carolina, and connecting Atlanta, Asheville, and Roanoke. Terranes of foreign rocks lie east of the Brevard zone. Discontinuous extensions of the Brevard zone even reach Staten Island, making part of the Big Apple a piece of the Old World.

While reptiles appeared during Carboniferous time, 360 to 286 million years ago, the North American and African plates began to rift apart, forming the present Atlantic Ocean. Since then, eastern North America has remained tectonically quiet while the North American plate has drifted west-southwest at the rate of about one inch per year.

We can also view Appalachian origins from a local perspective. Rather than immersing yourself in the technical details of the entire mountain chain, I encourage you to explore via hikes and geological maps the peaks, rocks, and folds in your own Appalachian neighborhood. Here is my geologic neighborhood.

A local set of corrugated strata often remind me of the power of tectonic collision. Two road cuts between Gore, Virginia, and Capon Bridge, West Virginia, expose layers of folded Devonian shale so severe, elegant, and compelling that at times I am hard-pressed to keep the old truck on the road — even though I steer by that spot at least once a month.

I live alongside Pine Cabin Run, a creek flowing over sedimentary rocks of the Devonian Chewing series laid down about 400 million years ago. Chewing rocks are part of the western half of the Meadow Branch syncline, a group of strata bent into a U. In order to visit my friends Mike and Annette at their cabin, I wind halfway up the North Mountain anticline, a set of strata bent into a ∩. Flanking this anticline are Silurian White Medina and Red Medina sandstones deposited 420 million years ago. Ordovician Martinsburg shale, a fine-grained sedimentary rock formed 500 million years ago, tops North Mountain. My westward drive to Romney, the county seat, passes over an unnamed anticline that forms Cacapon Mountain and then over a syncline underlying Cooper Mountain, both of which expose Oriskany sandstone from the Silurian (all of which you are

11

now equipped to interpret). On behalf of my old truck, I thank our erosive water for delivering today's gentle highlands; they are kinder on the transmission than the original rugged landscape would have been.

The Appalachian Mountains began to rise about 600 million years ago and reached their maximum height about 300 million years ago. Our mountains have been steadily eroding since Triassic time. Altogether, the Appalachian mountains have been uplifted out of the ocean for more than 500 million years, making Appalachia one of the oldest terrestrial environments on earth. By comparison, today's great mountain ranges — the Andes, Himalayas, and Alps — are infants, merely 50 million years old. Recognizing Appalachia's antiquity is crucial to understanding the range's biological diversity.

At the beginning of Mesozoic time, about 248 million years ago, the formerly joined ancestral continents of Laurentia and Gondwanaland went separate ways. Their resident land-dwelling animals became geographically isolated and began to follow different evolutionary paths. Most of the modern vertebrates of North America evolved from the primitive Laurasian faunal element — they are animals that arose in proto-North America. A few representatives of the Gondwanaland fauna, such as the catfishes and toads, colonized North America much later.

The Pleistocene period, 2.5 million to five thousand years ago, brought heavy rains and erosion to warm, southern areas and continental glaciation to cold, northern zones. The last two million years saw eighteen to twenty glaciations, each glacial cycle lasting about one hundred thousand years. Typically, brief (fifteen thousand years) warming phases, called interstadials, alternated with long (eighty-five thousand years) glacial conditions. The last glacial period, called the Wisconsin, began thirty thousand years ago and reached a glacial maximum eighteen thousand years ago. This last cooling saw the vigorous, two thousand-feet-thick Laurentide ice sheet polish rocks, excavate lake basins, and scrape away soils before it ground to a halt in central Pennsylvania.

The ice front stood at its southernmost extension for about four thousand years. During this period the species composition of plant communities beyond the ice sheet was stable. Within forty miles of the ice front, grasses and shrubs grew; farther south, throughout central and southern Appalachia, pine and spruce boreal forests dominated the landscape. At the height of the Wisconsin glaciation, deciduous flowering plants completely disappeared from the Appalachian Mountains, possibly surviving in small populations in the lower Mississippi Valley and southern coastal plains.

The Wisconsin ice margin, which I use to separate northern and southern Appalachia, began retreating about fourteen thousand years ago, receding into Maine twelve thousand years ago. Only in the last ten thousand years have soils developed in many glaciated areas of northern Appalachia. As the ice retreated, deciduous plants slowly recolonized northern Appalachia, and the coniferous boreal forest shrank to one-third its former size.

Throughout the last twelve thousand years, the Appalachian forest has presented a changing assemblage of tree species dispersing northward, thereby breaking up the Pleistocene flora. Each plant species advanced in response to changes in its own environment, at a rate independent of other species. Spruce reached New England eleven thousand five hundred years ago; alder, fir, and jack pine appeared one thousand years later; white pine, birches, and maple recolonized nine thousand years ago, and hemlock and oaks showed up shortly thereafter; and hickory did not appear there until five thousand years ago. American chestnut dispersed slowly northward, arriving in New England only in the last one thousand years. In general, tree species returned to northern Appalachia from widely scattered refugia, like the eastern coastal plain, Gulf Coast, and Arkansas, via different routes, and at different speeds.

All this geologic and climatic history presents us with an interesting irony: Appalachia is an extremely old mountain range that has accumulated a great variety of species, many of which are ancient. But the species comprising any particular community may have only a short shared evolutionary history. Thus, mutually

13

complementary adaptations, the sorts of traits that result from long-term, shared coevolution, as displayed by tropical organisms, are rare among Appalachian plants and animals. Biologically, Appalachia is more tossed salad than long-simmered stew.

3
Forest Design

On the hill above my lab, some old pines senesce. Interspersed among the pines are young maples and oaks, signs that this woodlot is changing from a coniferous to a broad-leaved stand. In my part of Appalachia, this particular replacement is predictable.

The structure of a forest — both the three-dimensional architecture and the kinds of species that comprise the forest community — changes over time. Through ecological time, whether measured in terms of several years or a few generations, new plant assemblages replace old ones in a process called ecological succession. Within limits and in a given region, the timing and sequence of the turnover of plant species are more or less predictable. In central Appalachia, a simplified succession might include the following stages, or seres, each named for its dominant species: grasses-ferns, blackberry-black locust, pines, oaks-hickories, and hemlock.

Classical succession theory holds that the end product of this process is the climax plant community, in which the numbers and types of plants do not change over the long term. In this view, successional change eventually yields a self-reproducing, stable community because until climax is attained, old individuals of dominant species render the site unsuitable for juvenile members of their own species. Some plant ecologists estimate that it takes two hundred to one thousand years for succession to achieve climax in Appalachia. Others wonder whether succession ever really leads to complete stability because neither biologists nor their funding live long enough to determine the significance of subtle long-term changes.

17

For all practical purposes, modern ecologists have abandoned the classical theory of succession. In lieu, one current hypothesis states that succession is a result of evolution for avoiding competition between species. In essence, some plant species colonize new habitats because they tolerate environmental extremes but thereafter are excluded from later seres by competition from other plant species. In another modern hypothesis, environmental catastrophes play a dominant role. Disturbances such as forest fires, windthrows, and rock slides set succession back to early seres and thereby help maintain biological differences among patches of vegetation. Periodic disturbance produces a flora rich in disturbance-adapted species. Such plant species possess traits such as high tolerance of environmental extremes, low tolerance of competition, fast growth rates, high reproductive potential, and short life span.

If we look even closer, climax becomes a heuristic device only arbitrarily distinguishable from early seres. The composition of an apparent climax community may be influenced more by the frequency of disturbance than by any inexorable laws of species replacement. Frequent disruptions result in mixes of species that are fleeting in time and space. If the interval between disturbances is short enough, the landscape will never host a climax community. Even relatively undisturbed sites do not yield complete predictability of their climax communities because seemingly minor historical events, such as the type of seed trees in an area, have greatly influenced present composition. In general, plants shift through succession from primarily herbs to trees, from annuals to perennials, and from synchronized to widely timed reproduction.

Species vary in how they colonize disturbed habitats. American beech, a climax species that grows slowly and waits persistently for an opening in the canopy, produces large seeds that germinate in shaded litter. Yellow birch annually broadcasts lightweight winged nutlets that succeed only if they land in a canopy gap, a disturbed site where they face little competition from other plants. Moderately moist forests, with a low frequency of fire and long intervals between disturbances, may be the only Appalachian plant community where the shade tolerance exhibited by beech is a characteristic strategy.

18

Not only do the species of plants and their life histories change with succession, but the three-dimensional structure of the plant community shifts as well. I am reminded of this as I walk across our lower field and enter the forest. The forest edge is thick with stems and leaves from ground to canopy. After I scramble through the brambles and vines, though, the inner forest opens up. Once inside, my shoulders brush against leaves of dogwood and witch hazel, trees that never exceed about fifteen to twenty feet in height. But few leaves hit my waist. This experience reminds me that the eastern deciduous forest has a definite spatial structure.

Through several decades of succession, the leaves of a forest assume several horizontal strata. To understand what causes this layered look, imagine a mature forest. Before Europeans settled North America, the eastern deciduous forest was a nearly unbroken expanse of trees. Interrupted only by occasional burned sites, windthrows, and rivers, the forest probably approached maturity more closely than we allow it to today. In that natural state, the fully developed deciduous forest took on a layered constitution: a bunch of tall trees with a dense layer of leaves at the top called the canopy; a haphazard carpet of green plants on the ground called the ground cover; and a sparse, less discrete layer of leaves on short trees and shrubs between the two called the understory.

The canopy, some fifteen to fifty yards high, is a continuous ceiling of sun-adapted leaves on the largest trees. The canopy includes the leaves of trees such as oaks, hickories, maples, white ash, black walnut, American beech, basswood, tulip poplar, eastern hemlock, and, formerly, American chestnut.

Understory shrubs and trees, which may be six to fifteen feet tall, intercept flecks of light penetrating the canopy. Never growing high enough to join the canopy, the understory includes woody plants such as flowering dogwood, maple leaf viburnum, common witch hazel, redbud, sassafras, and American hornbeam. These leaves form a loose, scattered layer.

Understory trees and shrubs depend on sunflecks, patches of direct sunshine that contribute up to 80 percent of the light penetrating the forest interior. Across this horizontal plane, light intensity varies greatly. Immediately beneath the canopy, each specific point at any given time can be either in a gap and illuminated or under a leaf and shaded. As the light rays approach the ground, they diffuse and coalesce, creating a horizontally more uniform layer of light. One theory suggests that plants of the understory have evolved to grow up to, but not exceed, this intermediate horizon of even light. A competing hypothesis states that a flush of germination following a disturbance such as a forest fire yields a stand of trees of similar height. A forest disturbed in the last thirty years or so would have an evident understory stratum because of the synchronized growth of such a flush of young trees.

The forest's bottom layer, the ground cover, consists of short, shade-tolerant plants that grow up to about three feet tall. Common plants of the ground cover include mosses, ferns, and herbaceous wildflowers.

Within the soil of a forest, fungi, algae, and even the trees themselves play hidden roles. In the Appalachian Mountains and probably in forests throughout the world, trees have benefited from a subtle ally — an underground forest. We have only recently come to appreciate that most higher plants have evolved a facultative, and sometimes obligatory, intimate relationship with fungi, an association called mycorrhiza or fungus root.

Mycorrhiza is the "organ" through which many plants absorb water and nutrients. This union is especially important for the uptake of certain insoluble nutrients, such as phosphorus. In poor soils, mycorrhizae compensate for the nutritional deficiencies of their hosts. Mycorrhizal plants grow satisfactorily on soils with low concentrations of zinc and phosphorus, conditions that stunt the growth of noninfected plants. After colonizing the outer layer of young roots, the fungal threads, or hyphae, grow out into the soil. Because hyphae contact a greater volume of soil than do the plant's roots alone, they increase the absorptive capacity of the root system. In return, the plant transfers to the fungus some of the carbohydrate it produces. Thus, in this relationship both parties benefit.

In addition to mycorrhizae, a complex community of free-living fungi reside in the forest's soil. The greatest diversity of fungal species inhabits the organic upper layer of soil, which includes the surface litter and the horizons of decomposing organic matter. Down through the underlying mineralized soil, the diversity of fungi decreases rapidly. Most species of free-living fungi achieve their maximum density in only one horizon, suggesting that competition between species has segregated the various species of soil fungi.

Even though little light penetrates the forest's soil, it hosts a teeming algal community. Forest soils contain up to 136,000 cells of algae per gram of soil. Closer inspection reveals two categories of algae within the forest's soil: ephemeral species, which appear suddenly, multiply rapidly, then disappear; and perennials, which persist through all the extreme conditions of the soil environment. Algae contribute organic forms of carbon and nitrogen to the soil and even stabilize soil against erosion.

Slime molds in the forest's soil accelerate decay, thereby recycling nutrients. A slime mold is a fungus-like organism that features both animal (feeds as a moving blob) and plant (reproduces by spores) attributes. A field study of five species of soil-dwelling slime molds found that each species existed in patches, suggesting that, as with fungi, competition between species has shaped the structure of the slime mold community. It seems no group of organisms, even those in the forest soil, is immune from interspecific competition.

Ecologists have determined that trees influence each other underground. Each tree species produces its own unique blend of root exudates, substances released into the surrounding soil by healthy plant roots. Exudates contain carbohydrates, amino acids, organic acids, and inorganic ions. Some chemical exudates seem to inhibit the growth of other plants, while others may be absorbed as nutrients by neighboring trees. An evolutionary question begged by this latter possibility is, "Who is nourishing whom, and what is their genetic relationship?"

The idea that ties together such diverse topics as vertical stratification, mycorrhizae, and slime mold communities is the concept

21

of ecological succession. As the woody plants in my field shift from blackberries to black locust and red cedar, then to oaks and hickories, the three-dimensional structure of the forest changes from dense and uniform to open and layered. Likewise, the ground cover changes from grasses and annual weeds to perennial wildflowers and ferns. As I wander through the woods trying to understand the design of Appalachian forests, I grow increasingly impressed by the power of the concept of ecological succession to explain a good chunk of it.

4

Creating Diversity

Within the borders of Great Smoky Mountains National Park grow 1,400 species of wildflowers. Thirty species of birds breed in one spruce-fir woodlot in Maine. At least twenty-one species of lungless salamanders (not just any type, but terrestrial vertebrates without lungs!) prowl the hollows of West Virginia. If you look, you will find similar diversity in deciduous trees, ferns, shrews, and darters. How has it come to pass that no other region in North America hosts such living diversity?

A new species arises when one group of interbreeding individuals, a population, becomes physically isolated from the rest of the group, impairing reproduction between individuals of the two groups. Over many generations, the separated populations accumulate observable differences. Should the two groups reestablish contact, the odds of interbreeding would depend on how much they diverged during the schism. Evolutionary biologists think it usually takes hundreds or thousands of generations before divergence precludes interbreeding. Called allopatric speciation, this process is thought to be the primary way new species arise.

Assuming allopatric speciation, a landscape that offers more opportunities to fracture populations should host more speciation events than an environment that allows the free mingling of individuals. For complementary reasons, species whose individuals disperse poorly become subdivided more readily into isolated populations than efficiently moving organisms. In other words, all else being equal, slow, plodding organisms yield new species faster than ones

25

that move quickly over vast distances. Birds have speciated more slowly than salamanders in part because flight thwarts reproductive isolation.

A region's antiquity also promotes high biological diversity. Old areas have been available for colonization by immigrating species for a longer time than new sites, and more species evolve over a vast stretch of time than over a short period.

Worldwide, centers of great biological diversity are often topographically complex and very old: mountain ranges, coral reefs, and tropical jungles. It is consistent that northern Appalachia is both ecologically younger and biologically less diverse than the central and southern zones. With land masses uplifted long ago from marine waters, and their surfaces unscoured by continental glaciation, central and southern Appalachia and their adjacent refugia have offered the longest continuously available terrestrial habitat in North America. The past 500-plus million years have provided more than enough time for the evolution of many new species.

Let's explore such an adaptive radiation among perches, fish species of the family Percidae. Perch dispersed to North America from Asia via Beringia, a land bridge that connected Siberia and Alaska during the Pleistocene epoch, one million years ago. Darters, a branch of that original percid colonization, arose in and are still naturally restricted, or endemic, to North America. Darters are small, two- to three-inch fishes that rest on the bottoms of streams. The approximately 145 species of modern darters evolved relatively recently, probably no earlier than the late Pleistocene. The Tennessee River basin, which is the theater of the greatest explosion of darter species, currently sustains fifty-two species. Within the basin, the largest concentration of extant darters resides in the Appalachian regions of eastern Tennessee and northern Alabama. By contrast, the much larger Missouri River system has only nineteen darter species.

On any given day, darters swim only a short distance. Their broad-bottomed shape, supportive ventral fins, and lack of a swim bladder complement their sedentary life on the stream bottom. Members of the darter genus *Etheostoma* have adapted to upland

26

streams with hard substrates and fast flows. Because of their limited power of dispersal and restriction to headwaters, individuals of the same *Etheostoma* species that live in different streams may seldom interbreed. Consequently, marked genetic differences could accumulate between headwater populations even within small geographic areas.

Two *Etheostoma* species illustrate such ongoing evolution. The orange*throat* darter is restricted to headwaters by downstream competition with the orange*belly* darter, a situation that severely curtails the flow of genes among populations of orange*throats*. This isolation has allowed significant genetic differences to accumulate among the populations of orange*throat* darters.

The story of speciation in lungless salamanders (family Plethodontidae) is more complex. Although sparse in northern Appalachia, salamanders appear to have evolved relatively undisturbed for millions of years south of the Pleistocene ice front. As was the case for darters, topographic diversity and limited mobility combined to allow the formation of new species of lungless salamanders. The landscape of central and southern Appalachia — numerous disconnected mountains separated by narrow, often river-filled valleys — has enforced genetic isolation among populations restricted to different hilltops, allowed divergent evolution, and led to today's high endemism of plethodontid species. Let us focus on one such species swarm.

In the Great Smoky and nearby mountains, Jordan's salamander exhibits different color patterns on different peaks and has thereby earned different names: Metcalf's salamander has a black back and gray underside; the red-cheeked salamander is black with bright red patches on its cheeks; the red-legged salamander has black flecks and gray patches; and so on.

All of these salamander populations live primarily in spruce-fir forests, which, in southern Appalachia, exist as isolated habitat islands at high elevations. Perhaps as recently as the retreat of the last glacier, populations of Jordan's salamander became isolated on separate mountains. While the climate remained cool and their low elevation habitat was probably continuous, Jordan's may have looked alike everywhere. As the climate warmed, the spruce-fir forests and their salamander associates dispersed up the mountains, until each fir-salamander community became trapped in the unique habitat of a single peak. Adaptation to the singular environment of each peak, plus a possible contribution by random genetic changes unrelated to the environment (genetic drift), presumably have led to divergent forms in isolated populations. From one ancestral species, Jordan's salamander, many new species of woodland salamanders are just now evolving. The high number (about twenty-five) of salamander subspecies endemic to southern Appalachia reflects this ongoing speciation.

The darter and lungless salamander stories are relatively well known, but the speciation of many other Appalachian organisms reflects the same constraints of physical barriers, limited movement, and the evolutionary divergence of populations that have become reproductively incompatible. The snowshoe hare, which seems to require the shelter of dense stands of red spruce, does not venture below the three thousand foot elevation. Its southernmost population, located in West Virginia, is 200 miles from the nearest neighboring hares in eastern Pennsylvania. Because of their reproductive isolation, West Virginia hares may be on the way to becoming a new species. Hares at this southern outpost not only change color at the same time as northern individuals, but also exhibit explosive population cycles with periods of nine to eleven years that coincide almost exactly with those exhibited by populations in New England and eastern Canada. The latter are six hundred miles away! What causal connection could possibly exist between populations separated by such a vast distance? Here we face yet another mystery.

Allopatric speciation — which includes roles for antiquity, topographic diversity, physical isolation, limited movement, genetic and morphological divergence, and finally reproductive incompatibility — can result in high diversity only over a vast geographic area. This process by itself would yield just one or a few species per taxonomic group in each habitat island. The hallmark of Appalachia, however, is that many species exist at each site. Therefore, sometime after new species arose, they must have come together to occupy the same piece of ground. Recurrent continental cooling and stream capture appear to have contributed to the overlapping ranges of salamander and darter species, respectively. Long-term climatic changes have also mixed species of plants.

In the Pleistocene, salamanders were forced down from the uplands by cold temperatures. When the climate warmed and the ice retreated, salamanders followed their thermal limits upward. Each species colonized several hills, mixing several species on each hilltop. Here, in turn, they underwent a round of isolation and speciation.

Climatic change has also induced species mixing among plants. The boreal coniferous forest, dominated by spruce and fir, extends southward along the frigid crest of the Appalachians into North Carolina. The boreal islands in the Great Smoky Mountains, rich in endemic plants and animals, are surrounded by a sea of deciduous trees growing at lower elevations. Some northern tree species — common juniper, spruce, gray birch, and quaking aspen — have representatives in the region's southern reaches. These trees apparently dispersed into central and southern Appalachia during the Pleistocene and have persisted ever since as isolated colonies in high, favorable sites. In this way, within a fairly small area, boreal and temperate species became mixed.

The bunchberry is my favorite local example of glacially induced plant mixing. This miniature member of the dogwood family grows in such diverse locations as Admiralty Island in southeast Alaska and Ice Mountain, a site at less than one thousand feet elevation in eastern West Virginia. On Ice Mountain's steep, north-facing hillside, cold drafts issuing from the gaps among sandstone boulders create a series of cool microsites. Here, bunchberry and a few other boreal species have persisted since the ice age.

In contrast, some tree species show significant evolutionary changes down the Appalachian backbone. Normally a boreal species, balsam fir (*Abies balsamea*) extends southward through the Appalachians. On some peaks in Virginia and West Virginia, another species of fir (A. *intermedia*) differs only slightly from northern balsam firs. Farther south, firs in the Great Smoky Mountains show

29

even greater differences and are called Fraser fir. Presumably, during glaciation the balsam fir dispersed southward and during interglacials dispersed upward, leaving isolated populations on cool, southern peaks. Thus, Fraser fir appears to be a young species endemic to southern Appalachia. Derived via an intermediate step from the boreal balsam fir, Fraser fir now grows among trees of the eastern deciduous forest.

Because the high-altitude habitats of southern Appalachia resemble those of the boreal north, the two areas continue to share a large proportion of species. On the basis of overall appearance and species composition, the spruce-fir forests of southern Appalachia are part of, yet distinct from, the great northern boreal forest. Restated from a different point of view, the coniferous forests of today's high Appalachian peaks are somewhat altered relics of the widespread boreal forests of the past.

Possibly because of such climatically induced species mixing, the southern Appalachians are poor in endemic trees. No tree genus is endemic to southern Appalachia, and only ten species are endemic: Fraser fir, Carolina hemlock, Table Mountain pine, yellow buckeye, cinnamon clethra, Fraser magnolia, Catawba rhododendron, kelsey locust, clammy locust, and mountain stewartia. Thus, trees of northern and southern origins are thoroughly mixed along the Appalachian continuum.

Turning from Appalachia's forests to its streams, we find that many fish species are endemic to only a single drainage. Consequently, the southern Appalachians harbor an extremely diverse fish fauna: One recent list totaled 398 fishes, the most common families being minnows, suckers, catfishes, sunfishes, and perches (including darters). The high species diversity of Appalachian fishes results in part from two phenomena: dispersal between bordering drainages and stream capture.

During the Pleistocene, headwater tributaries lying farther from the ice were less severely affected by faunal extinction than streams closer to the glacier. The more distant streams served as refugia, areas where organisms persisted until the climate returned to favorable status.

When climate warmed, species moved between the mouths of subbasins, enabling species exchanges among the Tennessee, Cumberland, and Mississippi rivers. The Mississippi River basin was probably the site of origin of most of the freshwater fishes east of the Rocky Mountains.

Stream capture also contributed to high fish diversity. By stream capture, I mean two headwater streams cutting toward a common divide, eventually meeting and breaking down the ridge, and forcing one stream to yield its water and fishes to the other. The Greenbrier River, a tributary of the New River in West Virginia, expanded north at the expense of some southern tributaries of the Monongahela system. Specifically, multiple piracies beheaded Glady, Laurel, Dry, and Gandy forks of Shavers Fork along Lynn Divide. By stealing the Monongahela's tributaries, the Greenbrier has accumulated a grand variety of fishes.

Central and southern Appalachia support a huge number of plant and animal species. The ridges and hollows split populations of slow-moving organisms, which allow biological differences between populations to accumulate over many generations, all of which facilitate the evolution of new species. Organisms from more northerly climes were forced southward during the last glaciation and dispersed upward as climate warmed, becoming stranded on mountaintops. Whether created *in situ* or accumulated from without, different kinds of living things became close neighbors by processes such as glacier-induced migrations and stream captures.

My half-day hikes often pass through several sets of hollows and peaks. The tulip poplars and black walnuts of the hollows grade into the oaks and hickories of the slopes, then into the spruce on the peaks. Many a time I have forgotten about my sore feet by concentrating on the changing plants, conjecturing about the roles of allopatric speciation and glacially induced mixing, and wondering how close I am to truly understanding the mystery of Appalachian biodiversity.

5

Catastrophe and
the Appalachian Quilt

I n ecology, as in other areas of inquiry, answers to even the most elementary questions hinge on the breadth of the observer's vision. Take, for example, the question of how the males of a particular bird species, like the wood thrush, distribute themselves across a landscape. They could appear uniformly distributed when viewed on the small scale, being spaced evenly by their mutual territorial repulsion. Since the birds' territories only occupy certain habitats, the individuals could also appear clumped in discrete groups if viewed at an intermediate scale covering several hills. Finally, the birds could appear randomly dispersed across a large geographic region where the habitat blocks are scattered haphazardly.

To understand why the Appalachian Mountains have continued to host so many species, we need to apply this practice of observing the forest at several scales. Although viewing through a continuum of scales provides the most realistic impression, it also proves unmanageable, so we'll simply examine the extremes: surveying some of the broad causes of biological diversity, such as environmental gradients and ecological disturbances; then narrowing our scope to explore small-scale factors such as canopy gaps.

As you climb a mountain, the temperature gradually cools. This thermal gradient helps determine which plants grow where on the slope. Moisture gradients similarly influence plant communities. In the oak forests of Virginia, several trends become obvious as you move from moderately moist to dry sites: the canopy coverage, stand height, and total area of the trees' bases decrease, while in the shrub level these features increase.

At the continental scale, environmental gradients contribute to the maintenance of plant diversity. The boreal forest covers a huge area across southern Canada and southward along the high ridges of Appalachia. Dominant boreal trees include balsam fir; black and white spruces; red, white, and jack pines; quaking and bigtooth aspens; paper birch; and balsam poplar. Farther south, the broad-leaved trees of the mixed deciduous forest take over. The mixed deciduous forest may assume several forms, including northern hardwood, oak-chestnut, oak-pine, mixed mesophytic, and cove hardwood forests. Mesophytic refers to a medium level of moisture. A cove is a bowl-shaped valley with rich, damp soil. One way of appreciating the great diversity of communities within the mixed deciduous forest is to compare three of its subtypes: the northern hardwood forests of New England, the mixed mesophytic forest of central Appalachia, and the cove hardwood forests of southern Appalachia.

The northern hardwood, or transition, forest combines features of the boreal woodland and the deciduous forest of southern Appalachia. Common in New England and at high elevations in the southern Appalachians, the northern hardwood forest contains only a few dominant species: red maple in wet spots, beech in drier conditions, and yellow birch on rock slides.

The mixed mesophytic forest of central Appalachia supports a marvelous diversity of tree species. Commonly, three dozen species are prominent in a mature community. Canopy trees include white basswood, beech, sugar maple, tulip poplar, red and white oak, hemlock, magnolia, white ash, and black cherry. Tulip poplars inhabit lowlands, hemlocks can monopolize ravines, and oaks dominate drier ridge tops.

The cove hardwood forests of southern Appalachia exhibit the greatest diversity of tree species in North America. Within a single stand, eight to ten tree species may share dominance in a total assemblage of forty species. Trees common in southern cove forests include tulip poplar, sugar maple, yellow buckeye, basswood, beech, yellow birch, red oak, black cherry, and Carolina silverbell.

In addition to the contributions of altitude and latitude, ecological disturbance and the introduction of exotic species contribute to high biotic diversity. At some sites, episodes of fire and windstorm may actually be more important in determining tree species composition than long stretches of tranquility.

Fire, so important in conifer-dominated systems such as boreal forests and southern Appalachian pine forests, also plays a role in the drier parts of deciduous forests. Fire alters light intensity, water and nutrient contents of the soil, microclimate at the soil's surface, and reseeding sources. Repeated fires favor species with fire-adaptive traits, such as serotinous cones that release seeds when stimulated by the heat of a fire, resprouting by roots, and even increased flammability of the plant community as a whole.

At first glance, fire appears to be a force imposed from without. However, the quick buildup of combustible organic matter and the fire-dependent reproductive strategies (e.g., serotiny) suggest that some plant species actually encourage fire. For example, fire aids reproduction of Table Mountain pine by destroying competing vegetation and forest litter while releasing seeds from the pine's serotinous cones. Without fire, the cones of Table Mountain pine remain closed for two years. At two years, 40 percent proceed to open even without fire; the rest stay closed holding viable seeds on the parent tree for up to ten years. The serotinous cone is an adaptation designed to release seeds into habitat cleared of competitors.

From an ecological point of view, fires truncate succession, restarting it at an earlier sere, or successional stage. From a landscape perspective, small, localized fires create forests composed of stands at various stages of succession. In presettlement Wisconsin, forest fires recurred at intervals ranging from several decades to a century, apparently precluding a widespread mature forest. In contrast, New England forests burned less frequently, allowing large areas to attain greater maturity. In the Great Smoky Mountains, a natural fire-return interval of ten years favored fast-growing, thick-barked tree species over slow-growing, thin-barked ones. Apparently, thick bark enhanced survival. With the advent of fire suppression in the 1940s, thin-barked species were suddenly allowed to grow large enough to resist fires. The longer the period of fire suppression, the greater the proportion of the forest claimed by thin-barked, slow-growing trees.

Fires scattered through time and space create a diversity of habitats for other organisms. A succession of animals depends on the succession of plants that follow fire. Deer mice are common for about seven years following a burn but decrease thereafter, whereas moles increase in number as the plant community matures.

Windstorms, occasionally blowing down large expanses of temperate and boreal forests, also help to maintain biological diversity. Collapsing trees contribute to soil mixing and create pit-and-mound relief, which provides a variety of microenvironments for seedlings of various species. In southern Wisconsin, severe thunderstorms cause catastrophic windthrow. Trees left standing along the gap's edge are suddenly less supported and more susceptible to falling domino-style. Since a return to climax takes two hundred to three hundred years, 17 to 25 percent of this forest remains in subclimax stages, with each sere supporting its own characteristic species of plants and animals.

The invasion of exotic species provides another type of large-scale disturbance that may contribute to high biotic diversity. (But I'm not saying that we should introduce new species.) Until the early 1900s, the American chestnut was the most common tree species in many parts of Appalachia, often forming 40 to 60 percent of the canopy. Chestnuts fed squirrels, bear, deer, wild turkey, and people. Chestnut logs, almost impervious to rot, were used to construct homesteads. Old chestnut split-rail fencing graces our farm in West Virginia, and chestnut joists support our cabin's flooring — all still going strong. Chestnut blight, first detected in 1904 in New York City, swept through the northeastern forests, then southward through Appalachia. First noted in West Virginia in 1912, the blight appeared in the southern Appalachians by 1925. By 1930, the disease had infected 80 to 90 percent of the American chestnuts in North Carolina. The blight's spores, carried by breezes, birds, and insects, enter healthy trees through wounds in the bark. The fungus then clogs the plant's vascular tissues. Although some roots survive, the blight kills most shoots before they are large enough to bear nuts.

Before the blight, the oak-chestnut forests — composed of several species of oaks, American chestnut, red maple, and black cherry — were extensive. After the blight, native species of oaks (chestnut, red, white) and hickories (pignut, shagbark) partially filled the canopy gaps. Acorns replaced chestnuts as the major food for wildlife. Within half a century, the great mixed deciduous forest of eastern North America changed from oak-chestnut to our oak-hickory forest.

Each of the many large-scale disturbances varies in frequency, predictability, area, and severity. As if that is not complex enough, the type and frequency of disturbance gradients often parallel environmental gradients. For example, the severity of windthrow is greater at high, wet sites than at low, dry ones. Such co-varying factors make accounting for the causes of biological diversity a huge challenge.

Think of our contemporary Appalachian forest as a patchwork quilt in which each piece has a different disturbance history. A few rare patches have gone undisturbed for one thousand years and host a mature forest; other stands have been disturbed every few years and support pioneer species; most patches, though, have been disturbed within the last one hundred to two hundred years and sustain an intermediate sere.

Biological diversity depends on the preservation of this heterogeneous matrix, not just the virgin old-aged communities. (Clarifying again, I'm not saying that it's not desirable, for a whole host of reasons, to preserve old-growth.) Successional patches of burns, fields, and brambles are important to animals such as white-tailed deer, red fox, and songbirds. Within limits, natural and human-caused disturbances contribute to the diversity of living things in Appalachia.

Tremendous diversity exists not only in large regions of Appalachia but within smaller areas as well — on a single hillside, along a stream, and even under a single tree. What maintains many species in small patches?

A temperate forest may contain more than twelve species of nonwoody plants, or herbs, per square yard. Subtle differences in topography, nearness to canopy openings, temperature, and sunlight account for much of the diversity of the ground cover. In the spring, shoots of many forest herbs expand and occupy the same layer. In the four to six weeks that pass between the last hard freeze and canopy leaf-out, the herb layer is richest in light, heat, moisture, and nutrients. Although their leaves may fill the ground cover, herbs apparently compete less for light than trees that leaf out later.

When a tree falls, it leaves a mound formed by the roots and attached soil and a pit where the roots used to grow. These local topographic differences contribute to herb diversity. Mound-and-pit microsites differ from the surrounding forest in moisture, acidity, temperature, and litter depth. At an even smaller scale, characteristics of the mound differ from those of the pit. In one New England site, mounds and pits cover 20 to 50 percent of the forest floor. Such a mosaic maintains populations of mosses, ferns, wildflowers, and many other ground cover species.

Standing trees create still more microhabitats for plants of the understory and ground cover. The trees alter the amount of light and moisture reaching the soil, thereby determining the rate at which the soil dries out. Trees contribute minerals dissolved from the leaves and stems to the soil at the tree's base. By inhibiting young individuals of the same species, trees of the canopy contribute to biological diversity. Seedlings face stiffer competition beneath adults of their own species than under other species, and fungi are more likely to kill or weaken seedlings that sprout under trees of the same species than under adults of different species. Further, the larger resistant trees may host diseases or pests that infect smaller individuals already weakened by competition.

Sassafras provides an excellent example of this growth suppression strategy. Sassafras invades abandoned fields, expands clonally from root sprouts, and persists as a relatively pure stand through various successional stages. Sassafras leaves, litter, and roots release a variety of plant poisons that exclude ten plant species, including several annual herbs. Seven other plant species thrive beneath the sassafras canopy. The latter seven appear to succeed because of their perennial growth cycle, which somehow makes them more resistant to the chemical interference. Plant poisons selectively harm some species, thus incidentally favoring others. One major drawback results from inhibiting growth of one's own species: dominant species may be unable to replace themselves. In this way, growth suppression may preclude a forest from ever reaching maturity.

Tree seedlings in mature southern Appalachian forests face the greatest chance of surviving if they sprout in small canopy gaps created by the death of one or a few trees. In cove hardwood forests, the species of the replacement tree usually bears no relationship to the species of the fallen tree. Unpredictability rules in part because most tree species reproduce by mass seeding of light gaps, a roulette process. In virgin forests, one dead tree is often replaced by a single successor that comes to occupy more or less the same space in the canopy. In this way, shade-tolerant species persist by efficient seed dispersal and fast growth.

As I lumber up the hillside behind my cabin, I am impressed by the variety of ferns and wildflowers. I must typically take several steps along the slope before I come across a second individual of a just-sighted tree species. Then, as I crest the ridge my gaze sweeps across a patchwork quilt of forest stands, each at a different stage of succession. I revel in this diversity.

6

Balds

Scattered throughout the higher reaches of southern and central Appalachia lie discrete areas without trees called balds. From an ecological perspective, a bald is a patch of naturally treeless vegetation occupying a well-drained site below tree line in a predominantly forested region. At least eighty of these inexplicable breaks, ranging in area from two to twenty acres, are strewn from Virginia to Georgia, most at elevations above four thousand feet. Similar treeless communities appear in the Ozarks, Nevada, and New Zealand, where they might be called slicks, knobs, or barrens.

Balds take on a variety of forms. Grass balds, also called meadow balds, are devoid of shrubs and support herbaceous vegetation such as mountain oat grass. Grass balds are common in sections of the Blue Ridge, particularly in North Carolina. In some places, grass balds merge into heath balds or barrens — mountaintops covered with a variety of densely growing heath shrubs and other low-growing plants, commonly huckleberry, blueberry, mountain laurel, and mountain azalea. In moist areas, alder balds support a tangled jumble of thick, shrubby, green alders three to four feet tall.

No neat, widely accepted theory explains the origin of balds. When Europeans settled the Appalachians, at least some contemporary balds were bare of trees. Some ecologists propose that Native Americans cleared trees and then periodically burned the areas to encourage the growth of mountain oat grass. Others suggest that Indians, particularly Cherokees, cleared some sites as sacred places. A third hypothesis holds that early European settlers cleared balds to

41

graze cattle. Even biotic causes such as attacking insects and brows-ing native mammals have been implicated. Climatic factors, such as injury due to winter ice, wind-throwing of trees, and drought have all been suggested. These points of view are consistent with the fact that balds often occupy rounded summits exposed to desiccating southwesterly winds. Natural fire and specific soil types have been ruled out, though, because neither burn evidence nor a consistent pattern of soil types exists among the balds.

A more complex hypothesis posits that about four thousand years ago a long period of hot, dry weather killed the spruces and firs near their lower limits, allowing beeches and maples to replace them. A cool trend, which continues to the present, caused these latter species to perish. Why spruce and fir did not reestablish themselves in the clearings is unknown. Without competition from trees, grasses invaded most of these sites, producing grass balds. Rhododendrons from the forest understory invaded a few of the high-elevation grass balds, creating heath balds.

It is consistent that some biologists have observed that, when plotted altitudinally, most balds occupy the border of two forest types. This suggests that balds develop along the tolerance limits of the dominant tree species. For example, in southern Appalachia, most balds lie near the upper limits of beech, buckeye, and red oak, and at the lower limits of red spruce and Fraser fir. If climate changed at this boundary, trees would reinvade the site very slowly because the wind, drought, and temperature extremes of the open bald would kill seedlings. Another possibility is that as the climate cooled during the Pleistocene, balds grew larger because deciduous trees retreated downhill faster than spruce invaded the vacated sites.

One final possibility — and this runs anathema to ecologists hungry for generalizations — is that different kinds of balds have different causes of origin, even that each individual bald has resulted from a unique combination of causes. The bottom line is that, even though we do not know what causes balds, all hypotheses share the idea that a disturbance has not been followed by succession.

42

What maintains balds? We are not even sure that they are being maintained. Although a few might be expanding, many seem to be shrinking. Our uncertain knowledge reflects the fact that the edge of a bald is constantly threatened by the invasion of woody plants. The war between the opening and its forest envelope keeps the size and species composition of a bald dynamic.

Several theories attempt to explain the persistence of apparently stable balds. The possibilities include that thick mountain oat grass prevents tree seedlings from getting a foothold, harsh weather prevents tree colonization, and the trampling and feeding of grazing animals, such as bison, cattle, and sheep, reinforced early successional communities. In heath balds, the dense network of rhododendrons' roots and leaves may exclude most herbaceous plants.

Some balds seem to be shrinking as herbaceous plants, which prepare the site for woody species, invade from cleared fields farther downslope. Such uphill immigrants include mountain oat grass, certain mosses, and bracken fern. Where seed sources are available, spruce is invading some grassy balds. Some balds seemed to shrink when livestock ceased grazing on mountain summits. If this last observation is true, some balds will vanish during the next century.

So, here is a mysterious Appalachian scene that embraces everything from archeology to zoology, with healthy doses of botany, geology, and meteorology thrown in. The exceptional nature of balds underscores the importance of identifying what creates and sustains them. Comprehending treelessness will help us understand the existence of, and thereby protect, our dense, diverse eastern deciduous forest. What fascinates me is the possibility that each bald may have been created and is currently being maintained by a unique mix of causes — and therefore is following its own successional path.

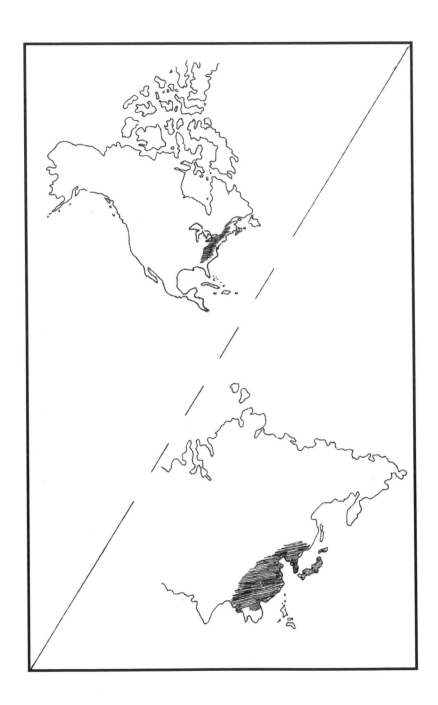

7

The Asian Connection

H ere's a claim that may surprise you: The forests of eastern Asia and southern Appalachia are so similar that if you were swept from one to the other, you would be hard pressed to tell them apart. These regions share many similar plants and some animals, even though intervening areas host vastly different organisms. Living things with fractured geographical distributions are termed disjunct. In this chapter we explore this unexpected connection: the Asia-North America disjunction.

The disjunction, usually at the genus and species levels, involves more than fifty genera of Appalachian plants that are restricted to eastern North America and eastern Asia and, except in fossil form, are absent in between. Among some genera, several Appalachian species are geographically separated from Asian relatives: hickory, tulip poplar, sassafras, yellowwood, coffee-tree, silverbell, witch hazel, and stewartia. Within other tree groups, such as the maples, dogwoods, persimmons, hollies, sumacs, snowbells, Hercules-clubs, and sweetleafs, the disjunctions affect only certain pairs of related species. Two observations are telling: (1) many disjunct genera contain few species, and (2) all are confined exclusively to eastern North America and eastern Asia. If not for these two facts, we might have dismissed the separations as due to random chance alone. This frees us to pursue a more interesting explanation.

Among trees, two pairs of related species, tulip poplar and Carolina hemlock, present particularly striking disjunctions. There

45

are only two species of tulip poplars, one in China and one in the United States. Likewise, the closest relative of Carolina hemlock, a local tree peculiar to the southern Appalachians, is in eastern Asia. In both the tulip poplar and hemlock genera, each North American species differs only slightly from its Asian twin.

The understories and ground covers of the two regions also share many plants. More than two-thirds of the total orchid genera of temperate North America have representative orchid species in eastern Asia. At least eight of these genera consist of disjunct species pairs. In contrast, not a single orchid genus grows exclusively in North America and Europe. Similar Asia-North America disjunctions are also known for ferns, ginseng, mayapple, Jack-in-the-pulpit, skunk cabbage, lichens, and mosses.

Let's focus on two small regions of China and North America. The floras of the eastern Chinese province of Hubei and our Carolinas share many families and genera. About 75 percent of their plant families are represented by at least one species in each region. Mimicking the continental pattern, many of the state and provincial disjunct species are closely related. In addition to likenesses, the floras of these two areas differ in that each has evolved some of its own endemic plant species.

Although less common, some animal distributions are also disjunct. The copperhead has a species in the same genus in southeastern Asia. The paddlefish, hellbender, and alligator also have disjunct Asian relatives.

So, here we have a paradox: Eastern North America was most recently continuous with the continents of Europe and Africa, yet Appalachia is floristically more similar to eastern Asia.

The most widely accepted theory to explain this puzzle suggests that the isolated plants remain as survivors of an ancient circumpolar plant community that died out in Europe, western Asia, and western North America. The Beringian land bridge linked Russia and

Alaska beginning in the Miocene epoch, about 9.25 million years ago. This timing precluded extensive migrations between Asia and America via Beringia before the Miocene. Yet one-half to two-thirds of the Chinese plant species originating in the late Cretaceous, 70 million years ago, and one-fourth to one-half of the plants arising in the late Eocene, 40 million years ago, are nearly identical to their nearest relatives in North America. The fossil record shows only a few Chinese species similar to those of North America after the Eocene. Therefore, today's disjunct plants must have been continuous between eastern Asia and eastern North America long before land connected Russia and Alaska. The floras must have connected via Europe.

The disjunct genera of eastern Asia and eastern North America must represent remnants of ancient plants that were once broadly distributed throughout the Northern Hemisphere. The two floras remain similar today presumably because neither site experienced extensive Pleistocene glaciation and both have shared a similar climate.

Not only do these two regions have similar plant genera, they also reveal four compelling ecological parallels. First, both are dominated by woody, broad-leaved, deciduous plants. Second, their non-woody plants have underground storage organs and bloom in the spring. Third, herbs are either early-leafing ephemerals or shade-adapted perennials with buds that overwinter in the soil. Finally, in both areas the kinds of plants change predictably along environmental gradients. The similarities in plant categories, life histories, and individual sizes and shapes reflect evolutionary descent in similar environments from a set of common ancestors, an evolutionary process called parallelism.

Today, eastern Asia is the foremost center of remnants from the widespread ancestral plant community that covered the northern hemisphere; eastern North America is second, featuring roughly half as many tree species from the ancestral community. By comparison, eastern Europe and western North America have about one-fourth as many remnant taxa as eastern Asia. Some tree genera are widespread in all four regions, but eastern North America and eastern Asia share the most tree genera, sixteen.

So Appalachia features blocks of African rock yet hosts many plants of Asian connection — this is quite the cosmopolitan place.

The Players

8

The Improbable Lady's-slipper

S tealing through the pine thicket to spy on the incubating broad-winged hawk, hiking up Pine Cabin Run to study nest-building chubs, and hunting for morels — all these activities have been interrupted, commandeered would be a better word, by a lady's-slipper. That flash of pastel, which I usually detect peripherally, demands my focus. After an internal struggle to continue my rounds, I accede, take a seat, and at least for a while, babble to the flower about how pretty it is. After a few seconds of ogling, I am reminded that I am witnessing a highly unlikely event, and this, in turn, usually triggers that smug satisfaction of being in the right place at the right time.

Although orchids may not abound at any one spot, around the world there are a great many species. In fact, Orchidaceae is probably the largest family of flowering plants on Earth. With twenty-five thousand species in eight hundred genera, the family boasts fully 10 percent of all species of flowering plants, a whopping share of the modern plant world. With all these species to draw from, it is no surprise that the orchid family has evolved the most varied floral structures in the plant kingdom. And orchids continue to evolve today.

Orchids arose in the tropics after Gondwanaland — a land area thought to have contained the landmasses of the Southern Hemisphere — broke up in the early Cretaceous, 120 million years ago. West Gondwanaland, which later split into South America and Africa, became the center of flowering plant evolution. Although orchids are cosmopolitan, they remain most diverse in the tropics. Most orchid evolution took place after the Paleocene, 55 million

51

years ago, when lush blankets of vegetation encircled the northern hemisphere. That relatively continuous environment allowed some species of orchids to take on a circumpolar distribution.

Although many tropical species grow upon plants, especially trees, all northern temperate orchid species root in the ground. About one hundred species, of which half are relatively recent immigrants from the tropics, live in the continental United States. Most native North American orchid species grow in the rich, shaded humus of the eastern deciduous forest; there are thirty species along the Blue Ridge Parkway alone. As with trees, a few orchid species clinging to the high peaks of southern Appalachia are relics of the boreal forest.

Appalachia hosts three subfamilies of orchids: the Spiranthoideae, which includes downy rattlesnake plantain and nodding ladies tresses; the Orchidoideae, which is basically an African group and includes showy orchis; and the Cypripedioideae, which includes the subjects of this essay, the lady's-slippers. The lady's-slippers' genus, which contains at least 110 species worldwide, is not ancestral to any other group of living orchids, but instead went off on an evolutionary tangent that preserved its own unique features.

Allow me to introduce several Appalachian lady's-slippers. Probably the most common orchid in North America, the pink lady's-slipper, also called pink moccasin-flower and stemless lady's-slipper, dwells in high, dry woods. Early in the spring, each plant produces two large, light green leaves, and a leafless flowering stalk that emerges rapidly from between the paired leaves. Sometime between April and July, depending on elevation and latitude, the plant produces one flower with purplish petals and a pink labellum, which is a lower lip extending into a saclike pouch.

Yellow lady's-slippers, or yellow moccasin-flowers, grow as clones, which are groups of asexually produced, genetically identical individuals. As the most widespread species of the genus, the yellow lady's-slipper ranges throughout the eastern United States except the southeastern coastal plain. A crab spider in matching yellow hunts on these flowers. Frozen and camouflaged, the predator grabs visiting would-be pollinators.

The showy or queen's lady's-slipper is our largest and most spectacular native orchid. Its white sepals and petals contrast with a pink-mouthed labellum. It grows from New England southward through the Appalachian Mountains.

All Appalachian species of lady's-slippers emit odors that attract insects. Sources of the essence include petals, sepals, and labella. Both the pink and showy lady's-slippers release a sweet scent; the yellow smells strong and spicy. The former two species are visited by large solitary bees; the latter by both social and solitary species.

With attractive colors and appealing fragrances, lady's-slippers entice insects to enter their flowers in search of pollen or nectar. They find neither — and here the plot thickens. After a nectar seeker enters the flower, the port's one-way funnel-like construction prevents a quick exit by the same route. Specifically, the margins and hairs of the aperture point inward and thwart the insect's escape. To egress, the insect must shove its way under the stigma, the female organ, where it will leave pollen grains from a previously visited flower. Then the insect must squeeze beneath an anther, the male organ, where clumps of sticky pollen grains adhere to its back. Light penetrating a translucent patch on the back wall of the pouch draws the visitor to where the margins and hairs turn outward and allow it to escape. This order of events makes self-pollination unlikely.

Although scientists knew as early as 1793 that some species in the orchid genus *Orchis* do not reward pollinators, biologists have only recently explained how the system works. Bumblebees visiting orchids expend time and energy but gain nothing for their efforts. Only bees that twice fall into the same unrewarding trap will transfer pollen between flowers. All else being equal, individual bees that avoid orchids should have more time and energy available for their own reproductive activities and, thus, produce more offspring than tricked bees. It thus seems that the pollination of today's orchids depends on insects whose ancestors were favored by natural selection to actually avoid orchids. Here is a paradox.

If natural selection favors individual bees that are not deceived, or deceived less frequently, bees should pollinate lady's-slippers less effectively with each passing bee generation. Although we know that in some areas many pink lady's-slipper flowers go unpollinated and experience low fruit set, we do not have crucial long-term data on pollination frequency, and so cannot address this issue.

Using a different approach, let us examine this seemingly counterproductive pollination system from each party's perspective. From the insect's point of view, it is called "mistaken pollination." Visits to a flower are mistakes by the pollinator caused by unrewarding flowers mimicking rewarding ones, in this case via colors and smells. From the plant's point of view, though, no mistake is involved; so-called "chance pollination" is an adaptation maintained by a low recurrence of fertilization.

A degree of naïveté by the insect is requisite for the pollination of nonrewarding flowers. After one or a few mistakes, though, many pollinators avoid such flowers. As a result, seed set is better when pollinators have just emerged from metamorphosis — while they are still naïve — than when they are experienced. The reproductive capacity, and thereby population density, of lady's-slippers are limited by the pollinator's learning ability. For chance pollination to work, orchid densities must be low. If plants grow in a dense stand, there are more chances for negative reinforcement of the insect, leading to less efficient pollination, than if the orchids are sparse. This paradoxical pollination system is the first improbable step in a lady's-slipper's life.

The second oddity involves germination. The seed capsules of orchids contain thousands of tiny, dustlike seeds, a condition called microspermy. Orchid seeds, among the smallest produced by any flowering plant, rarely are longer than one-twelfth of an inch and may be as small as one-hundredth of an inch. Their tiny size allows orchid seeds to float through the atmosphere for vast distances, a trait that may have contributed to the cosmopolitan distributions of some species.

Each seed, a small round mass of cells within an outer transparent coat, lacks endosperm, the food-storage tissue of common seeds like corn. How do tiny seeds with no food germinate successfully?

They have help. Throughout the plant kingdom, microspermous plants are either mycorrhizal or parasitic. Orchids exemplify the former — they maintain a mutually beneficial relationship with a fungus. For a seed to find the correct fungus requires widespread dispersal, accomplished by legions of small, lightweight seeds.

North American lady's-slipper seedlings lead subterranean lives for several years. The pink and showy lady's-slippers do not produce a green leaf above the ground until their third year of life. Because an interred life precludes photosynthesis, lady's-slippers seedlings are unable to grow without a fungal "infection".

In contrast, some other orchid species have seedlings that grow at the surface. Such seedlings can photosynthesize and may grow slowly without mycorrhiza, although even here at least some fungal participation seems to help. In general, species of sunny, wet habitats have green seedlings that grow rapidly; species of the forest, like our lady's-slippers, produce slow-growing underground seedlings.

The health of young orchids seems to depend on the mycorrhiza. The fungus invades the entire root system of its host. The host's roots digest part of the fungus and nutrients collected by the fungus. A hormonal feedback ensures that neither party dominates the relationship: Fungi secrete a substance that stimulates the orchid's root to produce orchinol, a compound that, in turn, inhibits fungal growth. The few individual lady's-slippers that squeeze through the bottleneck of germinating with the proper mycorrhizal infection settle into a pattern of slow growth and long life. Even as adults, some individuals return to subterranean life, then emerge a few years later and flower.

Now when I trip over a pink lady's-slipper in the woods, I feel awe over the sheer improbability of it all. First, bees have to be tricked into visiting nonrewarding flowers — not just once, but twice. And second, one of a million helpless, dustlike seeds must land by raw luck on a spot with not only the right conditions for germination, but the appropriate fungus for root infection and underground life. Although this sequence of events strikes me as colossally improb-

55

able, the roulette has obviously been working. The next time you bend down and mumble compliments to its pretty flower, think of the odds that plant has beat. You might come to admire that lady's-slipper for reasons more profound than its delicate pastel.

9

Sexual Decisions
of Jack-in-the-Pulpit

J ack-in-the-pulpit, a knee-high, deciduous, perennial herb of eastern North America, is one of over one hundred related species
found mainly in the temperate forests of China, Japan, and India.
Only two species of this disjunct group inhabit North America.
Widely distributed from Maine to Florida and west to the prairie's
edge, Jack-in-the-pulpit thrives in the moist, species-rich woods
of Appalachia, in some places forming dense populations of up to
five plants per square yard. This arum, a member of the plant family
Araceae, is a typical forest herb in that it has an extended juvenile
period and a long life span, low rates of growth and adult mortality,
and clonal reproduction. Jack-in-the-pulpit survives the winter as
a dormant corm, or underground stem, and as the canopy closes in
the spring, a bud emerges from the soil, leaves expand, and a single
unusual flower unfurls. A very exceptional flower, indeed.

This plant offers two lessons about sex. First, why reproduce
sexually? Jack-in-the-pulpit populations usually harbor a fungus infection that reduces the area and longevity of its leaves, thereby reducing the plant's acquisition of resources. Infected plants produce
42 percent fewer asexual progeny (cormlets), all of which are infected; all seeds (sexually produced) from both infected and healthy
parents are uninfected. These observations are consistent with the
hypothesis that pathogen attacks have favored the evolution of sexual reproduction. Sex is an evolutionary counter to disease.

The second lesson is about changing gender. The flower develops at the end of a fleshy column and is surrounded by a modified leaf, or spathe, that wraps around and forms a hood over the bloom. The floral spike bears flowers with either anthers, the male organs, or stigmas, the female organs. During any given season, each plant functions as either a male or as a female. A single individual plant can change sex from year to year — female one year, male the next.

Small flies, specifically several species of fungus gnats, are tricked into pollinating the flowers, from which they apparently receive no reward. As they look for mushrooms in which to lay their eggs, the flies are lured — probably by smell — into the flowers. Once inside, the fly is trapped and can only move downward. Pollen grains cling to the gnats' hairs and bristles, and pollination occurs when the gnat visits another flower. Flies can escape male flowers through a gap where the spathe folds over upon itself; female flowers lack this feature, so flies die within.

In some locations, female plants produce few seeds, a sign of inefficient or unreliable pollination. Due to forest fragmentation, fungus gnats may be less common today, and therefore less effective at pollination than in presettlement days.

The fruit takes most of the summer to mature, first enlarging and greening, then turning into a bright red berry by late summer. A fruit cluster may have one to many berries. The seeds within the berries disperse in the autumn when the stalk breaks or animals pick the berries. Seeds germinate the following year.

Stored in the thick corm, the plant's food reserves will be used for next year's leaves. Because reserves are not used for growth or repair of tissues in the current year, neither the plant nor its leaves grow after they develop in the spring. Possibly because these plants cannot repair themselves, the leaves, corm, and green berries are protected from herbivores by crystals of calcium oxalate, sharp little points that embed themselves in the grazer's mucous membranes.

By first frost, the embryonic cells of next year's leaves and flower have formed within a bud at the top of the corm. Dormant corms reveal their future clearly: Large corms will produce two leaves and bear next year's female flower; smaller, one-leaved corms usually produce male flowers; the smallest corms will form no flowers at all. In essence, by late summer the plant has made a developmental decision about which sex to be the following year based on the level of its reserves. In the closely related Japanese species, corm weight is also strongly related to sex: 91 percent of corms weighing 0.5 to 0.8 ounce yield males, 65 percent of the corms weighing 0.9 to 1.2 ounces develop into females, and virtually all corms heavier than 1.3 ounces become female. Gender expression appears related to size or physiological condition, and since individuals grow with age, over a lifetime they tend to change sex from male to female.

In making its sexual switches, the plant's growth seems to follow an internal debate: "Should I produce one or two leaves? Should I produce a male or female flower, or none at all?" This mock monologue is laced with contingencies: "If I am a medium-sized plant and have had a good year, I will produce buds for two large leaves and a female flower, but if I have just barely replaced my reserves, I will form just one leaf and a male flower bud. If I have had an outright bad year, I will not produce a flower at all."

Such fictional introspection also applies to the Japanese relative. When females of the Japanese species were transplanted to a site with poor growth conditions, most switched to male the following spring. When males were cultured under excellent growth conditions, most developed as females the next year.

In natural populations of Jack-in-the-pulpit, individuals change sex frequently. At one site in New York, 8 percent of non-flowering plants, 64 percent of the males, and 63 percent of the females changed their sex from one year to the next. Thus, there are two patterns of sex change: going from no flower to male to female with steady growth, and changing back-and-forth between male and female with reversals in body size. Both of these sequences are examples of sequential hermaphroditism, one of the rarest sexual breeding systems in plants. Among plants other than Jack-in-the-pulpit, only a few species of orchids, the striped maple (another Appalachian species), and two species of juniper also practice sequential hermaphroditism.

Back at the New York site, 60 to 80 percent of the female plants failed to set seed. When these same plants were artificially pollinated, seed set increased by a factor of ten, suggesting that in this population seed production is limited by the availability of pollen rather than by the availability of nutrients. It is consistent that in areas where Jack-in-the-pulpit is not pollen limited, plants display signs of nutrient limitation, such as smaller size and a shift to maleness.

With that background, let us try to determine why Jack-in-the-pulpits change sex. The most widely accepted hypothesis, called the size-advantage model, includes two general predictions. First, sex will change if the age- or size-specific expectations of reproductive success are different for males and females. For example, plants will change from male to female if larger plants are able to produce more successful offspring from seeds than smaller plants can by producing pollen. And second, sex will change at the size where the reproductive successes for the two sexes are equal. Specifically, plants will change sex at the size at which the number of seeds produced by females equals the number of seeds fertilized by males.

An important element of this theory is the idea that females allocate more of their resources to reproduction than males do. Regardless of the plant's size, male flowers represent about 8 percent of the plant's biomass, whereas female flowers represent 10 to 20 percent of the plant's biomass in large and medium-sized females, respectively. Simply put, the physiological costs of reproduction are greater for females than males. A small individual would have difficulty paying the cost of being female. By reproducing as a male when it is small, the plant avoids prohibitive costs and frees resources for growth.

That makes good sense theoretically, but in some populations reproductive success appears linked less to plant size and limited more by available pollinators than the size-advantage hypothesis assumes. All Jack-in-the-pulpit populations exhibit a minimum size below which female reproduction is prohibitively costly. This threshold creates selection for sex-changing. But because seed production and sex ratio vary from year to year, the strength of the selection pressures for maleness vs. femaleness also fluctuate. Such variation makes it unlikely that in such areas Jack-in-the-pulpit will ever attain the simple nonreproducing-to-male-to-female sex-changing sequence described by the size-advantage theory.

In a population near Concord, Massachusetts, female Jack-in-the-pulpits do exhibit greater reproductive output with increasing plant size. This population conforms to the assumptions of the size-advantage model: it seems to be less pollinator-limited and more nutrient-limited. With this assumption of the theory met, ecologists calculated the theoretical size at which plants should sexually transform, i.e., the size at which 50 percent are of each sex. Sure enough, the optimal and observed switch points were similar: when a plant reached a height of about fifteen inches. The size-advantage model had predictive power for this population.

Plants that alter their gender seem to do so in response to environmental factors that vary unpredictably. The general tendency among many animal and plant species, including Jack-in-the-pulpit, is for stress to induce maleness, where stress is defined as conditions that reduce growth, survival, or ability to allocate resources to reproduction. Like Jack-in-the-pulpit, some hermaphroditic orchid species also function as females in sunlight and males in shade — with shade and sunlight being transient features in the forest. When neighboring trees of equal height knock into one another, abrasion of buds, leaves, and branches create and maintain "crown shyness" gaps. Much of the light reaching the ground passes through such gaps, which seem to be unpredictable through space and time. Individual Jack-in-the-pulpits are rooted in spots that provide a variable and unpredictable energy supply.

Many forest herbs are in the same unpredictable ecological situation, and yet, sexual hermaphroditism is extremely rare. Why don't more ground cover plants exhibit sex reversal? Three published hypotheses have been proposed to answer this question. First, the energetic costs of making the sexual change — retooling, if you will — may lead to increased mortality or time taken away from breeding. Second, anatomical constraints may hinder an evolution from individuals having separate sexes to those with sex reversal. And third, opposite selection pressures — favoring male versus female functions — may cancel each other out. I add a fourth: sex change may be more common than we are aware, just undetected.

In the last few years, biologists have discovered sex reversal in a wide variety of plants and animals. Wrasses on Caribbean coral reefs and snails in the Amazon also display reversible gender, apparently for the same size-based reasons. And here, beneath the canopy of our Appalachian deciduous forest, lives one of the Earth's stars of sex reversal, the Jack-in-the-pulpit.

10

Nuptial Gift of the Hangingfly

Herbs tickle my arms as I sit on the ground in a cove forest watching the sex life of the black-tipped hangingfly. I'm close enough to see the medium-sized (0.8 inch), slim, brownish body, long thin legs, and four narrow, black-tipped wings of each hangingfly. Named for their habit of dangling from foliage by their front legs, they hang with wings outstretched rather than folded over their abdomens. Hangingflies superficially resemble long, slender, delicate flies but are not true flies, which are members of the order Diptera; they just look like them. In central and southern Appalachia, you will find the hangingfly's story easy to follow — they fly slowly over short distances, catching prey and mating throughout the day.

Research on the black-tipped hangingfly's behavior has revealed a complex blend of courtship, nuptial giving, thievery, and sexual prevarication. Although the male and female hangingflies look similar, their behaviors are markedly different — and therein lies the tale.

The male hangingfly uses his strong rear legs to capture houseflies, daddy longlegs, and other arthropods. While holding prey with the prehensile segment of his last leg, he catches onto a leaf or twig. He prepares the meal by piercing the prey with his needlelike snout and injecting digestive juices that paralyze the insect and liquefy its innards. After a brief taste, the male hangingfly may discard the prey; but if he retains it, he begins making short (less than twelve feet) flights through the ground cover. After each flight, he hangs from a leaf or twig and everts a pair of abdominal glands that release a

67

pheromone, a specific molecule that carries a message to a receiver. (Some biologists have suggested that a man's sweat contains a sexual pheromone that excites women. Not so in my experience!)

A female hangingfly responds to the male's pheromonal invitation by settling beside him, then hanging by her forelegs facing him. She signals sexual readiness by lowering her wings, which stimulates the male to present his gift of food. Both are initially hesitant and noncommittal: While the female evaluates the prey by feeding on it, she keeps her abdominal tip pulled away from the male. The male retains a firm grip on the prey with both hind legs and one or two middle legs.

With these behaviors, each member of the consort pair enters a conditional contract: If the prey is unpalatable or too small, the female flies away unmated or after having allowed copulation for a short time, an average of only five minutes. If on the other hand, she finds the nuptial gift to be satisfactory, she allows a lengthy copulation. In this latter situation, mating lasts an average of twenty-three minutes, during which the female feeds on the offering. Female black-tipped hangingflies select or reject mates on the basis of their food offering — much like humans.

Dr. Randy Thornhill of the University of New Mexico has discovered a tense battle between selfish individuals underlying this apparent romance, each fly pursuing its own reproductive priorities. Another look at the hangingfly's mating behavior reveals the brutal details.

Hunting is a dangerous activity for hangingflies. It not only costs time but exposes them to the webs of predatory spiders. Hangingflies have evolved several methods to reduce these costs. Female hangingflies do not hunt when their own males are abundant. When they do hunt, they retain the prey items. In contrast, males discard about 32 percent of the prey items as unpalatable or too small. This intersexual difference suggests that females reduce their odds of falling prey by allowing copulation in exchange for food.

Trading a meal for sex makes the male more vulnerable than the female to predation by spiders. Males have evolved a strategy for reducing their risks during hunting. They may capture free-ranging arthropods, as reported above, or they may steal prey from other males. Although a male with prey is a potential theft victim while feeding, flying, and copulating, he is most vulnerable when releasing pheromone because at that particular moment he is physiologically programmed to receive a female.

Fully 50 percent of a male's time between copulations is spent searching for prey. Males that steal rather than hunt for themselves reduce that unproductive interval by 42 percent, thereby obtaining more copulations than nonpirates. Further, because thieves move about less than hunters, they are less likely to get ensnared in a spider web. Thus, stealing food brings two benefits to a male: increasing the rate of mating and decreasing the odds of being eaten.

How a particular male obtains prey, by hunting or stealing, seems to depend on what he encounters first, a free-living arthropod or another male hangingfly carrying prey. This mixed hunting strategy may have evolved because the male's success at stealing depends on the density and sex ratio of fellow hangingflies, both of which seem to vary unpredictably through time and space.

Male hangingflies employ two equally common styles of prey snatching. A male may (a) fly forcefully into another male or into a mated pair, then grapple for the prey; or the thief may (b) behave like a typical female and deceive the male into giving up his prey. Transvestites fly up to a pheromone-releasing male and lower their wings, normally the female's signal that she is ready to copulate. About one-third of the time, the male with prey flies away undeceived, but in the rest of the bouts he presents his gift to the female-mimic. With both males gripping the prey, the mimic begins to feed. While the courting male attempts to copulate, the mimic keeps his abdomen out of range, just as a female would. This may continue for a couple of minutes before the owner tries to retrieve the prey from the mimic's grasp. In about one-third of the cases, the mimic successfully secures a hold on the prey and flies off with it. Like food thievery, female mimicry leads to more prey and mates, and lowers the odds of getting snared by a web. Female-mimics succeed because the sexes are similar in appearance, giving courting males few cues to warn them of impending theft.

69

The relationship *between* the sexes is also fraught with tension. As I said, the average successful copulation lasts twenty-three minutes, after which the male normally terminates mating. In an ensuing struggle, the male tries to uncouple from the female and pull the food item from her grasp. After separating, the male feeds briefly on the prey, and if he finds that it is still satisfactory, he repeats the pheromone-emitting and mating sequence. In this fashion, a single prey item may yield up to three successive copulations. Prey items in the size range of 1.1 to 1.8 inches square are most frequently employed twice. Smaller prey do not offer enough nourishment for more than one meal, and larger food items are too difficult to hold during the postmating struggle. If the prey has little nutritive substance left, the male discards it and hunts for another. Males win 64 percent of the struggles for final possession of prey; females only 8 percent. In the remaining 28 percent of the battles, the prey items drop onto the leaf litter.

Male-terminated copulations result in maximum insemination and turn off the female's sexual receptivity. A mated female hangs from vegetation for about three hours and drops an average of three eggs onto the ground. Thereafter, females are ready again to eat and copulate.

Females, then, discriminate among males at two levels. If the meal is inadequate, she may reject the male before copulation, or if the courtship proceeds, she may terminate coupling before the male transfers a full complement of sperm. The duration of copulation is important because of the positive correlation between the length of time coupled and the number of sperm transferred. Five minutes of copulation, which typically accompanies a small nuptial gift, must pass before any sperm are transferred and before the female is stimulated to lay any eggs. For matings five to twenty minutes long, the number of sperm transferred increases with time elapsed; after twenty minutes sperm delivery ceases. Males with small or unpalatable prey mate only briefly and transfer little or no sperm, whereas males offering large tasty meals enjoy prolonged matings and maximum insemination. Natural selection has favored females that accept large, nutritious prey because this superior resource fortifies their eggs.

At first glance, the black-tipped hangingfly seems to be acting in a romance: males sally forth to capture prey, court females by offering these nuptial gifts, and then mate blissfully. However, competition and tension between and within the sexes are the real forces that shape this Appalachian scene. Capturing the arthropod gift involves risks that males try to avoid by stealing from each other, either by direct assault or by mimicking females. On the other side of the relationship, a female will not accept a male's sperm until she is assured of a sufficiently nourishing meal. After mating, the conjugal partners even struggle over the leftovers. Although left feeling robbed of a romantic tale, I receive a deeper satisfaction from understanding how complex — dare I say humanlike? — a small Appalachian insect can be.

11

Femmes Fatales of Twilight

S ummer in Appalachia has its share of magical moments. For me such a time comes when I squeeze out through my second story window, settle on the porch roof, and survey the firefly meadow.

> Here come real stars to fill the upper skies,
> And here on earth come emulating flies
> That, though they never equal stars in size
> (And they were never really stars at heart),
> Achieve at times a very starlike start.
> Only, of course, they can't sustain the part.

In his poem *Fireflies in the Garden*, Robert Frost is so taken by the spectacle that he flirts with equating fireflies and stars, but in a final line of reflection, demurs. Poetic license is fair, but he was wise to change his mind, for beneath the twinkling pageant is a society of liars and cannibals.

Fireflies make up a family of beetles that emit light from specialized tissue in the ends of their abdomens. Male fireflies typically crisscross an area, flashing rhythmically. Females remain stationary on the ground or in a bush and respond to males with their own flashes. When a male receives an answer, he hovers and orients his lantern toward the female. Eventually, he lands near her, and they mate.

Each firefly species has its own unique male signal and female response. Among species, the signals and responses vary in the color, number, duration, modulation, rate, and intensity of the light emissions, the rate of repetition of the pattern, and the speed, altitude, time of day, season, habitat, and maneuvers of flight. All this variety enables us human observers, with practice, to identify many species by their flash codes alone.

It seems counterintuitive, then, that only the timing of the flash has been shown to play a role in a firefly's ability to identify a member of its species. For males, the parameters of timing involved in this communication include frequency, duration, and pause between flashes. The most critical characteristic of the female's response is her delay in answering the male's flash. The time lag preceding a female's reply varies among species from three to nine seconds.

Before we allow this scene of firefly behavior to get more complex, let's explore a basic, no-frills example. Males of *Photinus pyralis*, the most widespread species of firefly in North America, begin flashing at dusk, typically about three feet above the ground. Each flash lasts about one-half second, and the male repeats it about every seven seconds. Emitted during the upswing following a short swoop, the flash looks like an upward arc of light. On the ground, receptive females answer with a one-half-second flash three seconds after the male's. His visual display is not meant to attract a female of his own species, rather to persuade a receptive female to reveal her location.

Add the research findings of Dr. James Lloyd of the University of Florida and the plot thickens. In a firefly meadow, males greatly outnumber females. Because competition for females is keen, a male spends much of his time searching for females. When answered, he must reach and mate the female before other males converge. Given this much, we could logically conclude that natural selection should favor males that locate, reach, and copulate with receptive females as soon as possible. The catch is that the male's bright advertisement and scramble for mates make him vulnerable to exploitation — by other fireflies.

Of the three major genera of fireflies in North America, two (*Photuris* and *Photinus*) carry on a complex, intriguing relationship. (A warning: Keep these two genera straight.) Let us first focus on the behavior of fireflies in the genus *Photuris*.

74

Prior to mating, a virgin *Photuris versicolor* female answers almost exclusively the triple-pulsed flash of males of her own species. About three days after mating, she takes a station on or near the ground, stands erect with her jaws open, and begins to mimic the flash response characteristic of females of other species. She even credibly imitates the other species' latency. No longer interested in mating, she is now a predator. When her successful flash response attracts a male of another species, she pounces and devours him. In such femmes fatales, mating seems to induce the switch from receptive virgin to voracious predator. Apparently, something transferred with the sperm initiates the transformation.

This type of predation, called aggressive mimicry, has been reported for ten species of *Photuris* fireflies. At least three more species are suspects. In fact, further research will probably reveal that most species of the genus *Photuris* can switch on predatory behavior.

The females of some *Photuris* species prey on males of more than one species. So far, the extreme example of this type of versatility is *Photuris versicolor*, whose females prey on males of at least eleven other firefly species. These virtuosos readily adjust both the form and timing of their flashes in response to all these different male flash patterns.

Females of various *Photuris* species have been caught ambushing male fireflies in Appalachian locations from Massachusetts to Georgia. As this story continues to unfold, aggressive mimicry will almost surely be found throughout the entire Appalachian chain.

Why do *Photuris* females prey on other fireflies? Fireflies spend their first few years of life as larvae in the soil, then live as adults for only one to four weeks. Food they acquired as larvae permits adult females to produce some eggs, but protein gained via predation augments their fecundity. Thus, through aggressive mimicry a female firefly increases the number, and possibly the quality, of the eggs she produces.

The risk of falling prey to aggressive mimics has led to the evolution of counteradaptations in males. *Photinus* males (that's the other genus) do not just fly directly to a responding female; instead, they fly close, hover, back away, reapproach, and flash repeatedly. The male's ambivalence reflects a conflict: Should he pursue a seemingly receptive female and risk the predator's jaws, or dally and lose the copulation to another male? The male's compromise: if he lands, he does so several feet from the female and then approaches cautiously on foot.

For the male, the risk of being eaten is significant. In *Photinus collustrans*, for example, males are answered by up to five times as many predaceous *Photuris* females as by females of their own species. In one study, 16 percent of the males lured by females were duped and eaten.

Aggressive mimicry by *Photuris* females may have influenced another aspect of the evolution of firefly behavior: it may be the reason that males of most *Photinus* species fly at twilight rather than at dark. If a *Photinus* male can spy the silhouette of a larger *Photuris* female, showing a shape and stance different from that of his own females, he can stop short of the poised jaws.

Photuris females of several species have evolved another predatory tactic — aerial predation. Guided by their prey's luminescence, *Photuris* females attack flying male fireflies at night. These "sidewinder hawkers" sometimes use the aerial strategy together with aggressive signal mimicry.

And it gets even more bizarre. The males of one *Photinus* species display an alternate mating strategy that exploits aggressive mimicry. The normal flash pattern of *Photinus macdermotti* males is two short flashes, two seconds apart. While he is on the ground courting a female, a male sometimes injects a flash into the last one-quarter of the interval between the flashes of an approaching rival male. The timing of these injections matches the flashes that the predaceous females of two *Photuris* species occasionally — and apparently by mistake — emit. Thus, the courting *Photinus* male appears to be mimicking the accidental injection flash of predatory *Photuris* females. Injected flashes slow the approach of converging males, thereby extending the first male's sexual monopoly of the female. This neat trick is an example of the mimicry of a mimicry.

Even the males of some *Photuris* species exhibit mimicry, although not for predatory purposes. Some *Photuris* males duplicate the male flash of species that may be prey of their own *Photuris* females. They restrict the decoy signals to the habitats, seasons, and daily periods of the prey. If a hunting *Photuris* female answers and approaches the imitating *Photuris* male, he quickly grabs and inseminates her. Thus, *Photuris* males exploit their own female's mimicry to increase the odds of gaining a copulation. Since mating causes *Photuris* females to change from male-seeking to prey-seeking, males pursuing this strategy run a serious risk of being cannibalized.

Variation exists here too. Males of *Photuris* species can mimic the male flash patterns of two or more *Photinus* species. Some *Photuris* males can shift back and forth between their own species' flash pattern and those of other species that are simultaneously active. This also seems to be a strategy for increasing the pool of potential mates.

Understanding the last layer of complexity requires Herculean concentration because it combines the ideas of injection flashes and males mimicking males. When a predatory *Photuris versicolor* female mimics the flash of *Photinus macdermotti* females, the predator may produce extra flashes that mimic the injected flashes used by males that are competing for females. Such injections are made during the last 0.6 second of the rival's flash pattern. By mimicking competition flashes, *Photuris* females draw more *Photinus* males to the general area and thereby improve their chances of a successful hunt. This is an example of a female mimicking a female mimicking a male that is mimicking a predaceous female.

How did such a complex, interdependent system of behavioral mimicry evolve? Apparently, a step-by-step evolutionary arms race has been responsible. Initially *Photinus* may have produced only simple flashes of fixed duration, whereas *Photuris* may have shown variability. The latter presumably demanded a higher order of neural processing by the female, which in turn may have allowed the evolution of changeable female responses, the prerequisite for predation. Opportunistically, the males of some prey species may have incorporated deceit in their mating signals to maximize their own mating success.

Here's a pleasing finish to the story. We have known for several decades that some firefly species of tropical southeast Asia flash in rhythmic synchrony. Congregated in trees, males emit a concentrated light beacon that attracts females through the thick jungle vegetation. As I was finalizing the original edition of *Hollows*, synchronic flashing was first being studied in Appalachia. Although local folks had long known of "the light show" in a clearing in the Great Smoky Mountains, biologists began studying it in 1993. *Photinus carolinus* males emit five to eight flashes in unison over four seconds, stop for fifteen seconds, then do it again. In this "concurrent rhythmic group flashing," many males flash repeatedly, regularly, and at the same time.

What is the adaptive significance of this synchrony? The researchers suggest that, as in the tropics, the bright light seems to attract females through dense forest. Perhaps the darkness between bouts allows males to see the female's weak flash. I offer a third hypothesis: the concentrated extra-bright light helps males detect predaceous females, thus representing a recent step in this predator-prey escalation. As with many traits, group flashing may have several functions, so all three hypotheses may have roles.

We knew all along that fireflies were not very much like stars. But when I contemplate my firefly meadow now, my mind vacillates between the romance evoked by twinkling lights and the logical fatalism provoked by ambush. The bard was right in withdrawing the parity, but for reasons far more intricate than he may have suspected.

12

Small Fishes
in Shallow Headwaters

As drivers of Appalachian dirt roads, we are at least subliminally aware of the schools of fish that dash madly about as we splash through a ford. The most common fishes (two or more fish species) flushed by our tires are members of the minnow, sucker, sunfish, and perch families. Within these comparatively few taxa, Appalachia's numerous small, steep streams have catalyzed the evolution of a great fish diversity.

Many fishes native to Appalachia live in the alternating pools and riffles of headwater streams. These habitats are shallow, subject to torrential spates and bone-dry droughts; the fish dwellers are exposed to predation by raccoons, snakes, and herons. How do small fish persist in shallow headwaters?

During spring and autumn, when streams flow abundantly, fish can move freely among pools before settling down for the season. Once established, fish seldom wander, even when moderate water levels allow them to explore other pools. One study found that after summer flash floods, 75 percent of the fish could still be found in their original, pre-flood locations. Darters and sunfishes in particular exhibit this kind of site loyalty.

If winters are so cold that fish risk being frozen in shallow water, they migrate from their springtime spawning grounds in shallow headwaters to deeper overwintering reaches farther downstream. Presumably, natural selection has favored young adults that return to

81

breed in their own home pool — one of the best indicators of future reproductive success is that one's parents successfully reproduced there. Each creek, even each pool in a single reach, probably holds a unique cocktail of chemical odors, part of which becomes indelibly imprinted in the memory of juvenile fish during their first summer. We know that coho salmon imprint on naturally occurring chemical cues for homing. The salmon's homing response is highly specific: molecules with atomic structures that differ slightly from the stimulating molecule do not elicit the homing response.

Assuming that small fish in Appalachian streams use chemical cues to return to their home pool, an important part of the story still remains a mystery — what molecules provide pool-specific cues? Root exudates, the organic molecules released by the roots of trees, are a possibility. The number of combinations of different organic molecules comprising the exudate constellation in soil and water must be enormous, and their tree sources remain relatively stable over the long term.

In Pine Cabin Run and thousands of other Appalachian headwaters, adult creek chubs prey on blacknose dace and cannibalize juvenile creek chubs. Adult creek chubs themselves fall prey to belted kingfishers and green herons. How do small fish in shallow headwater pools escape larger predators?

Where shelter is limited, adult creek chubs aggregate under cover during the day. At night, when the birds are gone, they disperse to find their prey. Where shelter is plentiful, adult chubs do not aggregate. Young chubs employ a combination of camouflage and stillness, finding cover beneath leaves and other small objects. As you might expect, in pools that host predators, prey density increases with the complexity of cover provided by rocks, limbs, and overhangs. Both predator and prey choose pools that minimize their odds of falling prey.

Countershading, body coloration that combines a dark back and light belly, also reduces the odds of being eaten. Viewed from below, a fish with a pale belly presents less of a contrast against the sky than one with a dark underside. The dark back camouflages a fish from aerial fish-eating birds. A fish with a light back and dark belly would be obvious to predatory fishes from all directions.

Yet another way to avoid being eaten is to hide behind another individual. The random movements and indistinguishability of individuals within a school preclude the predator from fixating on one individual.

A fascinating adaptation for reducing one's odds of being eaten is the alarm system, a method of communication in which a fish emits an alarm substance that elicits fright in pool mates. Two major groups of bony fishes — one including chubs, dace, and catfishes; and the other containing perch and darters — rely on alarm systems. Large, specialized cells, called club cells, produce the alarm substance, rupturing and releasing their contents when the skin is injured. Nearby fish of the same species smell the alarm substance and display a fright reaction. Each species, even each developmental stage, exhibits a fright reaction suited to its own specific predators. A species that normally schools may tighten, flee, and avoid the site of the stimulus. Other species swim against the bottom and stir up a cloud of silt. Some freeze on the bottom and rely on camouflage for protection. Adult creek chubs sink to the bottom individually, but juveniles flee as a school. Although individuals respond most strongly to the alarm substance released by other members of their species, fright reaction is not completely species-specific. The alarm substance of some fishes may elicit fright reaction in members of other, closely related species.

The fright reaction may even visually signal other members of the same species. For example, when two aquaria are placed together, an alarm-substance-induced fright reaction in one tank will trigger a fright reaction in fish of the adjacent tank, even though there is no exchange of water between the two tanks. Thus, this adaptation allows quick chemical and visual communication of danger among the fish in a pool.

The individuals of some species lose their alarm substance cells, but not necessarily the fright reaction, during the breeding season. Seasonal loss of the ability to alarm evolved to complement abrasive spawning habits. At the onset of the spring breeding season, male fathead minnows lose the cells that contain alarm substance. This allows males to clean a site and spawn by rubbing against pebbles without releasing alarm substance that would frighten away interested females. In the fall, males resume their production of alarm substance.

Since *Hollows'* original edition, ichthyologists have added several layers to this story. Alarm substance has now been found in marine fishes, specifically two species of gobies.

The alarm system functions across species. After detecting alarm pheromone released by fathead minnows, brook sticklebacks avoid the labeled area. The sticklebacks continue to stay away for several hours after the source of the alarm has left. Reciprocally, fathead minnows, and also finescale dace, avoid areas marked with the sticklebacks' skin extract. Because two-way information exchange has not been demonstrated, I decline for now to call this interspecific communication.

A third recent twist to this story is that alarm substance passes through predators. Fathead minnows show their typical fright reaction in the presence of feces from a northern pike that has eaten minnows. The minnow's alarm pheromone is incorporated in the pike's feces. The pike may also release minnow pheromone via urine, mucus, or respiration. Thus, minnows may be able to recognize a new predator based solely on the predator's diet. As an apparent counteradaptation to fecal recognition, pikes defecate away from their foraging area.

Fourth, the alarm signal functions as a learned response. Fathead minnows learn to recognize a predator when alarm substance occurs with the sighting of an unfamiliar fish. European minnows develop a fright response to pike if exposed to alarm pheromone and pike simultaneously. This learned response, which is specific to the predator species used in conditioning, not just to any large fish, is retained for at least sixty-nine days. The specificity of this response is adaptive because reacting to any large fish as if it were a predator would waste energy and lessen feeding time.

Lastly, the alarm signal system can even function without alarm pheromone. Naïve minnows present during the fright reaction of conditioned individuals begin showing the antipredator behavior and then respond when tested alone. Thus, avoidance of risky areas can be learned through cultural transmission without the stimuli of either predators or alarm pheromone.

The alarm signal system of fishes resembles warning signals of other animals — alarm calls of birds, tail flagging by deer, and alarm pheromones of tadpoles — in that they appear to be altruistic. Over the past several decades, biologists have been trying to understand how such seemingly sacrificial signaling systems could have evolved. If there is an evolutionary cost to the sender, such as producing and maintaining alarm substance cells or putting the sender at risk of predation, the trait is entitled to be called an adaptation. However, if the substance eliciting fright is merely a normal bodily fluid that leaks passively, it may not be eligible for the status. Because the club cells in the skin seem to have no function other than to synthesize and store alarm substance, I conclude that warning others has a cost.

The most likely evolutionary explanation for this adaptation seems to be kin selection. Recall that young fish return to their natal pool. Although fish in a school may not be full siblings, their site loyalty suggests that they are related. Kin selection could operate in a straightforward manner: individuals releasing alarm substance may increase the odds that nearby genetic relatives become aware of a predator. The alarm pheromone might even reduce cannibalism by inducing fright in a large fish of the same species, thereby saving siblings.

Kin selection is easier to invoke if genetic relatives are spatially near each other. Even if kin disperse widely and non-relatives school together, kin still might be able to favor each other. Recent evidence suggests that fish can identify relatives through chemical cues. In fact, in a wide variety of animals, an individual's odor is in part determined by its genes. Small fish in Appalachian headwater pools may be able to identify kin solely through olfaction, and then favor them with alarm signals. It is awesome to consider the possibility that scattered throughout Appalachia's hollows are brothers, sisters, and first cousins clustered in pools reciprocating favors while slighting unrelated poolmates.

The other day as I drove my old truck through the ford of Pine Cabin Run, I tried to follow the streaking dace, my mind checking off the components of this intricate scene. It was daytime, so the dace were safe from predatory creek chubs who lurked under the rock ledge. Their countershading made them doubly hard to follow as they zig-zagged randomly within the school. I wondered whether any of them might have burst a few club cells and released a little alarm substance. It's getting harder all the time to simply splash through the ford and step on the gas.

13

Darter Daddies

Darters, as brightly colored as rain forest butterflies and coral reef fishes, are the fish analog to lungless salamanders — both have radiated extensively in the fractured landscape of Appalachia.

Darters in the genus *Etheostoma* draw my attention because of their multifarious forms of parental care. Males alone care for the eggs after the females have deposited them. Some lay their eggs on plants, logs, and other exposed substrates; others form a multi-layered cluster of eggs on the undersides of flat-bottomed rocks; the remainder deposit eggs in a single layer directly on the undersides of flat-bottomed rocks. A fish in the last category, the tessellated darter, has intrigued me for several years, especially after I observed in them an unusual behavior among animals: males caring for eggs that were fertilized by other males.

The tessellated darter lives throughout the Atlantic drainages of Appalachia. Male tessellated darters defend flat-bottomed rocks as spawning grounds. When a ripe female approaches a spawning rock, the territorial male flares his fins and quivers his body, then leads her to his rock. Just before she reaches the rock, he scoots under it, inverts belly-up, and begins wiggling across the ceiling. Through this behavior, he seems to be advertising his willingness and ability to clean eggs. In response, she swims under the rock, and inverts and wiggles, probably inspecting the ceiling's quality. If the male's courtship is successful, the female begins depositing eggs, one at a time, directly on the bare rock ceiling. As she attaches each egg, the male

89

simultaneously fertilizes it. After the female deposits ten to fifty eggs in a loose two-dimensional cluster, the male chases her away and begins caring for the eggs. If still gravid, the female may approach another nest and mate again.

The male scrubs the eggs with his ventral fins while swimming upside down. At the nest's entrance and while right-side-up, he aerates eggs by maintaining his position with his pectoral fins and pushing water into the nest with his caudal fin. Both cleaning and aerating the eggs burn calories and preclude other activities, such as courting females. Thus, caring for one batch of eggs reduces the total number of eggs a male could potentially fertilize. So far, this scene does not challenge conventional evolutionary ideas. The quirk is that males routinely clean and aerate eggs fertilized by other males.

The first time I saw a male cleaning eggs I knew had been fertilized by another male, I could feel Darwin's grip squeeze my Adam's apple. It was hard to swallow. Weaned on neo-Darwinian paradigms, I started mumbling to myself on the streambank, alternately feeling excited and confused. The darter's behavior, if consistently displayed by other males of the population, could be an exciting exception to the dogma that the function of behavior is to promote individual reproductive success. Or it could be a distant outlier explainable by extending the concept of natural selection.

During the next three years I dissected the tessellated darter's social system, carrying out a series of experiments to uncover the causes of this altruism. I studied this darter in a small stream that offered only a few rocks suitable for spawning because most rocks were smothered by heavy silt. The silt blanket and a dense population of darters meant there were more adult males than suitable breeding sites. Consequently, only a few large, dominant, territorial males were able to secure a spawning rock. This left smaller males, which composed the majority, without rocks. Small, subordinate males, or floaters, spent most of their time roaming the stream in search of suitable nest rocks.

During his first day of fatherhood, a male scrubs the ceiling, aerates eggs, and repulses potential egg predators. Quite the model father, he swims only an inch or two from his brood. Mother, long gone, contributes nothing thereafter to embryonic survival. When the embryos reach two days of age, father begins to stray. During extended forays several times per hour, he visits a series of other nest rocks, bullies his way into occupied nests, chases off attendant males, and attempts to usurp fertilizations. Cruising male darters embody the tradeoff between monogamous commitment and promiscuous behavior (a conflict exhibited by some male humans).

What opens the door to daddy's profligate behavior? During the first few hours after fertilization, the egg membranes are pliable, and the eggs are only weakly attached to the ceiling. By one day of age, the eggs have become rigid, firmly glued to the rock, and resistant to puncture. Now the eggs are virtually invulnerable, and father can chase females elsewhere without risking his embryos to cannibalism.

After most cruises, father returns to his original nest rock within twenty minutes. Once every two or three days, a cruising male finds a receptive female and spawns again at another rock. Because this restarts his commitment clock with a new brood at a new nest, he abandons his previous clutch.

Father, however, could not remain away without harm befalling his eggs unless another process came into play. Within minutes after a territorial male leaves his nest rock, floating males enter it, invert, and begin wiggling over the ceiling. Floaters sometimes peck at attached eggs, appearing to test their edibility, but almost always give up after a few nibbles. Although floating males that occupy newly vacated rocks gain only a remote chance of attracting a female and fertilizing a few eggs, from an evolutionary perspective a little reproductive success is immensely better than none at all. Because the dominant male's eggs are arranged as a loose cluster in the middle of the ceiling, interstitial and peripheral spaces are available for the floater's spawning. Cleaning the first male's eggs is incidental to the second's cleaning the ceiling for his own spawning. Further, females are stimulated to spawn by a few healthy eggs. Caring for the first male's eggs, then, involves no obvious costs and some benefits for the subordinate male.

91

Dominant males cruise because spawning at more than one rock leads to greater reproductive success than fertilizing a single clutch. In essence, large dominant males sequentially monopolize a series of spawning rocks that are temporarily most desirable to females. Father can get away with abandoning his offspring because of the ready availability of surrogate egg-sitters.

Floating males ensure the survival of eggs they did not fertilize because, in the process of maintaining the ceiling for their own spawning, they incidentally clean and aerate the previously attached clutch. They also clean unrelated eggs to advertise to females that they are effective fathers. Thus, everybody wins. Although the behavior of small males initially appeared altruistic, a few critical experiments demonstrated it is consistent, albeit somewhat anomalous, with conventional evolutionary thought.

Since the original publication of *Hollows*, genetic analyses have confirmed that male tessellated darters defend nests containing offspring they did not sire.

Let us look at this problem from a broader, comparative perspective. The mottled sculpin, like the tessellated darter, also defends nest rocks in Appalachian streams. The list of similarities between the two fishes is long: suitable breeding sites are limited; there are numerous predators and cannibals of eggs; males are larger than females; large males monopolize the most desirable nest rocks; small males are relegated to less desirable sites; and males mate with more than one female. The most frequent egg predators are female mottled sculpins, whose large mouths make them efficient cannibals. Unlike male tessellated darters, sculpin fathers remain with their own eggs until they hatch.

Large male sculpins obtain large spawning sites, and females choose to spawn with large males who are most effective at repelling potential cannibals and least likely to abandon the nest. This is important to the female because she deposits all of her eggs for that year in one discrete hemispherical mass. Field studies have confirmed that sculpin eggs are lost to predators and cannibals less frequently when they are guarded by large males than by small males.

Even though tessellated darters and mottled sculpins share many ecological and behavioral traits, their levels of paternal loyalty differ because darter eggs scattered on a nest ceiling harden and adhere to the point of invulnerability, whereas a clump of sculpin eggs can be eaten in a single bite.

Through such experimental and comparative studies, small, easily overlooked fishes of Appalachian streams have stretched our concept of natural selection. Under unique conditions, natural selection can even favor adults that care for genetically unrelated offspring if the behavior enhances their own reproductive opportunities and entails little cost. In his essay "Altruism," Lewis Thomas reasoned that sacrifice is our duty to each other because, compared to other organisms, we humans share much of our DNA. The darter's act suggests an alternative: one human is more likely to help an unrelated human when the "altruist" gets something out of it — or at least when he loses nothing in the process.

14

To the Brook Trout, with Esteem

I both respect and pity the brook trout. On the one hand, a stream-dwelling population of native brookies elicits admiration, even reverence, for these fish have been self-supporting since their origin — no hatchery-reared fish here. Painful to say, they seem to be losing the evolutionary battle. Brook trout live only in cool, clean water, and that kind of habitat is dwindling. Consider this essay first as a tribute, second as a natural history, and third as an expression of righteous indignation for the plight of a small, noble fish.

A male brook trout in breeding condition — its striking olive body streaked with iridescent red, blue, and white markings — is one of Appalachia's most beautiful fish. The light-colored, worm-like markings on the brook trout's dark green back, evoke a second name, speckled trout. I saw my first native male brook trout decorated in breeding colors in Big Run near Spruce Knob, West Virginia. Viewed through binoculars from the bank, he was elegant, even cocky, hovering assertively as he patrolled his hemlock-shaded pool.

Originally distributed throughout northeastern North America, westward through the Great Lakes, and southward along the Appalachian Mountains, brook trout have been transplanted broadly by conservation agencies. The fish has acclimated to numerous other areas, including the western United States. Like darters, brook trout in Appalachian headwaters maintain separate and discrete populations. These populations probably have been isolated from each other for several thousand years, possibly since post-glacial warming forced them upstream. Such small, isolated populations are vulnerable to inbreeding and extinction.

The only species of the family Salmonidae native to the Appalachians and one of the most important sport fishes in eastern North America, brook trout now inhabit a few headwater streams from Maine to Georgia. Anglers hit large populations so hard that natural age compositions are radically altered. Small populations are especially vulnerable to depletion. As a fisher friend says, "They're dumber than dirt and will bite to the last fish."

Today's brook trout, essentially a Pleistocene relict, occupies a challenging niche: streams that are cold, steep, scoured, well oxygenated, clear, and infertile — and therefore niggardly with food. Although they dwell in some hard-water streams in fertile valleys, brook trout are more abundant in the soft water of infertile mountain creeks. Perhaps the most temperature-sensitive native mountain fish, brookies need colder water than brown and rainbow trouts do. Optimal temperatures range from 50 to 61 degrees Fahrenheit; they seldom inhabit water above 68 degrees Fahrenheit. These trout are also intolerant of silty or turbid water.

Most brook trout streams are unproductive ecosystems whose energy comes from surrounding land. Erosion-resistant Devonian shales and sandstones yield coarse substrates, scarce nutrients and little dissolved solids, and thus clear waters. In these forest-shaded, nutrient-poor streams, slow-growing attached algae provide negligible food. Here, trout tend to grow extremely slowly.

Brookies do not prefer these streams, but are forced into them. In central and southern Appalachia, the species' original range extended from about two thousand one hundred feet above sea level upward to the headwaters. By the turn of the century, brook trout had been excluded from the lower elevations by logging, railroad building, forest fires, overfishing, and transplanted exotic trouts. By 1910 logging companies were stocking trout heavily, a practice that in part allowed much of the brook trout's former range in the southern Appalachians to be monopolized by rainbow and brown trouts. In more modern times, acid rain has been added to the list of the brook trout's stressors.

As warm water, unsuitable habitat, and exotic trouts press the brook trout from lower elevations, freezing water temperatures exclude them from higher country. Appalachian brookies spawn in the fall, during September and October, and their eggs incubate through the winter. At high altitudes in winter, anchor ice and dwindling flows imperil the trout's gravel nests, or redds, exposing them to air and allowing the eggs to freeze.

Brook trout in headwater streams build redds in areas of upwelling spring water along the sides or tails of pools. After the female cuts the redd, the beautifully reddened male fertilizes the eggs as they settle into the gravel. Fecundity ranges from twenty eggs for a four-inch female to two hundred eggs for a seven-and-a-half-inch female. The eggs incubate unattended until spring. Embryonic mortality during long freezes contributes to weak recruitment in higher reaches.

Reproduction drains the fat reserves that could have helped a female survive winter. This is why non-reproducing females survive to spring better than reproducing females. Thus, female brookies incur an increased risk of death during the first winter after they spawn.

Within the gravel, newly hatched brookies depend on their large yolk sacs for nutrition. Larger eggs tend to yield larger fry. After emerging from the gravel in the spring, the fry feed on minute drifting prey, and by July they begin to capture insects at the water's surface. Shortly after emerging from the gravel, a young brook trout begins protecting its food source by defending a territory ranging in size from twenty-five to three hundred square inches. In economic terms, young brook trout can afford to aggressively displace others because the contested area yields more food than the costs of defense. This combative behavior forces weaker individuals into suboptimal habitat.

Brook trout are generally visual, opportunistic predators that eat any animal their mouths can grasp, including insects, crustaceans, fish, even small mammals — but their visual hunting is less effective when high, silt-laden spring runoff obscures prey. One study reported that creek chubs were absent from clear-water streams prowled by sight-oriented brookies, but were abundant in turbid tributaries. In this situation, turbidity promoted a stable coexistence between a predator and its prey.

In their mountain streams, brook trout grow slowly, mature at a small size, and maintain sparse populations. In these habitats, they typically reach only six and a half inches long by three years of age. In contrast, those in fertile streams grow faster, mature at the same age but larger size, and maintain abundant populations. In Pennsylvania, an infertile stream produced only 20 percent of the brook trout pounds per year that a fertile stream yielded.

Annual production of brook trout in a Minnesota stream was tied closely to the abundance of the fish's primary invertebrate food, a small, shrimplike amphipod. When land development intensified in the stream's watershed, the silt load increased, amphipod populations decreased, and the annual production of brook trout dropped by 44 percent — further illustrating the brookies' sensitivity to water quality.

In eastern Canada, some brook trout hatch in freshwater, migrate to sea where they grow to maturity, and then return to breed in freshwater. And yet exclusively freshwater populations exist in some rivers of the same region. In Canada, the brook trout is more properly called the brook char because it technically is a char of the genus *Salvelinus*, not a trout in *Salmo*. Seagoing, or anadromous, brook char remain near shore, close to their rivers of origin, and grow four to five times faster than fish remaining in freshwater. Fast growth at sea presumably reflects bountiful food.

As I said before, the exotic rainbow and brown trouts have displaced brookies in many stream reaches. Following severe winter floods in Minnesota, two year-classes of brook trout were lost at the egg and fry stages. Thereafter, the mass of brook trout dropped by 92 percent, and adults matured more slowly. This gap in the fish community was filled by rainbow trout that moved in from downstream. In this case, winter floods killed brook trout eggs. In contrast, spring floods would have depressed rainbow trout, whose eggs incubate in the spring. Over the course of fifteen years, this trout community changed from 100 percent brook trout to 70 percent brown trout and 15 percent each of brook and rainbow trouts. Brown trout's pugnaciousness and large body size gives it an edge in monopolizing foraging and spawning areas. Further, brown trout populations seem to better resist predation and angling pressures. These competitive advantages have enabled brown trout to gradually move upstream through many runs that originally belonged to brook trout.

As if that were not enough, acid rain clobbers the reproductive success of brook trout. The number of viable eggs decreases sharply at a pH of 5.0, and to a lesser extent at higher (5.5 to 6.5) pH levels. The growth and survival of young fish also drops at lower pHs.

Although challenged by chemical insults, brook trout are well adapted to swift mountain flows. In one greater-than-five-hundred-year flood in the Blue Ridge Mountains of Virginia, brook trout numbers were severely reduced in reaches scoured by debris flows, but they persisted nicely through stretches that experienced only high, fast water. Rapid recovery after flooding belies great resilience in their natural steep, turbulent mountain streams.

The worthy brook trout appears caught in a desperate evolutionary squeeze. Pressed from low elevations by warm water, exotic trouts, and effective anglers, excluded from upper reaches by freezing temperatures, and stressed everywhere by acid precipitation, native brookies have come to occupy dwindling, suboptimal habitats. Sandwiched and isolated, a few populations of native brook trout continue to persist.

The survival of the brook trout in Appalachia depends on what we do to help them. We can encourage our state fishery agencies to deploy liming devices. The released buffer will neutralize some of the acid entering streams. Converting electricity-generating plants to burn low-sulfur coal will reduce the acid in rain. I have seen modest movements in these directions. We can also sensitize state fisheries units to avoid dumping rainbow and brown trouts near brook trout populations. Alas, there is hope — if we continue working together.

15

A Lungless Salamander Trilogy: Primer

S alamanders, those moist, smooth, lizardlike amphibians, are hardly material for a Madison Avenue-style logo. Yet if asked which animal best symbolizes the Appalachian highlands, I would nominate a salamander. Of Appalachia's thirty-four species of "spring lizards," my candidate is one of the woodland species of lungless salamanders, members of the genus *Plethodon* in the family Plethodontidae. They, more than any other group of living things, reflect the quintessential features of evolution in the Appalachian Mountains. Their small size and limited powers of movement, placed in the context of Appalachia's fragmented topography, have led to a fascinating complex of species.

Plethodontidae is the largest salamander family: Of the 390 salamander species worldwide, more than 200 are plethodontids. In fact, new species of lungless salamanders are still evolving. In Appalachia, Jordan's salamander on one mountain is noticeably different from those a few summits away. All told, there are twenty-one high-elevation, geographically isolated populations of Jordan's salamander, each in the process of evolving its own unique body features.

Why have lungless salamanders undergone a major radiation in Appalachia? Lizards have been unable to build large populations in the cool, moist forest, possibly because they require direct sunshine to maintain their high metabolic rate. This apparently has left salamanders with little competition. Further, the plethodontid's rela-

101

tive independence from surface water has allowed it to move freely through the forest's ground cover. Together, freedom from competition and water have allowed lungless salamanders to spread successfully across the landscape. Once they were widely distributed, lungless salamander populations became fragmented by geographic barriers and changing climate.

Not only are plethodontids geographically widespread, they are also frequently numerous. For example, the red-backed salamander, which is the most abundant woodland salamander in North America, may live in densities of up to two to ten per square yard.

Lunglessness among plethodontid salamanders spans a continuum from aquatic to fully terrestrial species. The completely terrestrial woodland salamanders of the genus *Plethodon* do not visit streams or seeps to lay eggs. They deposit their eggs in moist, protected sites on solid ground where the female broods them for up to eight months. Upon hatching, a fully functional little salamander emerges. I devote the remainder of this, and much of the next two chapters, to the story of these completely terrestrial lungless salamanders.

Of the twenty-one species of *Plethodon* in eastern North America, only the red-backed salamander ranges extensively into northern Appalachia; the rest are restricted to non-glaciated areas. Only the red-backed forages on the surface during cool weather, a trait that may have allowed it to colonize vast stretches of formerly glaciated terrain.

You have probably been wondering how in the world an animal without lungs can breathe. Lungless salamanders absorb oxygen and expel carbon dioxide through their moist skin by the slow, simple process of diffusion. Envision diffusion as the process by which perfume molecules move, by bouncing around slowly and randomly, throughout a room filled with perfectly still air. Diffusion suffices only if the animal has a lot of surface area in comparison to its body mass — if it is shaped like a hot dog. A long, thin shape maximizes the flux of matter or energy between an object's interior and its exterior environment. In essence, the evolutionary jettisoning of lungs was permitted by a skinny body. A serious disadvantage of this breathing

102

style, though, is that the skin must be kept moist, which restricts the salamanders to moist environments. And this opens up a whole other can of salamanders....

Because above-ground activities such as foraging and courtship are restricted to wet nights, woodland salamanders spend long periods resting in the moist micro-atmosphere under cover objects, punctuated by brief periods of above-ground activity. Because *Plethodons* do not engage in activities that require a great deal of energy, such as running, prolonged fighting, or producing huge quantities of eggs, their low metabolic rate and large energy stores enable them to survive long stretches between meals.

After emerging from deep underground in the early spring, red-backeds often congregate in groups of two to seven under rocks and wood. On rainy and foggy nights, they crawl up from the forest floor to forage for small insects on plants. During such arboreal forays in darkness, red-backeds rely on odors alone to locate their motionless prey.

Through summer, as competition for food intensifies, individuals spread out uniformly. During summer droughts, terrestrial salamanders move little, foraging in areas under and bordering protective cover. Thus, the survival of a terrestrial salamander is in large part determined by its ability to defend its cover against competitors. By releasing and scenting airborne molecules and through aggressive behavior, plethodontids advertise and protect their humid crevices. The seasonal change from clumped to dispersed suggests that some individuals actively repel others from the shelters, an example of interference competition.

A salamander's abilities to communicate with other salamanders and to locate and assess stationary prey at night attest to a good sense of smell. An adult red-backed salamander can distinguish between its own home site and those of other individuals on the basis of olfactory cues in body secretions. Male red-backeds prefer substrates with their own excretory odors over those marked by unfamiliar members of their species. Chemical markings on the ground allow communication among red-backeds and between individual red-backeds and Shenandoah salamanders. Picture a male dog lifting his leg on a fire hydrant and you have the idea. The chemical enforcement of territorial boundaries confines the movements of each woodland salamander to a small area.

Through such territorial behavior, adult male red-backeds employ "dear enemy" recognition — individuals are less aggressive toward familiar territorial neighbors than toward strangers. Individual recognition reduces the odds of escalated contests between established neighbors. Salamanders leave their scent by touching chin and cloacal areas to the substrate; they detect other individuals by tapping their fleshy whiskers to fecal pellets. This ability to recognize specific individuals via smell is an unappreciated talent of many lower vertebrates.

So-called "fecal communication" has received much research attention since *Hollows'* original publication. In red-backeds, and probably all *Plethodon* species, members of both sexes use pheromone-infused fecal pellets to communicate. Females advertise, and thereby defend, their territories. Males use fecal pellets to mark territories, to avoid or display submissively towards burrows of conspecific males, and to confirm their own shelter. A male intruder is more aggressive when exposed to pheromone from a male of about equal body size compared to emissions from a larger male.

Fecal communication is used in courtship. Males that eat termites deposit feces that are more attractive to females than males on an ant diet. Compared to armored ants, soft-bodied termites are better salamander food because they are easier to handle, pass through the digestive system faster, and yield more assimilable nutrients.

The hypothesis is that females select males with termites in their territories so females can gain access to those preferred prey. Thus, females exercise mate choice by an olfactory survey of males' fecal pellets. During courtship, female red-backeds squash male fecal pellets, and then preferentially associate more around males with termite residues in their feces vs. males with ant-scented pellets. From a female's point of view, a male that forages more efficiently makes an attractive mate.

According to this "sexy feces hypothesis," male red-backeds respond to a gravid female's pheromone by quickly producing fecal pellets. In response, the female pushes her head into the pellet and then rotates her head, thereby gaining information about the male and his diet. Putting it all together, female red-backeds prefer large males that monopolize (1) large, high-quality territories, which offer both (2) preferred termite food and (3) large cover objects, that in turn (4) buffer temperature and humidity extremes.

In addition to chemical signals, red-backeds have a small repertoire of visual displays they use in territorial contests. Threat displays include "all of trunk raised" and "looking forward"; submissive displays include "lying flattened" and "looking away." Males are more aggressive toward each other than to females, whereas females display no such intersexual differences.

Fertilization takes place within the female's body — but the males have no penis. They solve this sperm-transfer problem by passing a spermatophore, a packet filled with sperm. During courtship, the male deposits a spermatophore on the ground. If his amorous actions and pheromones stimulate the female, she picks up the spermatophore in her cloaca, the common external opening of the digestive, excretory, and reproductive systems. She stores sperm in her cloaca until the eggs are ready to be fertilized, and then lays the clutch in a protected site.

Although salamanders in other taxonomic groups brood their eggs, this behavior is most elaborately developed in plethodontids. Brooding defends the eggs against predators, infection, and desiccation. The female also rotates the eggs to prevent yolk stratification, which causes birth defects and a low hatching rate. Brooding females rarely eat their own eggs unless the eggs are dead or infected. These the mother eats before the pathogen spreads to the rest of the clutch. A female Allegheny mountain salamander maintains throat contact with her eggs, her throat pulsations somehow contributing to egg survival. Laboratory experiments have shown that clutches attended by Allegheny mountain females are less susceptible to predation by other Allegheny mountain salamanders and ground beetles than are unattended clutches. Further, clutches deprived of females but protected from predation usually succumb to a fungal parasite. While brooding her eggs, a female Allegheny mountain eats little and consequently loses body weight. Brooding, like all adaptations, has costs and benefits for individual reproductive success.

Amid Appalachia's diverse animal species live these common yet inconspicuous amphibians: lungless, skin-breathing salamanders that recognize neighbors by smell; females practicing mate choice by inferring the male's quality by his fecal scent; accomplishing internal fertilization without a penis; and brooding their young. As you wander Appalachia's hills and hollows, turn over a rock or a log — strange delights await you.

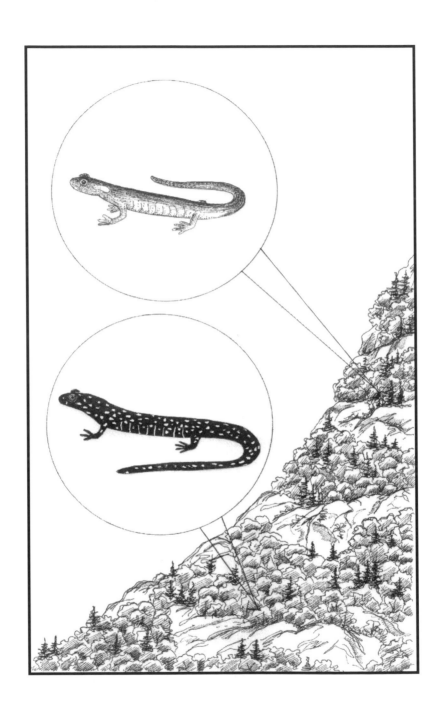

16

A Lungless Salamander Trilogy: Coexistence

Several species of lungless salamanders live in the same habitat, forage at the same time on the same prey, and use the same sites for brooding their eggs. In my hollow, the red-backed and slimy salamanders commonly live side-by-side. Yet a hallowed body of ecological theory and empirical evidence indicates that two or more species cannot exploit forever the same set of limiting resources. Either their resource requirements diverge through evolutionary time to reduce competition or one of the species becomes extinct. So how do several plethodontid species manage to coexist?

Several field studies have demonstrated that competition between species of plethodontids limits their coexistence. In West Virginia, the Cheat Mountain salamander dwells in habitat islands of spruce forests, relics of the formerly widespread boreal forest. In a few sites, the Cheat Mountain salamander appears to exclude the red-backed salamander. But over most of Appalachia, the Cheat Mountain cannot compete with the red-backed, so the Cheat Mountain has become extinct over most of Appalachia.

In the Great Smoky Mountains of North Carolina, the distributions of two other salamanders — the slimy, so called because of its slick, viscous coat, and the Jordan's — star in one of the great evolutionary acts of Appalachia. In southwestern North Carolina, Jordan's consists of twelve geographic isolates, which are local, genetically distinct populations of the single species. On some mountains, the slimy and Jordan's cohabit throughout the entire isolate;

in others the two species replace each other altitudinally with varying amounts of elevational overlap. It is as if in some isolates, the two species have evolved mechanisms that permit cohabitation over large areas, while in other areas competition seems to have been so strong that they can coexist only in narrow overlap zones.

In the Great Smoky Mountains, the altitudinal overlap between Jordan's and slimy amounts to only 230 to 400 feet of elevation, whereas in the nearby Balsam Mountains, the two overlap at least 3,900 feet. This comparative observation suggests that competition between the two species has been stronger in the former isolate than in the latter. This hypothesis has been tested: The experimental removal of Jordan's resulted in significant increases in the abundance of the slimy in both areas, but the increase appeared earlier in the Smokies. This outcome demonstrates that competition between species is stronger in the zone of narrower overlap, the Smokies, than in the zone of wider overlap, the Balsams.

In this experiment, both the Jordan's and the slimy benefited from the removal of the other. Yet there were a total of seven salamander species in the areas. None of the remaining five (other than Jordan's and slimy) increased in number after the removal of either of the two abundant species. Thus, we must not automatically assume that competition is significant in all instances of coexistence.

Another interspecific competition is playing on the north-facing slope of Hawksbill Mountain in Virginia's Blue Ridge. Most populations of the Shenandoah salamander inhabit small, isolated pockets of shallow soil tucked within the rocky confines of talus. Both the Shenandoah and red-backed prefer moist spots, but the Shenandoah tolerates dry conditions better than the red-backed. In drought, red-backeds, which live in deep soil, simply descend deeper. When forced to dehydrate, red-backeds lose more water, are less tolerant of the water losses, and do not survive as long as Shenandoahs.

Red-backeds are excluded from the dry talus slopes because they cannot traverse the rocks or tolerate periodic dry conditions in the shallow soil. As successful competitors for food, red-backeds employ aggressive territorial behaviors to exclude Shenandoahs from the soil of surrounding forests. The geographic distribution of red-backeds, then, reflects habitat selection, whereas the distribution of Shenandoah is best explained by competitive exclusion.

Experiments suggest that if red-backed salamanders were to suddenly disappear, Shenandoah salamanders would occupy the forest's soil. Competition between the species at the talus-soil interface currently prevents such ecological release. All sizes of Shenandoah emigrate from talus to soil, but only the largest, which are big enough to feed on prey that are too awkward for red-backeds, are able to invade more than a few meters into their competitor's territory. Even this incursion is only a temporary success, though, because the offspring of pioneering Shenandoahs, which eat the same-sized foods as red-backeds, lose in competition. Shenandoahs, then, survive only in suboptimal habitat where red-backeds cannot penetrate.

Red-backeds appear to be expanding their range at the expense of Shenandoahs. In the Blue Ridge, Shenandoahs live on only three mountains, each completely surrounded by red-backeds. This distribution suggests that current populations of Shenandoah salamanders are relicts of a formerly more widespread form that has been squeezed out of its original habitat, much like the Cheat Mountain salamander.

The talus habitat, left from the Pleistocene glaciation, is gradually disappearing. As soil washes into the talus slopes, red-backeds invade the fingers of soil and Shenandoah loses space and numbers. One comparison is particularly telling. Eight years after a severe drought, one population of Shenandoah salamanders finally recovered from a few individuals that persisted in soil patches. In soil patches of another talus pile, Shenandoahs became extinct. Together, interspecific competition and climate change can interact to cause the demise of a population or even an entire species. The Shenandoah salamander is experiencing an evolutionary bottleneck. Will it squeeze through and pop out the other side, or are these the details of a forthcoming extinction? Stay tuned....

In addition to this Hawksbill Mountain isolate, there are two other distinct populations of the Shenandoah salamander. Populations at Stony Man Mountain and The Pinnacle, in the Blue

Ridge about five miles from Hawksbill Mountain, are also surrounded by deep soil and red-backeds. Here, on a single mountain of the Blue Ridge, red-backed salamanders are playing out a similar scene of encroachment with yet another species, the Peaks of Otter salamander. Thus, three relict plethodons, the Cheat Mountain, Shenandoah, and Peaks of Otter, seem to be disappearing at the hands of imperialist red-backeds.

The red-backed salamander ranges from Nova Scotia to North Carolina, west to Ontario and Missouri, and continues to incrementally usurp the habitat of other salamander species. Some of the less competitive species have found temporary relief in relict habitats not accessible to red-backeds, such as talus for the Shenandoah and spruce forest for the Cheat Mountain. Others, such as Hoffman's and ravine salamanders, inhabit deciduous forests suitable to red-backeds and have been able to accommodate various levels of interspecific competition. Theoretical models predict that species of lungless salamanders will not be able to coexist indefinitely. However, because their extensive geographical overlap seems recent (i.e., post-Pleistocene), their long-term relationships may still be evolving. Some plethodontids compete for limiting resources, others do not. Of the former, some species pairs have been competing intensely and are diverging evolutionarily; others have competed only weakly and have veered little. Still other species are being competitively displaced, possibly to the point of extinction.

But the humbling fact is that after all of our ecological and behavioral studies, on everything from single-celled animals to salamanders and mice, we still cannot predict which species will win a particular competitive struggle. Are we probing something that is not knowable and therefore ultimately unpredictable? This possibility gives ecologists high anxiety.

17

A Lungless Salamander Trilogy: Mimicry

I n the Great Smoky Mountains, an amazing similarity exists between two salamander species, Jordan's and Allegheny Mountain. Both include some red-cheeked and some red-legged individuals. It's as if they are copying each other. The evolutionary cause of this improbable likeness lies in the tastes of salamander predators. Any meat-eating bird that feeds by scratching the forest floor will try to eat a salamander. The blue jay, brown thrasher, and wood thrush are all confirmed salamander predators. All species of woodland salamanders in the genus *Plethodon*, however, seem to be at least mildly distasteful to birds, and some are downright poisonous. Upon ingesting a "bad" salamander, the birds' reactions range from gagging to regurgitation. (Skin secretions of salamanders are reported to numb human taste, but I haven't had the temerity to lick one.)

In the continuum of salamander palatability, birds find the Allegheny Mountain tastier than Jordan's. Although not poisonous, Jordan's exudes viscous, noxious skin secretions, so experienced birds avoid it. Jordan's salamander is tastier than the poisonous red eft, but is passed over by most birds because of its bright warning coloration and overt defensive behavior. (You may know the red eft as the familiar, bright red juvenile stage of the red-spotted newt that wanders about boldly in broad daylight.)

In the Great Smoky Mountains, some isolates of Jordan's display red cheek patches. Four other Jordan's isolates in the Nantahala National Forest south of the Smokies have red legs. Some populations of the Allegheny Mountain possess, with varying frequencies, red legs, red cheeks, or both. Now for the most provocative observations: the red-legged form of Allegheny Mountain occurs only within the range of red-legged Jordan's; within the range of red-cheeked Jordan's, the imitator sports red cheeks. There seems to be a lot of copying going on.

If they have had previous experience with Jordan's salamanders, birds avoid the tastier but incognito Allegheny Mountain. Some bird predators transfer their distaste for red-legged Jordan's to red-legged Allegheny Mountain, avoiding them both. Likewise, birds that have been negatively conditioned by the unsavory red-cheeked Jordan's avoid red-cheeked Allegheny Mountain salamanders. The protective value of the Allegheny Mountain's false warning colors of red legs or red cheeks has been demonstrated experimentally. Simply, birds learn to associate red patches with unpalatability.

The phenomenon in which a palatable species evolves an exterior appearance or behavior that is similar to that of a distasteful or poisonous species is known as Batesian mimicry. Members of the tasty species thereby gain protection from predators. Allegheny Mountain salamanders with red legs, instead of the usual black, are interpreted as Batesian mimics of the range-sharing red-legged Jordan's. Analogously, red-cheeked Allegheny Mountain are Batesian mimics of the spatially overlapping red-cheeked Jordan's. The model is the large, black Jordan's salamander, which exists as twenty-one geographical isolates, and the mimics belong to the highly variable Allegheny Mountain salamander complex.

The mimicry between Jordan's and Allegheny Mountain salamanders appears to be a weak Batesian mimetic system. The system is based on only one model — Jordan's — which is only mildly unpalatable to begin with. The success of a Batesian mimetic system with a weak model depends on the availability of alternate food sources for the predators. The greater the availability of other foods, the less predation on the model and the greater the protection for the mimic. Another aspect of this system is consistent with weak Batesian mimicry: natural selection favors variable forms in the mimic — that is,

116

the mimic occurs in several color forms — when the model cannot support an extensive mimetic population.

The red-backed salamander and the red eft carry on another mimicry. In this system, the red eft serves as the model for an all-red phase of the red-backed. A classic example of warning coloration and behavior, red efts are extremely toxic to mammals and birds — their skin contains tetrodotoxin, a powerful neurotoxin and the strongest emetic known. This is why red efts can crawl around fearlessly during the day. As you would expect, where it coexists with red efts, the all-red color phase of the red-backed repels bird predators. The system is not quite this simple, though, because the red-backed itself is mildly distasteful, and therefore some predators might avoid it without the mimicry. However, it is fair to conclude that exposure to red efts reinforces the predators' avoidance.

With the red-backed mimic being distasteful, the red-backed-red eft mimetic system has another type of mimicry superimposed on its essentially Batesian foundation. Mullerian mimicry is the phenomenon in which unpalatable species mimic each other: Mullerian mimics share both warning colors and noxiousness. The selective advantage here is not in deceiving the predator but in training predators more quickly. In this case, the mildly distasteful red-backed is both a Batesian and Mullerian mimic of the highly toxic red eft.

From an original, ancient lungless salamander, a burst of adaptive radiation has rewarded us with diversity. Our fascination with these small animals rests in their habits of breathing without lungs, chemical recognition of neighbors, laying eggs on land, and egg brooding by females. Among some of the overlapping species, competition has led to coexistence; with others it is causing extinction. Further, in some cases of coexistence, evolution has led to complex mimicry. This small, undemanding creature, so instructive to those willing to look, embodies evolution in Appalachia. Fine logo material too, I might add.

18
Love Among the Frogs

The first colt's foot, eastern phoebe, garter snake — all help us chart the arrival of spring. Although I pay polite attention to these and other harbingers, a chorus of spring peepers is my personal watershed. In his essay, "The Day of the Peepers," Joseph Wood Krutch agreed: "I wonder if there is any phenomenon in the heavens above or in the earth beneath which so simply and so definitely announces that life is resurgent again."

Not just a single warm evening, which might be misleading, but an accumulation of a minimum number of degree-days incites the chorus to convene. As you might suspect, by having read this far into the book, the serenade hides conflict. Behind the music, war is raging.

Appalachia is not prime frog country. A paucity of standing water makes breeding habitat rare. Further, the ability of frogs to travel widely precludes the formation of the small, reproductively isolated populations that speed the evolution of new species. For these reasons, only fourteen species of frogs and toads inhabit southern Appalachia. These few species, however, enrich us with song.

Sporting dark mask-like streaks behind their eyes, wood frogs are the first to emerge in spring, after overwintering in logs and stumps and under leaf litter. Often with snow still on the ground, wood frogs converge on their woodland breeding ponds. Because they breed in ephemeral waters, the time they have is limited. By breeding in temporary waters early in the season, wood frogs reap the benefits of no predation by fish, fairly decent odds of metamorphosis before the pond dries, and attainment of large adult body size by the time land-based predators become active. These advantages presumably exceed the disadvantages of occasional freezing of adults and eggs.

Wood frogs arrive at their breeding pond with precise syn-chrony. One biologist witnessed the arrival of five hundred frogs within ninety minutes. Calling males float at the surface, sometimes in pools that still contain ice. Although each male's call is weak, the duck-cackling chorus carries a long way. Choruses are often intense. Males search, struggle among themselves, and intercept females as they enter the pond. Females are passive. After coupling, which may occur anywhere in the pond, pairs swim toward a single communal egg-laying site. Here, in full sunlight, females deposit their eggs di-rectly onto the growing egg mass. Late breeders add their eggs to the outside of the clump. The presence of eggs stimulates a female to release her own eggs. Over a hundred females may contribute to a single cluster, and most deposit their eggs on the night they arrive.

This explosive breeding is short-lived, lasting at most up to ten days, but often ending after a single night of mating. Essayist Annie Dillard's metaphysical exploration of fecundity well describes the wood frog's orgy:

"I don't know what it is about fecundity that so appalls. I sup-pose it is the teeming evidence that birth and growth, which we value, are ubiquitous and blind, that life itself is so astonishingly cheap, that nature is so careless as it is bountiful, and that with ex-travagance goes a crushing waste."

Within a clump, eggs insulated in the center are about six de-grees Fahrenheit warmer than those around the periphery, and in turn, eggs on the edge of a cluster stay warmer than single eggs. Dark embry-os absorb sunlight, and jelly envelopes around them retain the heat. In addition to passive solar heating, heat generated by normal metabolic processes increases the temperature of embryos. The temperature of the egg mass increases with the size of the clump. Within the cluster's warm microenvironment, embryos develop rapidly and normally.

Being one of the first females to breed brings thermal advantages. Because of their higher temperatures, eggs in the center of the mass have a 90 percent chance of hatching compared with 45 percent for peripheral ones. Further, central clutches have more eggs (1,125) than peripheral ones (750). Large females, which breed earlier, hold an edge: they not only produce more eggs than smaller females, but their embryos gain the thermal benefits of centrality. Selection pressure favoring early breeding is presumably countered by how quickly the frogs are able to emerge in the spring and when the ice melts at their breeding pond. The combination of a minimum temperature threshold and the ephemeral nature of their breeding habitat explain the wood frog's early, explosive, spawning behavior.

As I was writing the original *Hollows*, a couple of layers were being added to this story. Wood frog tadpoles and froglets recognize genetic relatives. For example, newly transformed frogs associate preferentially with full- and half-siblings over unrelated individuals. Such a provocative observation begs proximate and ultimate questions.

How do they do it? Laboratory experiments have demonstrated that neither familiarity nor a maternal factor, such as egg jelly, are needed for kin recognition. Rather, the cue, at least in tadpoles, seems to include both genetic and environmental factors. Self-learning of recognition cues, like specific genetically-determined chemicals secreted from skin and diet-influenced pheromones diffusing from feces, have been proposed.

Why do they do it? Several hypotheses are on the table: (1) Alarm pheromones protect kin from predators, as in fish schools (See chp. 12.). (2) Tadpoles secrete chemical growth regulators, which synchronize growth among school mates, narrow size differences within schools, and improve the antipredator values of the school. Synchronized growth of tadpoles, in turn, (3) synchronizes the timing of metamorphosis, and thereby swamps terrestrial predators.

A fourth hypothesis includes cannibalism. Wood frog tadpoles are efficient predators of all kinds of smaller amphibian eggs and tadpoles. In some natural wood frog populations in North Carolina, most tadpoles are not cannibalized because synchronized egg-laying and hatching yield little variation in tadpole size. However a small minority of adults, about 5 percent, lay their eggs a few days after the main orgy. These late eggs hatch when the older tadpoles are about one gram each, plenty big to eat new hatchlings.

Now let's combine the ideas of kin recognition and cannibalism: Cannibalism may be a selective factor that has favored the evolution of kin recognition. Not only would equality of body sizes and converging growth function as anti-cannibalism adaptations, but cannibalism could also have favored the ability to recognize genetic kin as a way of reducing the killing of relatives. In this story, temporary ponds and cold water are constraints; and explosive breeding, weak mate choice, cannibalism, synchronized growth leading to similar size at metamorphosis, and kin recognition evolved as a chain of integrated coadaptations, traits that reinforce the adaptive values of each other.

As swiftly as they arrive, wood frogs recede into the forest, where they spend the summer away from water. The next chorus issues from spring peepers in March and April, followed by cricket frogs, chorus frogs, and pickerel frogs. Bullfrogs drone on through summer. Spanning the late spring-early summer time slot is the gray tree frog, which breeds from April to late July. The gray tree frog is a small (1.2 to 2 inches from snout to anus) frog that typically calls from bushes and small trees near water. Suction cups on the undersides of its toes identify this creature as a tree frog.

Clinging to reeds, stems, and other suitable perches, male gray tree frogs use the mating call — a loud, resonant trill — to enforce spacing among themselves. They defend territories at least two feet across by using encounter calls, and occasionally by fighting off intruders. The encounter call sounds like an abbreviated cry from a rooster. Females are attracted by the males' chorus and trickle in singly during the long breeding season. In contrast to wood frogs, female gray tree frogs approach calling males and initiate the mating embrace with a nudge, after which the pair may remain coupled for over four hours.

Since the original *Hollows* was published, a twist has coalesced that offers closure to the tree frog story. In the eastern gray tree frog, males vary in how vigorous they call. Long- vs. short-callers differ in two important ways, respectively: 30 vs. 17 pulses per call, 1.5 vs. 0.9 seconds per call. Offered a choice, females mate with long-calling males.

In one study, male tree frogs obtained between zero and four matings per breeding season. This range is explained in part by the number of nights a male participates in the chorus. Number of nights participating is important because on any given night an individual male's call may be masked by the pervasive chorus, interfering with the female's ability to choose among males. Males that call on more nights have better odds of being heard by a female than males calling on fewer nights. In sum, a tree frog stud calls fast and loud on many nights.

Why do females prefer long calls? Among male tree frogs, aerobic metabolic rate is positively correlated with call duration and rate. Loud, long calling depletes a male's glycogen reserves quicker than soft, short calls. Females prefer metabolically costly calls presumably because they indicate that the calling male is in good physical condition. Thus, pulse duration and rate encode a male's condition.

But pulse duration and rate reveal something even more profound than the calling male's body condition. According to the "good genes hypothesis," female animals select males with superior genetic qualities. In laboratory experiments, the offspring of male tree frogs that produce long calls performed better, in terms of survival and growth, through their tadpole and juvenile stages than the offspring of short-call males. From a female tree frog's point of view, the male's call duration is a reliable indicator of his heritable genetic quality. So, within a given social environment, a female eastern gray tree frog shops among males, then chooses to breed with a male emitting a long, energetic call because it indicates a vigorous body and good genes. These findings are consistent with the good genes hypothesis.

As you might expect, females move toward louder calls more frequently than to weaker ones. In one field study, the sound level one yard away from good perches — ones that led to mating — averaged 89.5 decibels, whereas it was only 87.1 at poor perches. Poor perches may be near acoustic obstructions or may lack sound amplifiers, such as the surface of still water. Males occupy good perches earlier in the season and for more nights than poor perches.

This priority on calling sites places male tree frogs in conflict with each other. Dominant large males relegate many smaller males to inferior perches. In fact, only one-fourth to one-third of the males that call mate successfully. This explains the observation that male tree frogs caught in the act of mating are larger than single males.

Noncalling males, frogs that have lost vocal or physical contests, often remain close to calling males. Termed noncalling satellites because they hang around dominant males, these opportunists intercept and mate with one-third to one-half of the approaching females. A satellite remains motionless near a calling male until a female moves into the vicinity, then he swiftly grabs her. Calling males try to repel noncalling males by pulsed encounter calls, butting, and wrestling. When a calling frog vacates his perch, a subordinate male quickly occupies the site and begins calling, often within four minutes. Because males leave their perches to couple with females for over four hours, good calling perches become available to satellite males for lengthy periods. In essence, small satellite males sexually parasitize large vocalizing males of the same species. About 80 percent of the males are callers; the rest are consistently satellites or switch back and forth.

Each mating tactic of the male gray tree frog — calling from a territory, noncalling in a peripheral satellite position, and opportunistic switching — leads to at least some mating success. In such a mix, a male's best strategy depends on what others around him are doing. If a male is surrounded by calling territorial males, he might fertilize more eggs by forgoing the costs of fighting and behaving as a noncalling satellite.

What leads to the contrasting mating behaviors of the wood frog and gray tree frog? Wood frogs, explosive breeders in temporary ponds of early spring, form dense aggregations for highly synchronized chorusing and egg-laying. Females add their eggs quickly to the communal clump, ensuring that their eggs will be insulated by later clutches. Such explosive breeding systems place a premium on acquiring mates quickly, so female wood frogs do not exercise a great deal of discrimination in choosing mates. Males search widely, clasp every female frog, and do not defend a specific resource such as an egg-laying site. This combination of factors accounts for their explosive orgy.

Gray tree frogs, which breed in permanent warmer waters, call over a period of several months from established perches within defended territories. The territory provides space for a relatively undisturbed courtship and habitat crucial for egg survival. Because there is plenty of time for females to discriminate and choose large males, natural selection has favored small males that salvage at least some matings: they linger as satellites around their dominant counterparts and pick up the reproductive scraps.

Frog song can signal either a mad sexual scramble or slow, methodical courtship. Among frogs, both get the love job done.

19

Box Turtle's Independence

Few of us purposely search for box turtles, so it's no wonder we have few first-hand impressions of them in their natural habitat. However, most of us have vivid memories filed away of desperate swerves to avoid squashing their high domes on the road. Instead of allowing the image of a lethargic, indifferent creature to mislead you, envision these pedestrians as animals enviably insulated from the vagaries of their setting. In fact, land tortoises seem more divorced from environmental stresses than any other Appalachian vertebrate.

The turtle's habitat provides our first hint of its independence. Box turtles live in a variety of terrestrial situations — though permanent water does not seem to be a requirement. High densities of these reptiles commonly occur in woodlots with large trees, canopy gaps, and a diversified ground cover. The turtles bask in openings in the canopy and munch on a variety of short plants. The close ground cover of woody shrubs and leaf litter provide shelter. To feed and bask, box turtles also frequently enter open areas adjacent to the woods.

Much of what we know of box turtle biology comes from the labors of Charles and Elizabeth Schwartz, biologists who tracked tortoises for twenty years. By training Labrador retrievers to locate and retrieve turtles, they were able to study unprecedentedly large numbers. During nineteen years of the Schwartzes' study, the average size of the area a turtle covered routinely, or its home range, increased from 5.2 to 12.8 acres. Home ranges were essentially equal for males and females. Another study at a different field site concluded that box turtles restrict their movements to home ranges that average only about one hundred yards in diameter, which translates to about 2.5 acres. For comparison, the home ranges of snapping and wood turtles, two Appalachian relatives, average 8.4 and 3.2 acres, respectively.

When not traveling, box turtles rest in forms, depressions made in vegetation and the top inch of soil. During their active season, April to October, they remain in their forms until the morning sun warms them, then travel slowly and feed for about an hour. If it is sunny but cool, they bask; if it is hot they may crawl under a few leaves or a clump of grass. A turtle may meander up to seventy yards per day, or it may move just a foot or two before making a new form for the night. On any given day, one turtle might be active while another is quiescent. Some individuals are simply more sedentary than others.

Intuitively, it seems that resting forms should contribute to a turtle's independence from environmental changes because the form insulates the turtle's belly plate, or plastron, during hot days and cool nights. However, recent study suggests that there is no pattern in when or why turtles occupy their forms. Use is not related to an individual's sex or size, nor to a consistent difference in air or soil temperatures. Neither have we found an obvious reason for how long they stay in a form. In essence, each individual box turtle seems to have its own internal agenda, acting independently of the environment in determining when or where to settle into a resting form or how long to stay there.

One environmental condition turtles do respond to is a cold snap in autumn. Box turtles enter hibernation with the first killing frost. A wet fall without a sudden freeze provides good conditions for entering hibernation. Dry weather, which makes digging difficult, and a sudden freeze may trap some individuals above ground. Surprisingly, box turtles do not hibernate below the frost line, but remain dormant at depths of up to five inches below the leaf litter.

Since the original *Hollows*, I have learned some amazing facts about the box turtle's hibernation. Members of the genus *Terrapene*, which includes the eastern box turtle, hibernate in shallow terrestrial burrows that feature a vertical extension to the surface. In cold spells, turtles turn their heads farthest from the opening. In Ohio, the average turtle spends 142 days in a burrow under three inches of leaf litter with its plastron recessed two inches into the soil.

In such shallow retreats, box turtles are exposed to freezing temperatures, yet they usually survive. Able to supercool to only -1.1 C, this strategy cannot be its entire secret. (More on supercooling, a liquid cooling below its normal freezing point, in chp. 25.) In an astounding adaptation, the box turtle is able to survive the freezing of 58 percent of its body water for seventy-three hours, making the box turtle the largest animal known to exhibit freeze-tolerance (Again, more in chp. 25.).

In some areas, box turtles emerge from hibernation and move about on warm winter days. Final spring emergence occurs between late March and late April, an interval that roughly coincides with the last killing frost.

Most box turtles establish home ranges, but others are transients. Turtles found crossing roads, especially those we commonly see after warm spring rains, are likely to be transients. Only a few individuals wander, but those that do may fulfill the important function of transferring genes from one sedentary population to another, thereby reducing the harmful consequences of inbreeding. Of highway-crossing turtles, half are youngsters, small individuals less than nine years old, with equal numbers of each sex; the other half are mostly adult males. Transients move one way through the environment — no returning. Road kills, by the way, are particularly hard on this long-lived, low-fecundity species, so I seethe when a mountaineer cites his turtle-squashing score.

Box turtles mate from May through October. In copulo, the male's concave plastron complements the female's convex back shield, or carapace. His hind recurved first claws play a crucial role during mating: he wedges them between the female's upper and lower shells so that she can't clamp down on his penis. Even when they're not paired in hand, you can still tell the sexes apart by noting a combination of characteristics. Compared to females, males have a deeper depression in their plastrons; thicker, shorter, more recurved hind claws; and redder heads and eyes.

Hatchlings and juveniles are seldom found, so we know precious little about baby box turtles. The age of a box turtle is evident in some characteristics of its carapace. Individuals with shells up to 4.6 inches long fall within age class I. They are actively growing, show obvious new growth rings on their plastron and carapace, and are up to nine years old. Class II includes young adults that are 4.6 inches or longer. They show wear on old growth rings and have no obvious new rings, particularly on the plastron. They are ten through at least thirty-two years old. Sexual maturity appears to be related to size, not age. Individuals 4.7 inches long have well developed sex-specific characters, whereas the 4.3- to 4.7-inch size class includes both immature and mature adults. Old adults, in age class III, are also longer than 4.6 inches but carry worn, even smooth, uniformly colored carapaces. These old "bowling balls" are thirty-three to over fifty-one years old.

Some young individuals shift their residence before establishing a permanent home range. As a turtle grows, its home range enlarges, at least through the first two age classes. Specifically, the home ranges for Class I through Class III turtles average 4.2, 9.2, and 8.9 acres, respectively.

During the Schwartzes' long-term study, the turtle population fluctuated between four hundred and six hundred individuals, which, in the context of a wide variety of animals, is a fairly steady enrollment. Stable population numbers score as yet another indicator of independence.

Published reports suggest the box turtle's sex ratio favors males, but because males are more active than females, these estimates may reflect a sampling bias. Interestingly, where the Schwartzes used dogs to find turtles, the sex ratio was equal. Maybe to a dog's nose turtle essence is not sex-specific.

A box turtle's daily behavior seems to be divorced from the caprice of its immediate environment. The condition of a turtle at any particular time appears more an integration of its past experiences than a reflection of its present stresses. At least three adaptations create this apparent time lag. Most obviously, a box turtle's shell takes the edge off environmental extremes by buffering its body from environmental stresses such as heat and drought. During severe drought, the tortoises do not concentrate around creeks — they merely seek moist sites within their home ranges, make a form under a pile of leaves, and rest peacefully. Second, their forms and hinged plastrons protect and conceal them from what few predators they do have, such as raccoons. And third, box turtles have a low metabolism. Coupling that with omnivorous food habits, they enjoy a high supply-low demand economy and do not need to hustle. They eat insects, earthworms, strawberries, fruits, mushrooms, and many other foods, yet they burn these calories slowly. In these ways, box turtles enjoy a tremendous hedge against environmental stresses.

The box turtle's unique independence may result from the scale of time to which it responds. What you see lumbering across your Appalachian road is not an organism reflecting its present stimuli and immediate history, like the rest of us, but rather an easy-going, independent time lag living in the past.

20
Copperhead's Year

Along Pine Cabin Run — and probably throughout Hampshire County, West Virginia — I am one of those rare humans who is pleasantly surprised to encounter a copperhead. After summer rains, these vipers slither down the hill past our cabin on their way to local frog-hunting grounds. So, I come across them fairly often.

Before our daughter Leah arrived, Nancy and I would coax the serpents into a grain sack and covertly release them on a nearby hill. (I hope our neighbors don't ostracize us now that we've gone public.) Then two events converged: Leah learned to toddle, and I researched this essay. We were then confronted by a brutal tradeoff: accept the risk that Leah might be bitten, or kill the copperheads because, if released as before, they would return to their home range — our yard. We settled on the procedure of catching, bagging, and depositing the serpents in the freezer — admittedly not much of a compromise from the snake's point of view, but at least they seemed to die painlessly and yielded perfect study specimens. Now that Leah is a competent walker, we once again enjoy our copperhead friends basking out by the mailbox, where our daughter exhibits only naïve curiosity toward them.

Our risk of death by copperhead bite is far less than that by auto accident, yet of the two, the snake is the one that elicits involuntary shudders. This is perplexing. Although serpents are ingrained evils of our folklore, I will go out on a limb and propose that our reaction to them is learned, not genetically predetermined. After seeing this common reptile in a less evil light, you may even come to appreciate the copperheads you encounter in your Appalachian wanderings.

133

Copperheads spend about half of the year, from late October to mid-April, in hibernation. Dens where several snakes hibernate, called hibernacula, most frequently occupy rocky hilltops with a southern exposure, probably because such sites are warmer and drier than surrounding habitats. The snakes gather peaceably in the autumn, and within the hibernaculum, each individual benefits from the heat and moisture generated collectively. Copperheads coil together when hibernating. In some rock dens, copperheads, timber rattlesnakes, and black racers congregate in mixed-species groups. In this torpid state, their body temperatures may dip to thirty-nine degrees Fahrenheit.

Copperheads arouse in the spring when the temperature reaches forty-five to fifty degrees Fahrenheit. After exiting the den, they lie under nearby rocks that hold the warmth of the sun and provide insulation during cool spells. Some individuals remain near their den through the summer; others travel varying distances. Copperheads migrate seasonally between rocky hilltops and lower summering areas. One study found the average distance the snakes traveled between the den and summer sites was 0.4 mile for males and 0.25 mile for females. As summer approaches, copperheads either stay within a clearly delineated home range, near their overwintering site, or abandon the original area for another. Most individuals are "home-rangers," but of those that move on, males shift more often and farther than females. Home ranges average 1.7 acres for males and 8.9 acres for females, but the actual sizes vary with habitat. Within its home range, a snake seems to wander about in an irregular, circuitous course.

Copperheads have two mating seasons, one in the spring (Apr-May), just before females ovulate (May-Jun), and a second in the fall (Sep-Oct). Stored within the female's reproductive tract, autumnal sperm retain their capacity through winter and into spring. In this way, fall and spring ejaculates from different males can co-occur in a female during vernal ovulation, conditions leading to mixed-paternity clutches.

The snakes mate at night, the odor of skin apparently stimulating courtship. As with other reptiles, male copperheads have paired copulatory organs, called hemipenes, lodged at the base of the tail and covered with spines. The spines lock the male into the female and irritate the female's reproductive tract. By locking and irritating, the male precludes mating by other males, reducing competition from other males' sperm.

Since the original version of *Hollows* was published, herpetologists have come to a better understanding of male combat. During the mating season, large males occasionally entwine, lie outstretched, and struggle for five or ten minutes, each trying to achieve a superior position. Fighting males sway through the air, hooking, trying to force their opponent to the ground. Usually a smaller female can be found nearby. This ritualized male-male combat seems to have two functions, dominance over another male and mating that handy female. Where body lengths differ by 8 percent or more, the larger male always wins. Surprisingly, a loser does not re-challenge, but rather continues life as a subordinate, non-fighting snake. A loss seems to permanently override any advantage of body size, a behavior with interesting implications for mating.

Courtship is initiated by the male. His tongue-flicking is rapid, the paired tongue tips splayed more than while hunting. The male's touch-mounting, chin-rubbing, tongue-flicking, and tail-searching stimulate the female to sexual readiness. Not until the female stretches and actively gapes her cloaca does intromission occur.

Prolonged coitus extinguishes the female's receptivity. A mated female is unattractive to males five to seven days after copulation, and she usually remains non-receptive through the rest of that mating season.

Female copperheads exhibit a fascinating form of mate choice. During courtship, but before copulation, a female may display a behavior reminiscent of male-male combat. Specifically, in response to chin-rubbing by the male, she may lift her head above the ground, as a male would in the initial stages of combat. The male may respond to the female's head-lifting with a challenge display of his own. Within a few minutes, the female resumes her pre-courtship actions.

Some researchers have interpreted the female's behavior as an adaptation to discriminate between the winners and losers of prior male combat. That is, female copperheads mimic a part of male combat to elicit a reaction by the male, thereby allowing her to discriminate among males with winning vs. losing pasts. The male's response may also allow her to evaluate his body condition and maybe even his genetic quality.

When they emerge in spring, females carry small whitish eggs in their ovaries. During May, eggs grow, turn yellow, then are ovulated. The mature elliptical eggs average 1.4 inches long and 0.7 inch wide. To delay fertilization, female copperheads store clumps of sperm in stretches of their convoluted oviducts.

Like most members of the pit viper family, which includes rattlesnakes, fer-de-lance, and bushmasters, copperheads are viviparous — they produce living young whose embryonic development has been fostered by nutrients conveyed from the female's body. Females carry young internally through the summer, the embryos growing slowly during the 102- to 110-day gestation period. Compared to other copperheads, gravid females are docile and secretive, and more likely to be found in open or rocky habitats, where basking speeds embryonic development. Some pregnant females gather in small groups, but most remain alone. The typical female does not produce a litter every year, probably just in alternate years. After several weeks of development, the fetuses assume an elongate serpentine form coiled within the egg. Birth dates of the young vary from August third to November sixth, but at any one place, births are concentrated within a two-week interval.

The number of young in a litter depends on the size of the female. Females less than twenty-three inches long from snout to anus produce three to six young; those longer than twenty-five inches bear six to fourteen snakelets. Females in the east produce an average of slightly more than six young, several fewer than their midwestern counterparts. Newborn snakelets, called neonates, are about nine inches long.

The potential for problems makes birth a critical phase in the life of a copperhead. A neonate uses its egg tooth, a thorny, chisel-like projection on the tip of its snout, to puncture its flexible fetal membrane soon after birth. The egg tooth drops off soon after hatching. Once breached, the membrane collapses about the head. With nostrils exposed, the neonate remains coiled for several hours. If all goes well, a newborn copperhead can strike immediately after rupturing its fetal membranes.

Mothers stay with their snakelets for about a week, until they shed their natal skin and disperse. After birthing, the female becomes irritable and menacing, and advertises her unpleasant disposition by vibrating her tail, arching her neck, and darting her tongue.

Whereas the background hue of adults can vary from red to tan, juvenile copperheads display tail tips of bright yellow or yellowish-green. Initially used to lure small frogs, the tail's color and luring movements are eventually lost as the growing predator switches from frogs to rodents.

A copperhead spends most of its time in a flat resting coil — its tail outside, its head and forebody in an S-shaped loop near the center, and the remainder of its length wound compactly in one or two cycles. Entwined and concealed from potential prey, it waits in ambush for a meal, for several days if necessary.

Sight, scent, ground vibrations, and infrared radiation alert the snake to the presence of prey. Insects are probably located by chemosensory searching. The facial pit, between the eye and nostril, is highly sensitive to infrared wavelengths, such as thermal radiation emitted by warm-blooded animals. The paired pits, which are probably infrared imaging devices, not just heat detectors, allow copperheads and other snakes to locate prey in the dark.

Preparing for a strike, the snake brings more body length into the coil nearest its head, extending its reach. Slight movements — cocking the head, shifting the coils — are not readily noticed by the victim. A short jab, often at a distance of less than six inches, delivers the bite. The copperhead aims, opens its mouth, erects its fangs, and injects venom. Typically, the bite penetrates the prey's chest. Strikes

137

may be wildly inaccurate (to which I gratefully attest!). After striking, a copperhead immediately releases its prey and snaps back into a coil. This ensures that the prey, perhaps a sharp-toothed mouse, will not bite the snake.

It has been said for quite some time that snakes "taste" the air with their tongues. Since the original *Hollows*, we have learned that the forked tongue actually functions more as a sophisticated chemosensory edge detector. Whether following the scent emitted by an envenomated mouse or the pheromone from a member of the opposite sex, a forked tongue simultaneously samples two points along an aerial chemical gradient. Using its edge detector, a searching snake is iteratively correcting its direction of travel, shortening the length of its oscillating sweeps, and closing on the target.

The primary function of the copperhead's venom is to rapidly kill small prey; poisoning enemies is a lesser, secondary function. A defensive strike at a predator injects less venom, if any, than a predatory bite of a prey animal. A slightly viscous, watery liquid, often cloudy yellow in color, copperhead venom kills prey by inducing blood clotting, circulatory arrest, and respiratory paralysis.

The poison fang holds a fascination. The copperhead's axillary bone, to which the upper teeth are attached, can rotate almost ninety degrees. This twist permits the poison fang, which is just a greatly enlarged tooth, to be either erected or folded against the roof of the mouth. The poison fang has evolved from a solid cone to a highly effective hypodermic needle, with a hollow channel leading to an opening near the tip of the tooth. The fang's tip is solid. Compared to related species, copperheads have short fangs: For individuals of equal size, the copperhead's fang is about half the length of a rattlesnake's. Fangs have short functional lives; the snakes shed them almost monthly, swallowing them with food and passing them unaltered through the digestive tract. Several replacement fangs in various stages of development wait behind each functional fang.

Copperheads produce a relatively weak venom; most rattlesnakes have venoms two to six times more potent. Young copperheads inject two drops of venom, adults three drops, and exceptional individuals four drops. Among individuals, venom varies greatly and unpredictably in quantity and potency. One study found the strongest venom was three times as toxic as the weakest.

Although copperheads bite people more often than any other snake species does, their venom is not fatal to healthy adult humans. In uncomplicated cases, recovery occurs without the aid of antivenin. Copperhead venom acts on the blood, the walls of the blood vessels, and the central nervous system, causing, in succession, muscle twitching, swelling and discoloration, severe throbbing, numbness, respiratory congestion, intense pain, and vomiting. The bite causes no extensive hemorrhaging, and all body functions return to normal within a month.

It is interesting that poisonous snakes are immune to their own venom. Two venom-neutralizing proteins in the serum of copperhead venom counteract the lethal actions of its own species' venom.

Adult copperheads typically consume only about eight meals per growing season. Well adapted for fasting, they prey on large animals and store fat in their abdominal cavities. As sedentary animals whose body heat comes from their environment, their food requirements are modest. While digesting a large food item, a copperhead spends most of its time coiled beneath shelter.

Few animals prey on copperheads. Moles and opossums eat first-year young, and king snakes and red-tailed hawks take a few adults. Against such predators, a copperhead's most effective defense is to lie still and depend on camouflage. Irregular bands and blotches disrupt its body outline, minimizing initial detection by predators. If vulnerable and threatened, a snake rotates its head suddenly, faces the danger, and cocks its head back forty-five degrees preparing for a strike. When severely alarmed and ready to strike, the snake vibrates its tail against the surrounding leaves and twigs, producing a rattling or whirring sound. Caught in a predator's grasp, the snake's last resort is to spray musk from anal glands and defecate its cloacal contents.

As it grows, a serpent periodically replaces its inelastic skin. During an active season, copperheads shed two to four times, living an average of eighty-five days within each coat. Young that do not shed promptly stiffen inside their dry outer layer and cannot assume the compact resting coil. Shedding also beautifies: snakes are dull and dark before shedding, bright and vivid afterwards.

I n *A Country Year*, Sue Hubbell noted that there is no record of a human death caused by a copperhead bite in Missouri, and I have heard similar non-statistics cited for Virginia and West Virginia. Hubbell wrote calmly and with respect about sharing the Ozarks with copperheads, just another species with its own set of strengths, weaknesses, and desirabilities. I appreciate her point of view. You may not embrace the first copperhead you come across, but I hope this annual account eases the anxiety a bit. In the process, both snake and human will gain.

21

Oaks and Squirrels

During late summer and early fall, in years when acorns are plentiful along Pine Cabin Run, two or more squirrels work the big white oak brooding over my lab. The metal roof reports the rhythm of their labors. Last summer, after some listening practice, I learned to discriminate between the pings made by the cuttings of acorn husks and the plonks of acorn bodies, which in turn allowed me to estimate the number of bites it took a squirrel to exploit an acorn — about five. Over the years, I have noticed that my roof gets pelted only in certain summers, an important insight into the oak-squirrel association. As with most relationships, there are two points of view here: the oak's and the squirrel's.

Before diving into details, let me introduce two kinds of oaks. Species of the white oak group, like white, post, and chestnut oaks, sport leaves with rounded edges, in which the veins do not extend beyond the leaf margins to from bristles; their acorns mature the first fall after pollination in spring. In contrast, species of the black oak group, like red, scarlet, and black oaks, have leaves with bristles; their fruits ripen the second year.

Oaks fruit irregularly. In some years a white oak twenty-four inches in diameter might produce two thousand acorns, then several years may pass without any crop at all. Chestnut and scarlet oaks may produce a good acorn crop only once every four or five years. Long-term data from central Pennsylvania reveal the magnitude of variation. Over twenty-seven years, white, chestnut, red, black, and scarlet oaks produced between 0 and, respectively, 115, 101, 291, 42, and 108 pounds of acorns per acre per year; and produced no acorns in eight of twenty-three, fourteen of twenty-seven, six of twenty-seven, six of twenty-three, and ten of twenty-seven years. By major oak group, white oaks produced no acorns in seven of twenty-seven years, whereas it was four of twenty-seven for trees of the black oak group. All oak species combined produced no acorns in two of twenty-seven years. Such year-to-year variation in the quantity of nuts produced, known as mast-yearing, has been documented for a variety of nut-bearing trees.

Nut production also varies among neighboring trees during any given year. Within a single stand, some trees produce large crops while others produce none at all. In one study covering fourteen years, only one tree in twelve had good-to-heavy yields, and only during five of the years. Many of the remaining eleven trees produced only a few acorns.

What causes such variation in acorn production within a stand? Trees shaded by neighboring trees produce fewer good crops than those with crowns exposed to direct sunshine. The extent of crown suppression is only a partial answer, though, because thinning enhances fruiting in only some of the surviving trees. Other causes remain a mystery.

Getting back to year-to-year variation, spring temperatures strongly affect acorn yields. White oaks produce good crops of acorns in years when (1) late April features warm days with mean night temperatures of fifty-five to sixty-one degrees Fahrenheit and (2) thirteen to twenty days in early May are cooler with temperatures of forty-five to fifty degrees Fahrenheit. Conversely, a cool April and warm May presage a small acorn crop. When chestnut oaks are in flower in early April to early May, freezing temperatures greatly reduce acorn production. For these oaks, April and May seem to be important because female flowers emerge in late April or early May, five to ten days after male flowers. The early warm period increases the development of viable pollen while subsequent coolness enhances ovary development and fertilization.

144

Springtime weather does not affect the mast crops of all oak species in the same way. Recall that although white oak acorns ripen in one year, acorns of black oak species require two years to mature. A frost that causes failure in white oaks one year will ruin a nearby black oak's crop a year later. Mast failure in the black oak group is due to six consecutive nights of frost in May of the previous year. Oaks offset the consequences of irregular reproductive success, at least in part, by their extreme longevity. A six-hundred-year-old white oak, with a trunk a yard in diameter and fifty yards tall, has experienced many good acorn seasons.

Since the original *Hollows*, forest ecologists have learned that the amounts of acorns produced are more than simple responses to weather events. They also reflect a tree's reproductive history. Past acorn production impacts the current crop; more specifically, trees incur a tradeoff between last year's and this year's reproductive investments. Further, mast-fruiting species seem to store resources in some years to produce a big mast crop in other years. These patterns of tradeoff and storage are consistent with the hypothesis that mast-yearing is an adaptation, probably with the function of satiating seed predators.

The trick from the oak's point of view is to have at least some of its acorns germinate. Many forces mitigate against it, though. White-tailed deer, wild turkey, squirrels, and an army of insects and fungus leave few acorns embryologically intact. Further, acorns seem to have better odds of reaching adulthood if they take root outside the influence of their parent's canopy. Not only will the parent shade the seedlings, but experienced seed predators and adapted pathogens are likely concentrated there.

Squirrels enter the scene as acorn transporters. In gathering and caching nuts for their winter food supply, squirrels inadvertently improve the oak tree's reproductive success. A tree that produces occasional large crops may have its seeds dispersed farther than a tree that consistently produces a small crop. For a moment, make the simplifying assumption that squirrels bury nuts at a constant density in a rough circle around the base of a tree. Accordingly, a tree that produces twice as many fruits as its neighbor would benefit from having the nuts spread over twice as large an area. Since the radius of a circle with double the area is 1.4 times as long as the radius of a circle with half its area, a tree that annually alternates between large and no crops would theoretically have its nuts dispersed 1.4 times farther than a tree that consistently produced half as big a crop every year. Perhaps, then, oaks do not "fail" as such to produce mast in some years; instead, natural selection may have favored individual trees that produced few or no acorns in some years because this has increased the dispersal, and thereby survival of acorns, in years of high production.

Natural selection could favor mast-yearing for another reason. Poor years may depress the populations of seed predators, allowing trees to overwhelm the food needs of predators during peak years. In this sense, an oak tree may be "setting up" squirrels with a series of bad years to be overwhelmed by a flood of acorns in a good year. This could improve the odds that some seeds will escape being eaten and will germinate. The word "failure" may have crept into our interpretation because the "success" of "our" game species depends on mast.

Squirrels, however, do not care about the germination rate of acorns. They are simply obsessively pursuing their own survival and reproductive priorities.

Using its jaws like a crowbar, a squirrel inserts its lower incisors into a hole it gnawed and snaps off the shell bit by bit, exposing the meat inside. While gnawing, a squirrel seems to be ranking nuts by how efficient they are to gather. In general, a squirrel will choose to forage in a patch with abundant, low-quality food that yields a high rate of energy intake over a patch with sparse, high-quality food.

Gray squirrels exhibit definite acorn preferences. In one area, they prefer, in decreasing order, red oak, chestnut oak, and white oak acorns; and they choose all acorns over black walnuts and shagbark hickory nuts. Squirrels simply take less time to shell acorns than to hull walnuts or hickory nuts, netting more food value in less time (Think fast food.). Yet in another area, gray squirrels offered a variety of nuts consistently chose hickory nuts. The gray squirrel's site-

146

specific food preferences may reflect cultural traditions, local habits learned from elders, but based on long-term differences in the kinds and amounts of available foods.

Gray squirrels not only prefer particular foods, they also discriminate among trees within a species, and even among seeds on a single tree. Part of the reason lies in differences between the two oak groups. In general, acorns of the black oak group contain higher levels of lipid and tannin than white oak acorns. Lipids provide energy, tannins interfere with protein digestion. In this situation, the balance between lipids and tannins may determine the desirability of an acorn to a squirrel. As it turns out, acorns from lightly harvested trees contain more tannin, a poisonous acid, than nuts from heavily harvested trees. The desirability of a nut increases as its concentration of tannin decreases. Tannin acts as a natural insecticide that interferes with protein digestion of acorn-eating insects, so the variation of tannin content in acorns among and within trees may stem, at least in part, from the tree's evolutionary battle with herbivorous insects.

Surprisingly, in a controlled experiment, squirrels did not reject acorns infested with beetle larvae. The researcher concluded that gray squirrels cannot discriminate among unopened acorns based on their internal qualities. But an alternate explanation is that squirrels welcome beetle protein.

After a squirrel decides where to forage, it proceeds to store nuts for winter. Squirrels bury nuts to reduce competition from birds, mice, deer, and, of course, other squirrels. Squirrels consume or bury fruits of favorite species as they ripen in late summer and autumn, and then use them heavily thereafter while stocks last. Nuts of oaks, hickories, and walnuts make up at least 83 percent of their autumn and winter diet.

Through most of winter, gray and fox squirrels usually have plenty of stored nuts to eat. The survival bottleneck comes in late winter and early spring as caches are running low but fresh foods are not yet available. Squirrels often lose weight during this time. To get through winter, the animals employ a specific strategy of food hoarding.

147

Fox and gray squirrels bury individual nuts in widely scattered locations. This is called scatterhoarding. Animals that are unable to defend the food against competitors will likely store the food items in numerous, widely scattered, small caches. The optimal spacing of scattered caches reflects a tradeoff: the more scattered the caches, the fewer will be lost to competitors, but the more time and energy will be spent storing the nuts. The spatial pattern of scatterhoarded sites balances these costs and benefits.

In contrast, the red squirrel larderhoards conifer cones, storing all of its food in one large cache. Spreading its food over a large area would not reduce the red squirrel's losses to other animals that can open cones, such as mice, chipmunks, and other red squirrels.

Once nuts are buried, how do squirrels find them? Some animals, such as Clark's nutcracker, a jay of western North America, have the extraordinary ability to remember the exact locations of thousands of seed caches. Squirrels, however, do not remember specific sites. Resident squirrels remember a cache's general location, giving them an advantage over naïve newcomers. Squirrels locate individual buried nuts using their keen sense of smell. Experiments have shown that squirrels can smell the nuts that other squirrels buried, and even recover nuts through a foot of snow. Remarkably, fox squirrels can detect differences in densities of buried nuts, then concentrate their search in those high-density areas. This ability, plus their powerlessness to defend caches from larger species such as deer and turkey, may have led to the evolution of the scatterhoarding strategy of nut storage. Despite the squirrels' keen sense of smell, many acorns escape and sprout.

With their dependence on acorns, squirrel populations fluctuate with the mast crop, but with a time lag of one year. A good food supply in the fall and a mild winter result in earlier and larger litters the following spring. A poor mast crop leads to delayed, or even cancelled, spring breeding. When black oaks, beech, walnut, butternut, and hickory produce small crops, the harvest of squirrels by humans also drops the following year. Since 1930, squirrel populations in West Virginia have fluctuated radically, primarily as a function

148

of the previous year's mast availability, a measure that incorporates both mast production and winter harshness.

Oaks and squirrels are tight partners in a mutually exploitative relationship. The reproductive success of oaks depends on squirrels to disperse their acorns and plant them in favorable sites. Oaks accomplish this by producing good acorn crops only occasionally. In turn, squirrels depend on oaks for winter food, but pay the time and energy costs of scatterhoarding. Scatterhoarding and the squirrel's imperfect sense of smell ensure that at least some acorns endure to germinate. Thus, a causal chain connects springtime weather, pollination success of oaks, and annual variations of mast, with the squirrel's overwintering success, reproductive rate, and population density. The pings and plonks on my tin roof remind me of one of the great mutualistic acts of the Appalachian play.

22

Highlanders

I do not know when humans first set foot in Appalachia. Most anthropologists agree that we have been here since the last ice age, about twelve thousand years ago; a few argue for a far more ancient colonization, possibly one hundred thousand years ago. I cannot settle the question, but I can suggest a sequence of human habitation in the Appalachian Mountains: indigenous Americans, European settlers, and mountain lovers.

Continuing the confessional, a second issue I cannot resolve is how our mountains got their name. In one history, Native Americans named the mountains Appalachia, or "endless mountains." Alternate history posits that as Spaniards probed for gold in the 1500s, the Appalachee Indians of northwest Florida pointed towards the distant mountains, the southern Appalachians. A little later, European maps started carrying various forms of the name. Maybe both stories are true — perhaps it's best left a mystery.

In pre-Columbian times, eastern North America was covered by a seemingly endless forest. Closer examination may have revealed a mosaic of different forest communities interspersed with occasional openings. North American Indians used broadcast fire to clear the woods of underbrush and preclude the clandestine approach of raiding tribes. Because new grass attracted grazers such as deer, Indians used fire to maintain the wild game habitat along the forest-grass edge. They also may have used fires to drive deer to waiting hunters.

In the late seventeenth century, several tribes inhabited the Blue Ridge. The Cherokee, for example, were numerous in southern

Appalachia, especially between today's Asheville, North Carolina, and the Great Smoky Mountains. One census estimated twenty-five thousand Cherokee thinly dispersed through the region.

Humans have also occupied West Virginia for at least twelve thousand years. This time of first colonization, which is fairly typical of many North American sites, coincides with the existence of Beringia, a land bridge that connected Russia and Alaska during the last ice age. Most anthropologists think that Asians colonized North America ten thousand to fifteen thousand years ago. Based on gross anatomy, the closest relatives of Native Americans are Siberians. After crossing the north Pacific, the first people swiftly dispersed southward to inhabit the entire western hemisphere.

At first, American aborigines lived as nomads and hunted large mammals, but by 4,000 BC they adopted a semi-sedentary life-style. The hunting-gathering economy of pre-1,000 BC was gradually supplemented by small-scale horticulture. Around 800 to 900 AD, the Mississippian Mound Builders grew corn, beans, and squash. By 1,000 AD, dense populations of the Late Prehistoric Village Farmers lived in permanently stockaded villages and practiced intensive agriculture. Such evidence has led some archeologists to identify eastern North America as one of the world's four centers of plant domestication.

Paleontological evidence suggests that prehistoric Appalachian humans consumed a varied diet. During the Pleistocene, from about 1.8 million to ten thousand years ago, North America supported a community of large-bodied mammals as diverse as that roaming Africa. The southern Appalachians sustained ninety species of mammals, more than any other area of eastern North America. The large seeds of some North American plants, such as Kentucky coffee tree, osage orange, and paw paw, seem out of ecological context — no extant animals eat and pass their seeds. This incongruity suggests that recently extinct, large-bodied herbivores dispersed their seeds. Likewise, the extreme spininess of some trees, such as honey locust, does not make sense without invoking the existence of large mammals. It is not unreasonable to surmise that humans, an opportunistic omnivore, dined on this diversity.

Europeans began to move into Appalachia in the early 1700s. The first settlement in eastern West Virginia was built near Shepherdstown in 1719. Settlers invading the hunting grounds of the Kanawha, Mingo, Delaware, and Shawnee peoples found the forests little disturbed. The lush wildlife that provided sustenance to early European settlers apparently depended on habitat that the Native Americans had been sustaining with fires. Fires also helped maintain grassland corridors, such as the Shenandoah Valley that provided a major thoroughfare for the dispersal of settlers.

As seen through my zoologist eyes, European immigrants, like other dispersing animals, may have been escaping environments that limited their survival and reproduction. Restated in the words of history, people were eager to escape intolerance, taxes, and other forms of oppression. Playing a major role in the peopling of Appalachia were the Scotch-Irish or Ulstermen. Persecuted by the crown, they arrived *en masse* in Pennsylvania around 1682, where they settled outside German settlements, which in turn, were already located west of the Quakers in southeast Pennsylvania. This was only a temporary home for the Ulstermen, though. As game, land, and other resources became scarce in Pennsylvania and the French and Indian War of 1763 secured the countryside, a surge of Scotch-Irish homesteaders penetrated central and southern Appalachia. A few brave souls struggled westward over the Blue Ridge escarpment, but most followed the easier Great Valley route southward and settled lands from West Virginia through North Carolina.

The first Blue Ridge homesteaders raised their log cabins where they found water, gentle slopes, and fertile soil — generally on sites with bedrock of granite or basalt. In contrast, areas underlain by sandstone or shale generally offered thin rocky soil, steep slopes, and intermittent springs. The earliest arrivals cleared the broadest valleys and erected cabins. When the generous lowlands filled, the homesteaders' children and other late arrivals moved into the coves and hollows of higher elevations. Temperatures in the Blue Ridge averaged five to thirteen degrees Fahrenheit lower than adjacent lowlands, but precipitation and winds were greater. Accordingly, many homesteaders chose sites strategically located with protection against westerly winds but exposed to maximum sunlight. In these marginal sites, people scrabbled for a living. Even later homesteaders were left with only hillsides to clear, which quickly became infertile when their off-contour plowing aggravated erosion of the already thin soil. With this sequence of settlement, humans conformed to a pattern seen in other animals: dispersing individuals were forced to colonize increasingly marginal habitats.

The shell of a log house — a single large room, eventually with a stone fireplace and chimney — could be erected in one day by four men. Logs were notched to fit together at the house's corners, and the wide spaces between logs were filled with wood, rocks, mud, or anything that happened to be handy. Using German or Scandinavian building methods (our house's corners overlap in German design), these early settlers constructed sturdy log homes, many of which continue to nestle folks today.

European immigrants found one of the richest natural environments on Earth. Flocks of passenger pigeons darkened the sky; woodland buffalo, elk, and timber wolf roamed the mountains. Where *Homo sapiens* and the Pennsylvania long rifle moved in, though, these large-bodied animals disappeared. Woodland buffalo were wiped out by about 1800; elk and mountain lion disappeared by 1855; and wolves vanished by 1900. By the early 1900s, suffering from the combined blows of market hunting, lumbering, and farming, white-tailed deer became virtually unknown throughout the southern Appalachians.

In little more than a century, the settlers thoroughly logged the vast, eastern deciduous forest. Colonists cut trees to clear fields for agriculture and to feed the eastern lumber markets. Shipbuilding, with its demand for tall, straight wooden masts, became a major colonial industry. By the end of the eighteenth century, British shipwrights were importing a large proportion of their lumber from the American colonies. The greatest decline in forest area occurred between 1750 and 1850; by 1880 less than 35 percent of southern Appalachia's virgin forest remained. Around 1880, railroads opened the mountain summits to systematic logging. With help from the

154

rails, almost all remaining tracts of virgin timber were converted to lumber, turpentine, and ship masts. By 1920, all was gone except for a few hundred acres.

Today's "mountain whites" are descendants from migrants who settled in mountains such as the Alleghenies and Blue Ridge, and within the Unakas along the Tennessee-North Caroline border. With the prime land already taken, many latecomers moved westward, to Kentucky and beyond. The Cumberland Gap, found in 1750 by British surveyor Thomas Walker, funneled the westward dispersal. This natural breach, only one thousand six hundred feet above sea level, and other mountain gaps played major roles in the settlement of the United States.

The dispersal behavior of humans points to the possibility of different genetic predispositions for sedentary versus dispersing behaviors. Conjecturing, there may be a "wanderlust gene" in the human population. Daniel Boone, who in 1769 pioneered the Cumberland Gap by following a Cherokee and Shawnee hunting trail, may have had such a gene — two of Boone's preceding generations and one succeeding generation also sought the frontier. Boone's contribution was to hack out the 208-mile Wilderness Road, which allowed Carolina and Virginia families to pour into the lush lands of Kentucky.

O f the original *Hollows*, the following three-and-a-half pages received the most reactions — not surprising given it was a look in the mirror. Some wrote from distant Appalachian places, others sought me out after my illustrated talks. Some thanked me for making sense of their family's behaviors; others, just as thoughtful, excoriated me for relying on outdated references, overgeneralizing, and perpetuating myth. Few, it seems, fell in the middle. Praise or criticism, I thank you.

I based the original passage (pp. 137-140) on diverse publications, interviews of folks from Maine to Georgia, twelve years of work and play in central Appalachia, and several critical reviews of the evolving manuscript, so I cannot simply dismiss it. Therefore, at the risk of maddening some, here is the near-original passage, warts and all.

The story of pre-industrial Appalachian highlanders is one of hard knocks in a farm-and-forest economy. They girdled trees to clear new ground, producing quick canopy gaps. Plowing the soil with a bull-tongue, a wide blade attached to a plow, the highlanders grew staples of corn, cabbage, and beans. They raised tobacco and gathered ginseng for the market, harvested wild bloodroot and ginger for medicinal purposes, and grazed livestock on balds. Not long after they cleared their acreage, however, rains washed the topsoil away, and the land reverted to poor pasture or second growth forest. Forest nutrients that had been accumulating for eons left as muddy water.

For generations, highlanders scratched a living from steep hillsides and narrow valleys. This accounts in part for why highlanders held few slaves, an economic adaptation better suited for large flat fertile floodplains.

From 1700 to 1900, the fractured topography limited human intercourse (in both ways) much as it has isolated salamander populations since the last ice age. Each enclave superimposed its own vocabulary on the Queen's English. The dialect of mountaineers still includes words and phrases common to Elizabethan England, including the old Anglo-Saxonisms "hit" which means "it," "hisn" for "his," and "aims to settle down." Verbs are prefixed with "a," as in "I'm a-goin'." Some linguists consider mountain talk to be the closest surviving relative of the language of Shakespeare.

A constellation of interesting behavioral traits also arose. With the custom of settling close to kin and intermarrying, many valleys became the domain of a single family. Even though mountaineers knew well the consequences of inbreeding, first cousins still married, sometimes to the extent that entire districts were interrelated.

By the early 1900s, many mountain folk were still cut off from greater society. Five or six generations made do without improved tools, medical advances, and long-distance communication. Some mountaineers had never seen a town. The world as they knew it extended a few miles from their home. In Greene County, Tennessee, I have talked to people who were born, grew up, married, had their families, and plan to die in a single hollow. Here was an ethnic group that remained relatively unmixed.

The music of the southern mountaineer is uniquely American. Because a large proportion of mountain folk descended from Scotch highlanders, their music evolved from the ballads of England and Scotland. Tunes brought to the mountains by eighteenth century colonial settlers took root and flourished, shielded from the outside world. Though some of these tunes were already dead in Britain, they thrived in the southern hills. Appalachian people still have a native fondness for music and dancing, and they hold fiddler and banjo player in high regard.

Antic, bawdy, or mournful, many mountain songs were homemade, passed along by word of mouth. Appalachian songs packed a punch, a primordial intensity, that the mellow, sweet British versions often lacked. Mountain tunes were also freer, more spacious. The purest ballads came from the most isolated areas, with certain valleys in western North Carolina, southwestern Virginia, and eastern Kentucky being especially rich musically.

In the old country, whiskey-making was perfected by the poorer classes of Irish as a townsman's only weapon against the government. Immigrants brought this craft to North America, typically hiding the still in a rhododendron thicket along a run. The difficulty of getting surplus corn to market at least partly motivated whiskey production. Making moonshine, "blockadin'," was a family activity. Mountaineers still get excited over good, cold water, in part because of its crucial contribution to good moonshine. Dependable springs are guarded like reliable fishing holes and ginseng patches. I have heard men damned to hell for "ruinin' a good spring."

Clans were patriarchal. Intense individualism and clan loyalty led to a general disregard for the law. It is logical, therefore, that Appalachian frontiersmen were the first to establish governments of their own, in defiance of the king.

157

Some women married young, then proceeded to have many (e.g., seven to ten) children. High infant mortality ensured that hillside family cemeteries usually contained several children.

Because their small reference group was of overwhelming importance, extended communities did not develop. Human relationships were personal, based on kinship. Mountain folk were passionately attached to their homes. Emotional dependence, not shared activities, bound one to another — a relationship that led to insecurity in the face of broader challenges. Suspicion reigned, filling mountain societies with intense anxieties. This behavior contributed to wars between families.

Life on a small mountain farm was hard, and the occupants languished in isolation. As the nation as a whole progressed, the gap between townfolk and highlander widened. However destitute, they were seldom abject and never resorted to begging. Haughtily independent, they could not stand to be bossed. They were existence-oriented, not future- or improvement-oriented. They did not strive for objects, but for being liked and accepted within their reference group. This made them supersensitive to slights and criticisms.

Passive resignation was normal. Sharp limits in the amount and quality of land led to fatalism. In the mountains, nature did not yield, and the harshness of the land overcame the man. Mountaineers had little confidence in their own abilities to meet and overcome unfamiliar problems. A residue surfaces even now when I see local people offered an opportunity: they promptly cite an inability to handle the responsibility and decline.

The highlanders' behaviors seemed inconsistent. On the one hand, the average mountaineer was lean, inquisitive, and shrewd. Yet the individual felt little control over his or her own destiny and consequently planned little for the future. The mountain folk regarded hospitality as a sacred duty towards "furriners"; nevertheless, the average mountaineer was schooled to dissemble.

The highlanders' fierce independence and individualism, so adaptive in the habitat of an isolated mountain hollow, became a

158

stumbling block in the modern world where cooperation was essential in work, education, and progress. Possibly because it seemed irrelevant, mountaineers derided education. Folks signed contracts they could not read, leading to outside control of the coal and timber resources, and thereby of the land. Many landowners sold the mining rights when deep mining depended on the relative harmlessness of picks and shovels. Mechanized surface mining, however, brought disaster to their descendants. Miners diverted water, poisoned wells and streams, piled refuse, withdrew support timbers in mine tunnels, and cut roads. Courts upheld them in all of this. In particular, judges and lawyers protected the mine owners from the liabilities created by their actions on the bodies and property of workers and landowners. Absentee parties bought coal rights at fifty cents to a few dollars per acre and were free to do with the land as they saw fit. For many mountaineers, strip mining destroyed the economic base of their existence. To this day, mountain people have no national organization to represent their needs.

With poor diets and joint problems, mountaineers were not notably healthy. Many with physical defects and little or no education remained in the home hollow and reproduced. The high rate of illegitimate births apparently stemmed from the girls' desire for purpose and self-worth. In the mountains, birth control was poorly understood; poverty, self-perpetuating.

As I said four pages back, several recent authors and thoughtful critics have opened my eyes to a different picture. As I continue to learn, I have come to see that some of my statements may have been more relevant to people in isolated areas, like hollows without through roads, than throughout the highlands generally. Viewing life through one's local reference group and deriding formal education may have applied more in remote hollows than accessible towns. I see how my original words cast highlanders as a homogeneous population, with a uniform culture, in a coherent region, with a common history.

I was also overly influenced by the "invented Appalacia." Several modern historians assert that after the Civil War, Appalachians entered America's consciousness as a curious people of a distinct region through the writings of travel writers, home mission advocates, folk song collectors, handicraft leaders, and even a few regional scholars. These people promoted narrow views by: (1) generalizing about the southern Appalachian region, (2) valuing folklife as an instrument for advancing rural improvement projects, and (3) ignoring racial and ethnic minorities, even though African Americans comprised up to 12 percent of Appalachia's population. They perpetuated some well-turned phrases, like "strange land and peculiar people" and "out of step culturally and economically."

Appalachia has always been more diverse than life in isolated hollows, more varied than a single regional folk society. Although absentee economic interests manipulated state laws and local political agendas in the coalfields, this phenomenon was weaker in the Shenandoah Valley; although remote uplands may have hosted Scotch-Irish descendants, broad valleys and industrial towns were home to African Americans, Italians, and Poles; and although topographic constraints may have facilitated fatalism in remote areas, communities near roads provided more life choices.

My now twenty-two years of teaching, environmental protection, and playing in Appalachia support this more pluralistic view. Although my picture of folks characterized by musical talent, curiosity, shrewdness, orientation to the local reference group, fatalism, and derision of education is consistent with my experience with some people in some Appalachian places, I've also found optimism, motivation, dissatisfaction with current conditions, love of family, and a strong sense of place. Even in contrast to this book's organizing theme, I've personally benefited from altruistic acts unexplainable by the neo-Darwinian model of human behavior.

By the 1930s, one was considered poor if he or she lived in a log house, so most log dwellings were covered with milled wood to resemble the then-fashionable board-and-batten homes. Our log home bears the scars of this swinging pendulum. Built in the 1820s, the logs were left exposed for many years. Then, studs were retrofitted to hold weatherboard. Coming full cycle in the 1960s, the weatherboards were removed, reexposing the logs.

Through the years, the mountains have been a physical, social, cultural, economic, educational, and religious barrier. The late 1950s were bust years, part of a three-decade-long depression when people deserted the mountains for factories in Chicago, Cleveland, and Detroit. A modest reversal began in the 1970s.

Peopling the mountains today, in addition to the mountaineers' descendants, are educated drop-outs, weekenders, summer vacationers, retirees, and outdoor enthusiasts. What I call "mountain love" has motivated this third wave of Appalachian habitation. We mountain lovers are attracted to mountains because they help us find who we are — in the hills, our minds drift towards fundamental questions. What is the meaning of life? How can I make a difference? The convoluted topography invites exploration — eyes, ears, and nose become alert as we walk up the hills and down the hollows. Together, the sensuousness of the mountains and the curiosity they excite give strength and clear-eyed vision.

Annie Dillard expressed mountain love well when, finding inspiration in a valley of Virginia's Blue Ridge, she opened her senses to nature's excitement, transcended her daily blinders, felt the pulse of the seasons, and shrank before the overwhelming fecundity of life around her. Yes, humans have changed Appalachia — but the mountains have touched us, too.

Seasonal Acts

23
Autumn Leaves

I t happens every fall. I'm hell-bent on splitting a pile of wood, winterizing the old truck, or jogging from the house to the lab when I feel the tug. Resist as I might, my concentration wanes. I give in, and indulge in inspecting the colorful leaves. The meander takes me farther and farther from my task. During these rambles I am reminded of a favorite yet deceptively complex question, "Why do leaves change color and drop?"

When biologists confront "why" questions, two camps usually emerge and commence battle. One group argues that each feature of every living thing has a purpose, that in some way every trait is an adaptation that contributes to the survival or reproduction of the individual. The other school counters that some life processes have no reason for being, are adaptively neutral, just happen. (As you know by now, I sit in the former camp.) The recent history of evolutionary biology is punctuated with the ebb and flow of this debate. With these conflicting possibilities in mind, I'll weigh in with my interpretation of the meaning of autumn leaves.

Leaves change color, then fall. Let's consider these events in their natural sequence. We all know that leaves are green in the summer; what may be news is that summer leaves also harbor other pigments. July's dogwoods certainly contain chlorophyll, a molecule that reflects green light and plays a crucial role in photosynthesis, but they also contain carotene and xanthophyll, molecules that reflect orange and yellow light, respectively. Together, these three pigments allow a plant to absorb light of a wider range of wavelengths, and thereby enable the plant to capture more energy from sunshine, than if it had only one pigment. Because summer leaves contain all three pigments and yet are green, the green of chlorophyll must overpower the other colors.

The process of photosynthesis continually breaks down chlorophyll, but as long as the weather is warm, plants continue to produce it. Through the summer, plants maintain a fairly constant chlorophyll concentration and thereby go on reflecting green wavelengths. As the temperature drops, leaves absorb less water and minerals, and chlorophyll synthesis decreases. By late summer, chlorophyll is breaking down faster than it is being replaced. What little photosynthesis still occurs in the fall completely exhausts any remaining chlorophyll molecules. Suddenly, the other pigments are unmasked. Zooming up to the continental scale, the fall color wave advances southward at about forty miles per day. Though the yellow of October's hickories seems to appear spontaneously, it was there all along. From this perspective, the yellow and orange shades of autumn leaves, leftovers of a previously functioning biological mechanism, are manifestations of adaptive traits.

Red autumn leaves, on the other hand, develop in a different way. During the cool nights and sunny days of fall, leaf cells begin to synthesize a new kind of molecule called anthocyanin, which reflects red wavelengths, instead of chlorophyll. Anthocyanin accumulates in the sap of leaf cells. Anthocyanin's formation depends on (1) the breakdown of sugars in the presence of bright light and (2) a decrease in phosphate due to the plant's diminishing water supply. The brighter the light during this period, the greater the production of anthocyanin, the more brilliant the colors. The most flaming reds develop when autumn days are bright and cool, and the nights chilly but not freezing. In contrast to orange and yellow, we know of no purpose for the trait "red leaves." Thus, the redness of tree leaves in the autumn appears to be adaptively neutral — they convey neither advantages nor disadvantages to the reproductive success of the individual tree.

166

Since publication of the original *Hollows*, a tentative idea has surfaced on why leaves turn red in the autumn. Anthocyanin, a molecule the leaf makes fresh in the fall, screens out blue wavelengths that normally power photosynthesis in the chlorophyll-laden layers of the leaf. This observation suggests that by filtering out blue, the red pigment turns off the photosynthesis reaction, and this in turn facilitates the tree's recycling of nutrients from its leaves to seeds or roots. Thus, it is possible that red leaves may not represent, after all, a caveat to the neo-Darwinian dogma.

The second feature of a tree's seasonal change is its loss of leaves. For the past several years, I have watched a sugar maple sprinkle its leaves through still air. (I use the languid plume from my wood stove to verify total calm.) Leaves falling through quiet air betray an active process of self-amputation.

During summer, long days induce leaves to synthesize a hormone called auxin, which helps maintain cells throughout the leaf's stem that are firmly glued to each other and to the stem. Shorter days cause auxin production to drop, which allows the development of cells that only weakly attach a leaf stem to its branch. The resulting abscission layer consists of a band of cells that separate easily from each other — it is designed to fail mechanically. Imagine how easy it would be to topple a brick wall in which the bottom two rows were set without mortar. Similarly, with its abscission zone in place, a leaf will drop at the slightest breeze, or even, as was the case with my maple, just under the weight of the leaf itself. After separation, a thin layer of cork cells quickly seals the wound.

As an example of evolutionary convergence, some desert plants also amputate their leaves, even some branches, but as an adaptation to reduce water loss during drought.

I am again led to ask "why?" Why do trees shed their leaves? Leaves are thin, full of water, and thereby exquisitely vulnerable to freezing. In autumn, trees drain their leaves, but a tree covered with dry leaves would never do. Should fall gusts snap off drained leaves, a tree would face winter with thousands of open, hollow wounds. Water would enter these openings, so a single winter of alternating freezes and thaws would yield a tree that looked like a frazzled lightning target. Sealing the stem may also reduce water loss and pathogen entry. At least in part then, today's trees shed their leaves and seal the scars because this saved their ancestors from being ripped apart by wedges of ice.

Marcescent leaves, that wither but are not shed, offer instructive exceptions. In the autumn, little or no abscission zone forms in their petioles. Even though in winter these leaves look dead, like on a white oak, some tissue at the base of the petiole remains alive. Within this living zone, an abscission layer develops in the spring, then soon thereafter the leaves drop. So how do I explain the withered, brown leaves clinging to my white oaks in February? One hypothesis is that marcescence arose in southern climates as an evergreen trait, and that these tree species are still adapting to northern winters.

When you find yourself contemplating a blazing autumn hillside, consider two notions. Although the colors may inspire you to daydream, wax poetic, or paint a landscape, the reds may be irrelevant to their trees' reproductive success. Further, when those gay leaves flutter groundward, the tree is actively amputating its own members to prevent a shattering trauma. At least that's how the teleological metaphor would go. I offer these musings not to cancel mystery, which we all crave, but to foster a deeper understanding of the biological underpinnings of the autumn season in which we rejoice.

24

Window on Bird Politics

Busy birds come and go, helter-skelter, about my pile of sunflower seeds. One comes to expect this when birds have been conditioned by easy calories. When I watch casually, this is all I see. But when I critically examine the scene, I discover that my bird feeder serves as a window into a subtle world of dictators, parasites, and liars. Read this chapter on a cold winter day, feet propped up and hot chocolate at the ready, overlooking your stocked bird feeder. You will find your backyard birds engaged in intriguing politics.

In the winter, my feeder attracts single-species flocks of northern juncos, American goldfinches, evening grosbeaks, and purple finches, and mixed-species flocks featuring black-capped chickadees, tufted titmice, white-breasted nuthatches, and occasionally downy woodpeckers and brown creepers. A mixed-species flock includes individuals of two or more species. Although pairs of cardinals and of rufous-sided towhees occasionally visit, flocks bring most of my customers. The two reasons birds form into flocks — greater protection against predators and higher feeding efficiency — provide insight into the action at a feeder. Let us take a look at each.

Many of us have seen on television a film in which a lioness fixates on and then attacks an isolated zebra, the one that strayed from the herd or behaved differently. The pruning of marginal individuals favors the evolution of centripetal instincts. For this reason, flocks of small birds tighten in the presence of a raptor.

This point was driven home not long ago when I saw a flock of starlings flying in a highly synchronized formation. Based on their

171

tightness, I thought a predator might be nearby. Sure enough, a few seconds later, a sharp-shinned hawk glided into view. Under my breath, I hoped a stray would trigger a stoop, but on that day the squadron was disciplined.

In many bird species, when one member of a flock sees an aerial predator, it gives a special alarm. Chickadees and titmice respond to the cry by diving into bushes and remaining quiet for several minutes; downy woodpeckers and white-breasted nuthatches simply freeze on the tree trunk. Regardless of the type of response, alarm calls present us with an interesting evolutionary problem. Some flocks include both genetically related individuals and unrelated members of the same species. In such flocks, alarm calls alert not only genetic relatives, which would make the call explainable by kin selection, but also are heard by unrelated members of the same species. Thus, a warning caller could increase the fitness of unrelated flock mates. This would represent genetic altruism, reproductive selflessness, a phenomenon unexplainable by natural selection. How then do we account for alarm calls?

Perhaps the individual that sees the hawk and sounds the alert is manipulating its flock mates into heading for cover even though the responders do not know the predator's position. Then the caller could head for the far side of the flock. Thus, straightforward natural selection may have favored the behavior of alarm calling because the caller increases his own chance of survival to the detriment of its flock mates.

On the other hand, we know that some flocks reflect the action of kin selection. During winter, black-capped chickadees and tufted titmice, the nucleus of natural mixed-species flocks, forage with their mates and offspring. The high pitched alarm calls of chickadees and titmice are ventriloquistic, making the caller hard to locate. These observations suggest that chickadees and titmice may benefit from kin selection.

The great tit has added an intriguing layer to this story In Denmark in the winter, great tits give alarm calls without a predator being nearby, especially when food is scarce. Hearing this false alarm call, a bird leaves its feeding site for shelter, giving the manipulator access to the food. In this population, all great tits give false alarm calls — each individual is both manipulator and manipulatee.

I have long wondered if this is happening at my feeder. Several times per day, even though I see no predator, the juncos, sparrows, and other ground-feeding birds explode into the air and fly away. It is not unusual for one or two individuals to remain on the spot and continue feeding. Cheating has its limits, though, because false alarm calls are effective only as long as they are not too frequent.

Flocking also improves the odds of finding food. Look at the northern junco, which normally feeds on the ground below a feeder. Snowbirds feed in large winter flocks. They peck and scratch, and deplete a spot before searching elsewhere. Chase-offs by other juncos are common: a bird might deplete its own feeding spot, observe a neighbor feeding, make a quick approach to chase it off, and then feed at the conquered spot. If the site proves empty, the bird will make another approach-attack. Dominant displacers tend to be large, dark males.

The members of a junco flock conform to a stable pecking order. Within this society, subordinate individuals are at a disadvantage. They carry less body fat and thereby have less fuel for winter than dominant birds; they possess larger adrenal glands, which is an indication of a high level of stress; they feed at the periphery of the flock where they are more vulnerable to predators; and they burn more energy avoiding other birds.

Apparently, juncos find it more profitable to chase off subordinates and conquer feeding spots than to search for food independently. Most of the encounters below a feeder are of this parasitic type. Dominant junco shepherds use subordinates as their food-finding sheep. From the low-ranking bird's point of view, the food-finding ability of the flock reduces the odds of outright starvation — seeds are clustered, and groups seem to find them more efficiently than individual birds do. Regardless of an individual's standing, then, the benefits of flocking seem to outweigh the costs.

Large flock size improves an individual's feeding efficiency. As flock size of the yellow-eyed junco, a western relative, increases, individuals spend less time scanning for predators, which in turn allows more food pecks. This is also true in Wisconsin's mixed-species flocks of American goldfinch, pine siskin, and purple finch. Even though individuals spend more time in aggressive interactions as flock size grows, the mean rate of food pecks still increases with flock size.

The behavior of the white-throated sparrow, which breeds in Canada and overwinters in Appalachia, reflects the tradeoff between feeding efficiency and predation risk. Like juncos, white-throated sparrows form loose winter foraging flocks with dominance hierarchies. In one experiment, when birds of known rank were provided food at varying distances from dense shrubbery, individuals preferred to feed nearer the cover. They would nearly exhaust the food in secure areas before moving farther into the open. Dominant birds fed nearer to shelter than subordinates since their high rank allowed them access to preferred sites. Subordinate white-throated sparrows enjoyed high foraging efficiency but were relegated to more exposed sites where they faced a higher risk of getting caught.

The make-up of winter foraging flocks varies among species. The black-capped chickadee and tufted titmouse make an interesting contrast. During spring and summer, black-capped chickadees live as monogamous pairs and defend breeding territories that provide a rotten stump for a nest and enough caterpillars and other foods for parents and chicks. In September, the molting adults and their fledged young gather into a flock and repel other chickadee flocks from their communal territory, an area two to three times larger than the breeding territory. In winter, each individual chickadee takes on one of two possible behavioral modes. It either becomes a flock regular and spends its entire winter in a single flock, or it behaves as a floater that moves among three or four flocks. About 80 percent of the members of a flock are regulars, with an average of ten regulars per flock. Future mates pair when the flock forms in the fall, so it is a safe bet that a flock with ten regulars contains five mated pairs. Floaters, though reproductively mature, are prevented from breeding by dominant individuals.

174

Within a chickadee flock of regulars and floaters exists a clear-cut linear pecking order. Each member of the flock consistently either dominates or is subordinate to flock mates. Chickadee pecking orders, like those of the northern junco, are the same at or away from feeders. Within a flock, floaters rank below regulars of their own sex. Counterintuitively, should the male at the top of the pecking order disappear, the highest ranking floating male takes over as the dominant male of the flock. Likewise, should a high ranking female vanish, the dominant female floater assumes the regular spot. Each substitute acquires the mate of the bird it replaced. In chickadee society, vacancies are not filled by the next highest regular apparently because regulars are locked into their status by the rank of their mate.

Floaters do not fill every vacancy, however. If the mate of a newly inserted floater dies, a second floater will not pair with the first. Instead, the first reverts to floating. It seems that floaters only insert when a high-ranking bird of the same sex dies. Thus, regular, low-ranking widows and widowers remain mateless for the rest of the winter. Because only the top two or three pairs in a flock will gain a territory and breed, and because the fastest route to high-rank is via insertion as a floater, floating is actually more desirable than a low-ranking, regular position.

To reproduce successfully a chickadee should emerge from winter as a high-ranked regular. The chances of gaining a breeding territory, listed from highest to lowest positions, are high-ranked regular, high-ranked floater, low-ranked regular, and low-ranked floater. It makes sense, then, that this happens to be the order in which the slots of the flock fill as young birds arrive in the fall.

Contrast chickadee society with that of the tufted titmouse. Tufted titmice also form winter flocks in the fall, but their flock size ranges from only two to five individuals. Almost half of all titmouse flocks consist of only one adult male and one adult female. Further, since titmice do not float, the membership of a titmouse flock remains stable throughout the winter. The average territory of a titmouse flock covers thirteen acres and, like the chickadees', its boundaries

175

are stable and delineated early in the flocking season. On or near their territorial boundaries, the birds aggressively engage neighbor flocks — jeering loudly, erecting crests, and flitting about with quick spastic movements. Like juncos and chickadees, titmice exhibit linear dominance hierarchies within their flocks. Males dominate females, and seniority on the flock territory determines dominance within a sex. Again, titmouse ranks assigned away from feeders hold at the feeders as well.

When a winter titmouse flock disbands in March, the dominant male and female, who are mates, establish a breeding territory within the winter flock range. This pair will most likely be the only titmouse couple to breed within the flock range.

Chickadees and titmice often forage together in mixed-species flocks during winter. Flocks composed of black-capped chickadees, tufted titmice, and several follower species, such as downy woodpeckers and white-breasted nuthatches, are common in Appalachia. Birds form mixed-species flocks for the same reasons that members of the same species flock together. Feeding in mixed-species flocks proves profitable for sponging individuals. For example, white-throated sparrows chase off juncos, providing an interspecific example of the shepherd-sheep relationship. Reducing the risks of being caught by a predator works for similar-looking birds, regardless of whether they are members of the same species. Chickadees, titmice, and nuthatches are gray above, white below, and about the same size. Presumably, individuals of these three species look enough alike that birds hiding behind each other do not betray an odd size or color.

Carolina chickadees, though, seem to incur a cost by foraging with the more dominant tufted titmice. In an experiment in Ohio, when titmice were removed from such mixed-species flocks, chickadees began foraging in more titmouse-like sites and showed greater growth, an indication of better nutrition. Thus, dominance exists both within and between wintering bird species.

All these species — chickadees, titmice, woodpeckers, and nuthatches — fall prey to raptors and respond to each others' alarm calls. Within these flocks, chickadees and titmice give most of the

176

alarm calls. When a downy woodpecker forages with a chickadee-titmouse flock, the woodpecker spends less time being vigilant and thereby eats more. The core species seem to get nothing in return from the woodpeckers.

I invite you to uncover these and other intrigues by closely watching the action at your bird feeder. You may notice that winter-flocking birds are slow to visit a newly stocked station, but then descend in droves after that first visit. Even this simple observation allows two inferences. First, winter-flocking birds often overlook good food in new places, possibly because they have been conditioned by known patches of natural food. Second, that first visit by a single bird assures a visit by the entire flock, thereby demonstrating one of the big advantages of group living, namely that birds learn from each other where the food is. Do not underestimate the power of simple, local acts to illuminate the Appalachian play.

25

Thwarting Swords of Ice

Living things are made of cells. With an electron microscope, we can see that these tiny chambers hold criss-crossing tubules, packages of high-powered fuel, and bins of enzymes that could digest the cell itself — all suspended in jelly and wrapped in an ultra thin membrane. These fragile, interacting parts import and process food, consume and disperse oxygen, generate and export waste products, and by cooperating, build exact copies of themselves. Life is possible only if each component occupies its proper place in the subcellular neighborhood. The medium for this machinery is an exquisitely versatile fluid, water. Exquisitely versatile, though, only so long as it remains liquid.

Freezing weather challenges living things to keep the water in their cells from freezing. Vincent Dethier, an insect physiologist who made his mark by discovering how a fly is able to taste, went right to the problem. In his book, *The World of the Tent-makers*, he declared that the sword of winter is the ice crystal. If you want to get a feeling for the unyielding character of an ice crystal, deflect your breath, inch your nose up to a frosted window, and study the rapiers stretching across the pane. If these lances could gain a toehold inside a cell, they would displace specialized structures, shred tubules, and perforate the cell's membrane. Yet even on bitterly cold mornings, when dry snow squeaks under my boots and my mustache freezes solid, a variety of hardy animals keep the spark of life. How do Appalachian animals thwart these swords of ice?

Organisms employ two broad strategies to avoid frozen tissues. They either meet winter's full force head on or move to sites that do not freeze. Let's first focus on species that, like ourselves, face winter's Arctic blasts.

Those that continue to forage and avoid predators through the coldest months must be able to find food, generate body heat, and retain enough of that heat. If a bird or mammal has any hope of living through a West Virginia winter, it must consume seeds, dormant plants, or other winter-active animals. It is no coincidence that January's birds are primarily seed eaters — purple martins and ruby-throated hummingbirds are long gone. Birds and mammals produce heat primarily in their abdomen. Metaphorically, food fuels an abdominal stove. As long as the animal can find suitable and sufficient food, it can maintain its torso above freezing.

Shivering, the rapid contraction and relaxation of skeletal muscles, also contributes to heat production. Because shivering requires no external work, all energy so generated is released in the form of heat. In severe cold, shivering can elevate an animal's metabolic rate up to five times its basal level. We now think that many small birds, including titmice and chickadees, shiver continuously all through winter. Their pectoralis muscles, the major breast muscles that stroke the wings, produce most of the heat generated by shivering.

Heat generation alone, however, cannot sustain life. Winter-active animals must also be able to retain their hard-won warmth. Good insulators, such as fur and feathers, impede radiation and convection by trapping a layer of warm air around the skin. In some animals, a layer of fat under the skin serves as both insulation and stored energy.

Beyond the minimum requirements of feeding and generating and capturing heat, winter-active species exhibit more subtle adaptations. The first of these involves the animal's body shape. Heat is produced in the body's mass but escapes through the surface. In general, heat escapes more slowly from an animal shaped like a sphere (with a small surface area and a large volume) than from one shaped like a hot dog (large area, small volume). As a set, arctic animals are plumper than tropical ones: polar bears and Aleuts are rounder than orangutans and Masai. It is also no accident that igloos are hemispheres. The few long, skinny mammals in cold areas, such as weasels, pay a tremendous price in heat loss and therefore compensate by voracious predation. It is not quite that simple though, because although very few winter-active animals are hot-dog-shaped, tropical species come both skinny and round.

The principle that an animal's surface-to-volume ratio determines its rate of heat loss is illustrated within single species as well. The subspecies of the white-tailed deer living in Maine weighs up to three hundred pounds. In New York, white-tails weigh one hundred and fifty to two hundred pounds. On the Florida mainland, they weigh up to one hundred and fifty pounds, and on the Keys, only eighty to one hundred and ten pounds. Small animals in general, including southern deer, have a higher surface-to-volume ratio, and therefore lose heat faster, than large ones.

Because of their large surface areas and poor suitability for heavy insulation, limbs might appear to be thermal liabilities. In fact, legs and wings lose little heat. To minimize the loss of heat from extremities, animals come equipped with a fascinating set of blood vessels called a counter-current heat exchanger, in which arteries feeding the limbs pass intimately alongside veins returning blood to the torso. Heat passes by conduction and radiation directly from the warmer artery to the cooler vein. In this way, arterial blood with its oxygen and nutrients continues its surge to fingers and toes, while most of its heat short-circuits the extremities. Some duck legs have such efficient heat exchangers that blood arriving at the foot is just half a degree above ambient. This permits smooth function with little heat loss, even in icy water. Counter-current heat exchangers can also be found in beaver tails, the legs of deer, and human arms.

Small birds such as chickadees have such high surface-to-volume ratios that they cannot generate enough heat to compensate for the heat lost through their skin. Instead, they save fuel by allowing their body temperatures to drop at night. In one experiment, the body temperatures of chickadees exposed to freezing dropped by 23 degrees Fahrenheit during the night. Nocturnal hypothermia, the second strategy for facing Artic's blasts, seems to be a normal part of the bird's winter life. This adaptation saves birds up to one-fourth of the energy required to maintain normal body temperature.

Insects, in contrast to the animals discussed so far, do not generate body heat. Even so, many insects, including larval tent caterpillars and adult paper wasps, live through winter without being compromised by ice crystals. Millions of years ago, insects evolved the third strategy of coping with winter's bitterness, supercooling.

The molecules of a liquid constantly ricochet off each other in random fashion. Normally, as a liquid cools, its molecules slow their bouncing and eventually reach a point where they move so sluggishly that their mutual repulsion is exceeded by their mutual attraction. At this point, the molecules of the liquid line up in a definite geometrical pattern, forming a crystal. Once that initial crystal forms, it serves as a seed for the alignment of other molecules. The crystal grows rapidly, and the liquid turns solid. Apparently, mixing a liquid increases the chances that its molecules will randomly conform to the critical angles required to form that first crystal.

If, however, a liquid cools slowly and without agitation, its molecules may not strike each other at just those specific angles. Cooled slowly and carefully, a liquid's temperature can drop far below its freezing point without starting the crystallization process — the liquid supercools.

Insects exhibit the knack of supercooling the water in their cells and blood. The key is subduing the odds of forming that first seed ice crystal. They accomplish this by remaining absolutely motionless. Nudge a supercooled insect, though, and it instantly freezes solid. Plants can also supercool. Liquid in the cells of the shagbark hickory does not freeze until its temperature drops to − 42 degrees Fahrenheit. Other trees and shrubs may persist unharmed down to − 53 degrees Fahrenheit.

Insects employ the fourth mechanism to avoid frozen cells. As winter approaches, the cells of some insect species synthesize and concentrate an antifreeze called glycerol. Like the antifreeze in your car's radiator, glycerol lowers the freezing point of water. In *The Days of the Year*, Hal Borland reported mourning cloak butterflies flying in New England during the warm days of winter. You can witness a similar sight through the open winters of central Appalachia. One of the few butterfly species that overwinter as adults, mourning cloaks probably combine the tactics of supercooling and antifreeze synthesis to persist through winter in a state of suspended animation.

Some insects are actually more like mammals with abdominal stoves. Clustered in a tight sphere, a honeybee colony functions as a heat-generating superorganism. Bees in the core produce heat and rotate with peripheral individuals that temporarily serve as insulation.

A few insects even seem to defy the laws of physics. In Maine and Vermont, two types of winter moths can fly through freezing air. Adults in the subfamily Cuculinae emerge in the fall and fly during the winter when ambient temperatures approach 32 degrees Fahrenheit. Some species warm by shivering at temperatures as low as 26 degrees Fahrenheit and continue to shiver until their thoracic muscles reach 86 degrees Fahrenheit, the minimum for sustained flight. For these species, prolonged shivering, a one-twenty-fifth-inch-thick layer of insulating pile on the thorax, and reduced heat flow from thorax to abdomen allow them to fly in subfreezing conditions.

Another group of winter moths, in the family Geometridae, is even more amazing. Also emerging in the fall, they fly from late November until the first heavy snowfall. These small-bodied moths cannot generate their own heat, yet they fly in temperatures at or above 26 degrees Fahrenheit — without employing shivering, basking, insulation, or high thoracic temperatures. In fact, they fly when their muscle temperatures are below freezing! Further, they do not have specialized enzymes that operate at subzero temperatures. We just don't know how they do it. The moth befriended by Robert Frost in his poem "To a Moth Seen in Winter" was probably one of these winter-active species. Alas, it was perfectly normal and did not go loveless as he lamented.

In contrast to heat-producing birds and mammals, other vertebrates, including fishes, amphibians, and reptiles, do not produce significant amounts of internal body heat, and consequently, their body temperatures reflect ambient conditions. Formerly and inaccurately called cold-blooded, these vertebrates exhibit two overwintering strategies for avoiding frozen cells: moving to a site that does not freeze or depressing the freezing point of cellular water.

The gray tree frog overwinters beneath leaf litter and survives freezing, whereas the leopard frog, which overwinters in aquatic sites, lacks such a cold-tolerance. How does the tree frog survive freezing conditions? The key is that the tree frogs accumulate glycerol in their body fluids, whereas leopard frogs do not. Leopard frogs, in contrast, hibernate in small pits at the bottom of ice-covered ponds, lightly covering themselves with silt and remaining capable of some movement. The pit is larger than its frog occupant, presumably allowing free movement of water and gas exchange through the animal's skin.

While I was drafting the original edition of *Hollows*, physiologists were unraveling a new overwintering strategy. Wood frogs overwinter at or just below the soil surface, under leaf litter of the forest floor, like the box turtle. Thus exposed, wood frogs freeze.

In contrast to the gray tree frog, which gains its freeze-tolerance from glycerol that it synthesizes from glycogen, the wood frog uses glucose as its cryoprotectant. Each has advantages: Glycerol reduces the rupture of red blood cells, but glucose is rapidly produced, easily transported, and fuels anaerobic metabolism.

This fifth strategy of facing Artic blasts is freeze-tolerance. Defined as survival with extracellular ice under natural temperatures and exposure periods, freeze-tolerance has been documented in five species of frogs (spring peeper, eastern and Cope's gray tree frogs, and chorus and wood frogs), one salamander (Siberian salamander), one snake (common garter snake), and three turtles (painted turtle, eastern and western box turtles). Of these, freeze-tolerance has been most studied in the wood frog.

184

Normally, a wood frog's body fluids supercool before freezing. Freeze-tolerant frogs can stay supercooled at 27 degrees Fahrenheit for up to twenty hours. In autumn, as wood frogs slowly cool to high subfreezing temperatures, like 28 degrees Fahrenheit, ice crystals start to form in body fluids pooling in spaces between cells. Within minutes of ice onset, wood frogs begin distributing glucose to body tissues. To move glucose from the site of glycogenesis, the liver, requires efficient cardiac function in the early stages of freezing. In the first minute of freezing, heart rate nearly doubles to eight beats per minute, slows after one hour of freezing, and then stops at near-complete ice formation at about twenty hours.

Fast cooling injures wood frogs because the production and distribution of cryoprotectant are inhibited. In the laboratory, injuries to red blood cells and the neuromuscular system were reduced in experimentally glucose-laden frogs, suggesting that rapid cooling injury results from inadequate production and distribution of glucose. In fast cooling, glucose mobilization is hampered by heart failure.

Quick freezing of supercooled body water starts when the frog makes direct contact with ice crystals. Animals may freeze at high subzero temperatures due to such transepithelial ice inoculation. A frog's supercooled body fluids begin to freeze in less than thirty seconds after direct contact with external ice crystals.

The wood frog is one of the few species of land-hibernating frogs and toads that can tolerate ice in its body fluids. Freezing of body fluids is fast and extensive — two-thirds of its total body water may freeze. Upon dissection, large amounts of ice can be seen in the abdominal cavity, subcutaneous spaces, and spaces within organs. Frozen wood frogs, which show neither breathing nor heart movements, rely on anaerobic metabolism.

In addition to producing and distributing glucose during cooling, the wood frog's organs dehydrate, which prevents ice-caused mechanical injury. In laboratory experiments, the organs of slowly cooled frogs retained less water than in rapidly cooled frogs. The water seems to move from organs to body spaces, and then freezes.

Together, the two adaptations of producing cryoprotectant glucose and drawing water from organs promote survival of freezing by wood frogs. Slow cooling is critical to freeze-tolerance. Rapid cooling inhibits both glucose mobilization and organ dehydration during freezing, probably due to heart failure.

In spring, heart beat resumes within one hour after thawing, with near normal functions in a few hours.

The second broad strategy for precluding the formation of ice crystals in cells is to overwinter in a place that does not freeze — either migrate or hibernate. A discussion of migration could easily fill an entire chapter, so I will treat only the latter topic here. Hibernation is one of those biological concepts that is attractive and intuitively understandable, but as we shall see, difficult to generalize.

Let us consider the groundhog, a true hibernator. A hibernating whistle pig remains rolled in a ball, with head between hind limbs, unresponsive to disturbance, for six months. While normally at 99 degrees Fahrenheit, the hibernating woodchuck's body temperature drops to between 43 and 57 degrees Fahrenheit. Its breathing slows to a point that cannot be detected by sight alone. In July, adult groundhogs start accumulating a fat layer that grows to one inch thick by autumn. They hibernate when they have amassed the requisite amount of fat — in New York that is about mid-September. They store no food in the burrow; fat is their only fuel. During winter, a groundhog burns 33 to 40 percent of its body weight. In one study, adults that weighed 9.2 pounds in September averaged 5.5 pounds when they awoke in March.

The only other Appalachian mammals that clearly hibernate are several species of jumping mice, chipmunks, and some bats. All other mammals display varying levels of metabolic depression — they may sleep for long periods but do not lower their metabolism as severely as true hibernators. Raccoons, for example, often den in hollow trees, do not cache food, and usually remain near their dens during the coldest three or four months. Because the raccoon's abdominal stove burns enough fat to remain above 95 degrees Fahrenheit, a raccoon may lose up to half its body weight in a severe winter. Although commonly thought to hibernate, black bears in North Carolina and West Virginia are not true hibernators because they rove about and feed during warm spells.

If an animal can generate heat in its belly and find fuel for its abdominal stove, is aided by body roundness, insulation, and heat exchangers, and can hold on to enough heat to move its muscles smoothly, it is a candidate for an active life through winter. Lacking any of these adaptations relegates a species to inactivity via supercooling, antifreeze, or freeze-tolerance, or to overwintering in a site that does not freeze. Those plump chickadees cleaving sunflower seeds at your feeder, that "poor, cold" duck paddling through an icy pond, and those insects that mysteriously take to wing on the first few hours of a mild winter day bear witness to the marvelous adaptations that sustain life through a cold Appalachian winter.

26

Spring Tensions

That first waft of warm air, the pale green brush to a hillside, the first warbler singing in a treetop — all excite our senses and push aside the day's problems. It is fitting that the opening movement of Aaron Copland's "Appalachian Spring" captures the timid, cautious mood of the first few days of resurrection.

Then comes the onrush. From a biological point of view, things change faster in spring than at any other time. Along Pine Cabin Run, phoebes flick their tails, hickory leaves unsheathe, and creek chubs vie for headwater pools. With a big shudder, my living neighbors shake off winter and begin anew. But spring emergence is fraught with tension. Timing is everything.

The first warm sunshine of February rekindles the flow of sap on the south side of trees, and leaves soon begin to unfurl. In a locally predictable sequence, the leaves of various tree species emerge over the span of a couple of months. The timing of leaf-out appears to vary from year to year — late April one year, early May the next — but our printed calendar offers only weak relevance. The immediate stimulus for leaf emergence is actually the cumulative thermal sum, or the amount of ambient heat available in the spring after a requisite cold period. When we relate the timing of leaf-out to thermal sums rather than to the days of the month, we find it consistent over the years. (When I speculate with my neighbors up the hollow about whether spring has come early or late, I know I'm applying the wrong yardstick, but I enjoy the rite just the same.)

Most of the plants of the forest floor respond acutely to lessening sunshine as trees leaf out. The seasonal light hitting the forest floor runs out of synchrony with the temperature cycle. Ground cover plants receive strong sunshine or warm weather, but not at the same time. The woodland herbs of early spring display their flowers during the brief window of time between the first prolonged period warm enough for pollinators and the closing of the canopy. The heydays of herbaceous wildflowers end as the canopy closes above.

Early-blooming, ephemeral herbs of the Appalachian forest include spring beauty, round-lobed hepatica, cut-leaf toothwort, squirrel corn, Dutchman's breeches, rue anemone, and bloodroot. Many of these early-spring bloomers have white, bowl-shaped, sun-following flowers with reflective petals, and fuzzy pollen-producing and seed-bearing organs. These flowers stay warmer than the surrounding air because they reflect visible light and other forms of radiation onto the flower's sexual organs. Such tiny parabolic solar ovens speed the development of pollen, seeds, and fruits, and aid the survival and reproduction of visiting insects by providing them with a warm microenvironment. These wildflowers need the full energy of bright sunshine to grow and bloom, and so retreat as the canopy thickens.

Some of the extremely early bloomers actually produce their own heat. With short bursts of intense metabolism, the eastern skunk cabbage warms its flowers to as much as 31 degrees Fahrenheit above the ambient temperature, allowing them to melt their way through ice and snow. Because skunk cabbage plants generate heat, they get a jump on flowering and seed production. The spike of flowers inside the skunk cabbage's hood is warm to the touch, and the hood, which resembles styrofoam, insulates the flower spike. The warmth inside the flower and the plant's characteristic smell of feces and decaying flesh lure insect pollinators. The heat may help to volatilize the odorous molecules. After pollination, the plant maintains a tropical climate for embryonic development.

The temperature of a skunk cabbage's flower spike varies little because a built-in thermostat helps regulate the plant's metabolic rate, and thereby its body temperature. In fact, the metabolic rates of skunk cabbage's flower spike and warm-blooded animals of similar weight are about equal, suggesting that both plants and vertebrates independently evolved the ability to generate heat via the common route of elevating their metabolic rates.

The sequence of wildflower bloom in West Virginia from late winter through mid-spring, goes something like this: skunk cabbage, blood root, spring beauty, hepatica, Dutchman's breeches, squirrel corn, violets, star chickweed, trilliums, crested dwarf iris, columbine, and fire pinks. Our trees also bloom in a definite order: downy serviceberry, flowering dogwood, black cherry, eastern redbud, and tulip poplar.

I find it curious that all the individuals of a given plant species do not emerge at the same time. For example, at a specific site, Jack-in-the-pulpit individuals may emerge within a two-week period. Why don't all members of one species emerge simultaneously? Herein lies a conflict, as you will see in the following musing.

When in the spring an organism mobilizes its biochemical resources and begins nudging, probing, and stretching strikes me as a period laden with tension. The timing of emergence reflects a tug-of-war between competing priorities. Each plant must accelerate its metabolism, which is probably a non-reversible physiological change, and emerge from below ground without knowing what the weather will be like in the near future. Presumably, each species of plant has evolved to leaf out within a certain time frame, determined by some combination of day length and thermal sums. From an evolutionary point of view, the timing of leaf emergence seems to reflect a trade-off between the potential photosynthetic gains from early leaf-out and the probability of leaf damage by late frosts. Leaves should open when the benefits gained from photosynthesis equal the costs of replacing frozen leaves. However, individual plants that bloom during their species' flowering peak often suffer low rates of fertilization and seed production, possibly because the pollinators are swamped. The ultimate currency in this cost-benefit transaction is, as always, the number of successful offspring the individual organism produces.

Consider bloodroot, an herbaceous flower of the forest floor. Individual plants that emerge early might risk being frozen before pollinating insects are active. Late individuals risk unfurling their leaves after the canopy has opened, thereby missing opportunities for photosynthesis. Late plants also may fail reproductively because other flowers may have already rewarded, and thereby trained, the pollinators to visit them. Theoretically, within a specific area, bloodroot should emerge collectively within a short period of time, and these temporally clustered plants should experience the greatest survival and reproductive success in the long run. Most of the time, that is. The catch comes with the nonsynchronous individuals during unusual years. Nonconformists occasionally gain huge reproductive advantages over normal individuals. Early individuals benefit if spring comes early. Following similar logic, a late-emerging plant has high reproductive success in a late spring because all of its competitors have been frozen out, leaving all the pollinators to the latecomer.

Nonconformist flowering may stem from differences that convey no effect on reproductive success, that is they are adaptively neutral, or they may represent genetic adaptations for different dates. Variation of the second type reflects the action of natural selection and is therefore fascinating to me.

As I have said, even though emergence within a brief window of time yields excellent odds of pollination, fertilization, and production of viable seeds, a plant may occasionally gain even greater fitness by operating outside the norm. The question arises of whether a plant should conform, play with normal odds to gain a modest payoff, or be a nonconformist gambling against low odds for a huge payoff. Natural selection may have led to a diversity of emergence times because every once in a while nonconformity paid off handsomely for the ancestors of some of today's flowers. This tension is the irony of spring.

27

Dawn Chorus

At least once each spring, as dawn breaks, I hike up to our pine thicket and practice the brand of stump-sitting espoused by Charles Fergis, naturalist and curmudgeon of Pennsylvanian Appalachia. In his book, *The Wingless Crow*, Fergis suggested that stump-sitting would release me, allow me to open my senses to nature's bounty, permit me to see and feel new things. But try as I may, I am a lousy stump-sitter. Invariably, any sensory free association I manage gets cut short by a sound or movement. More often than not, the distracter is a little bird high in the canopy that calls, then answers itself, a male red-eyed vireo competing for its slice of the dawn chorus. This common Appalachian bird illustrates the wonder of bird song. As I listen, I wonder why he sings, what is he saying, to whom, how? Rational inquiry takes over; I step down from metaphysical stump-sitting and reenter science.

In monogamous bird species it is almost always the male that sings, to attract a mate or to proclaim his nesting territory off-limits to other males of that species. He thereby monopolizes an area with enough food for himself, his mate, and their offspring. In general, males aggressively guard only those areas with tangible resources that are defensible at reasonable cost.

Natural selection seems to favor individuals that defend areas large enough to include just enough resources for their family's survival. However, a few ornithologists argue that some birds defend superterritories, areas that provide more than enough resources, as a way to reduce the reproductive success of less aggressive individuals.

195

The idea is that by monopolizing more space than needed, a male bird limits the food available to potential competitors. There may also be another reason for superterritories: to repel, or to reduce the odds of being distracted by close neighbors, and thereby avoid being surprised by a predator. Like international boundaries, the borders between bird territories often remain stable even though their occupants change. If a resident disappears, a single substitute replaces it and inherits the territory and the established neighbors.

Although male birds usually direct their territorial aggression at other males of the same species, some repel members of other species. Territoriality between species can evolve if two species, such as red-eyed and Philadelphia vireos, compete for the same resources. Both of these species have highest breeding success in areas they occupy jointly, so a male vireo must repel members of both species from his territory. Some ornithologists have suggested that *interspecific* territoriality is just misdirected *intraspecific* territoriality, and therefore not adaptive. I disagree: The frequency and regularity of aggression between these two vireo species are signs that natural selection maintains this behavior.

Definite benefits accrue with larger and better territories. Male field sparrows with larger territories weigh more and mate more frequently than males on smaller territories. On average, such benefits go to older males because they occupy their territories for longer portions of the year than first year males. In many species, clutch size varies as a function of territory quality, as indicated by the amount of food or availability of refuge sites. Presumably, a female lays the optimal number of eggs for her territory — the number of offspring the pair can feed. Thus, the kind and amount of resources within the defended area become crucial determinants of the reproductive success of both partners.

The songs of dozens of males of several species drawing attention to their territories collectively comprise the dawn chorus. During the height of the breeding season, the dawn chorus can be deafening, seemingly chaotic. Like the crescendo in Rimsky-Korsakov's *Scheherazade*, sophisticated structure underlies the cacophony.

196

Male birds sing at relevant loudnesses. Among songbirds in general, the sound power of songs, which averages about 0.5 milliwatt (mW) per acre of territory, matches their territory sizes. According to this relationship, song sparrows, red-eyed vireos, and black-capped chickadees defending territories of 0.3, 0.8, and 9.0 acres, respectively, are predicted to produce about 0.15, 0.40, and 4.5 mW. These energy levels should reflect optimal solutions that just cover the birds' courtship and territory needs.

Most birds sing in the morning when there is little wind or convection. Calls voiced around sunrise broadcast up to twenty times farther than songs of equal amplitude proclaimed at midday. Many birds sing from treetops, again to take acoustical advantage of a favorable microclimate. Like light, sound can be blocked, deflected, or absorbed to create a sound shadow. Near the ground, steep temperature and wind velocity gradients cause such sound shadows. Since greater height reduces the effects of these near-surface refractions, singing well above the ground increases the broadcast coverage.

There is a competing hypothesis on why male birds reach their song peak in the early morning. A male great tit directs song at his female as she emerges from the nest cavity in the morning — this stimulates her to copulate. Thus, the females' daily cycles of sexual receptivity may influence the timing of Appalachia's dawn chorus.

Two dominant variables influence identification and localization of sound in a forest: changes in volume and reverberations. Fluctuations of loudness, caused by the scattering effects of turbulent air, vary in strength with weather conditions. The degree of volume distortion determines how intelligible the call is. Reverberations, caused by surfaces that scatter sound, also interfere with the receiver's ability to recognize a call. However, a benefit of echo is the camouflage it provides the singer through ventriloquism. Ventriloquists produce sound whose source is hard to locate, presumably to make it harder for a predator to locate the singer.

Communicating animals employ special tactics to reduce sound degradation. First, they call when and where degradation is least, such as from treetops in morning. Second, birds may sing in patterns that differ from the sounds created by scattering. Finally, singers incorporate redundancy into their signal. Repetitions allow the receiver to predict the entire signal from part of it or to average the sound. However, broad leaves and other surfaces that reflect sound cause severe reverberations in deciduous forests, so long-range callers here usually avoid signals that sound like reverberations, *i.e.*, those that vary in either volume or pitch. In general, forest-breeding songbirds also avoid rapid repetition in their long distance communications. For example, when communicating with others up to ten yards away, chickadees use the "gargle" call, which sounds like a small bird rinsing with mouthwash. Over greater distances, though, the birds employ the long, plaintive "fee bee."

Even though they could potentially use a huge range of frequencies, birds sing only at certain pitches. The sound window used by forest birds (1,585 to 2,500 Hz) is limited at the low end by the frequencies of wind-generated noise and at the high end by the pitch of insect song. Birds exploit this range even though lower wavelengths actually carry farther.

Within this frequency span, many male birds sing at the same time. To avoid the worst interference, species drop in and out of the chorus at different times of the day. Some warble in feeble predawn light, others sing when the sun is well overhead.

To further preclude audio interference, male birds avoid singing at the same moment others call. The males of the least flycatcher and red-eyed vireo communicate with short advertising songs of similar pitch repeated through the day. When they breed in the same place, the flycatcher and vireo avoid superimposing songs. Forbearance is more marked in the flycatcher: he avoids starting his song while an adjacent vireo is singing. Specifically, the flycatcher inserts its short (twelve seconds) song in between the longer (forty-six seconds) songs of the vireo. Other Appalachian birds have solved this problem in a similar way. The wood thrush, eastern wood peewee, tufted titmouse, white-throated sparrow, and great crested flycatcher tend to avoid singing during the songs of other species, usually by beginning their song immediately after the neighbor has stopped. Singers must also solve this interference problem within their own species. In one experiment, male ovenbirds overlapped an artificial ovenbird stimulus song in only 10 of 251 trials. Further, most of the ovenbirds sang during the first tenth of the silent interval in order to avoid interference.

Male birds master a repertoire of stereotyped songs — one endlessly repeated song will not do. The number of song types varies greatly both between and within species. Three hypotheses, which unfortunately are not mutually exclusive, attempt to explain the evolution of large repertoires. A long song list may indicate a male's superior age, experience, and territory. Males with large repertoires may be more successful in copulating with their own mate and neighboring females than are males with a small repertoire. In laboratory experiments, female canaries that listen to playbacks of many song variations build their nests faster and lay more eggs than females exposed to less variety. In red-winged blackbirds, the larger the male's song repertoire, the more females he attracts to his harem.

In several bird species, there is a positive correlation between male repertoire size and the number of copulation solicitations displayed by females. Soliciting copulation includes crouching, wing-fluttering, and back-arching, all interpreted as an invitation to copulate. In Norway, the copulation-solicitation display of female great tits is more strongly elicited by large than small repertoires. Specifically, an average of four displays answers one male song type vs. fourteen are solicited by five. A large repertoire may even predispose a female to extrapair copulation, i.e., cheating with a male neighbor.

A second hypothesis states that large repertoires contribute to territorial defense. Labeled the Beau Geste hypothesis, it claims that a territorial male can inflate the apparent density of singing males at his spot by singing several distinct song types. Prospecting males then avoid such an acoustically dense area. However, so far, the Beau Geste hypothesis has been only partially supported by experimental data.

A third hypothesis has emerged since the original edition of *Hollows*: Variable song reduces the habituation of listeners. As with the Beau Geste idea, support for this "antimonotony hypothesis" is mixed. On the negative side, in the Carolina wren repertoire size does not seem to reduce habituation to male intruders. On the positive, a female may prefer a male that sings a variety of calls because she is constrained by a basic property of all central nervous systems, habituation. A female bird may respond well to variable sounds simply because her nervous system is stimulated less and less by a repeating, unchanging stimulus. How do you respond to a variable-pitched teacher vs. a monotonic talking head? Male song repertoires may have evolved to exploit the pre-existing susceptibility to boredom inherent in the vertebrate nervous system.

Some species of birds exhibit local dialects. Neighboring birds may sing similar or identical songs, while just a mile or two away the call of the same species may sound noticeably different. Like human language, bird dialects do not blend at boundaries to form intermediates, and their basic pitch and rhythm are stable over many years. Although local subdialects may involve as few as two to five birds, a specific accent usually characterizes several hundred individuals.

Some evidence indicates that dialects are population-specific. The "gargle" of the black-capped chickadee is a sputtery, explosive, complex threat emitted when males from neighboring flocks meet along their mutual territorial boundary. Syllables at the end of the vocalization are shared among several small interbreeding groups, but introductory syllables usually differ, even at sites less than four miles apart. Flock members also share a great similarity in the "dee" elements of "chick-a-dee" calls. These findings, in view of the flocking and mating adaptations of chickadees (See chp. 24.), suggest that each interbreeding group develops its own unique dialect.

Why do birds have dialects? Perhaps young males copy the songs of established neighbors to gain an advantage in territorial defense or mate attraction. Male ovenbirds, yellow-breasted chats, indigo buntings, and white-throated sparrows respond more aggressively to the recorded songs of strangers than to those of established neighbors. In other words, males habituate to familiar songs. Such "dear enemy" recognition saves resident neighbors the time and energy of expensive contests. Copying the local idiom may allow a young, new male to establish a territory relatively painlessly, as other males would mistake him for an older resident male. Thus, song dialects may reflect mimicry within a species that leads to social elevation. This hypothesis holds merit. In southern Michigan, first-year male indigo buntings that matched the songs of adult territorial neighbors had greater success in mating, nesting, and fledging young than first year males that did not match those songs. No disadvantage fell to the males being mimicked.

Something as simple as imperfect learning may account for dialects. The inaccuracy by which young birds copy older birds may cause gradual cultural changes that eventually lead to marked spatial differences. This leads to the hypothesis that adherence to a dialect is not an adaptation, just an incidental byproduct of fallible learning.

Some young songbirds overlearn songs. Young male swamp sparrows produce four to five times more song types than they will eventually use in their adult repertoire. Through a process of attrition, the excess is discarded during the crystallization of the final adult song. According to one hypothesis, overproduction may compensate for unpredictable opportunities to learn from older male models.

It makes sense that in some situations song learning depends on socialization fairly late in life, not simply on hearing a song at the birthplace. For example, young rufous-sided towhees and indigo buntings disperse from their birth site, then settle and begin singing like their new neighbors.

Birds have developed foolproof ways to recognize each other's song. In experiments, white-throated sparrows identified their neighbors after hearing only the first three notes of a five-note song. Ovenbirds also discriminate between the songs of nearby residents and those of noncontiguous males, but by using the singer's location as the main cue. When a neighbor's song was played from the territorial border farthest from the neighbor's usual location, the ovenbird responded as if it were defending against a stranger. Unfamiliar songs would presumably be sung by a transient, unsettled male looking for a territory. Such "dear-enemy" recognition saves the costs of territorial contests with established neighbors that present little threat.

In a compelling aside, the study of bird song may eventually help cure certain human brain diseases. Until recently, neurologists accepted the dogma that vertebrate brain neurons form early, and from then on the adult animal has a fixed number — lost neurons are not replaced. As I was drafting the original edition of *Hollows*, a team of biologists discovered that in the adult canary brain, new nerve cells replace older ones. This finding set the precedent that neurons born in adulthood travel through the brain and take their place in neural circuits involved in learning.

The volume of the part of the canary's brain that controls singing changes seasonally: it's at peak volume in spring, shrinks in summer, then expands in fall (when it learns and rehearses new songs). Fresh neurons in the fall replace those that died in summer. The new nerve cells originate from stem cells in the brain's fluid-filled cavities.

Neurogenesis, the production of neurons, has also been found in adult chickadees, but in brain sites responsible for spatial learning. In autumn, when chickadees are busy hoarding food, they grow new neurons in the brain center that deals with spatial memory. Locations encoded in these new neurons help chickadees find their seeds months later.

If found in therapeutically relevant numbers, such stem cells could represent a potentially limitless supply of neurons for repairing a damaged brain. Imagine your grandfather's brain self-repairing its own Parkinson's or Alzheimer's pathology!

The last time I settled onto my favorite stump, I felt overwhelmed by the skill of a red-eyed vireo. His pitch and simple expressions carry through broad leaves; he sings most assertively at dawn when broadcast conditions are best; he recognizes his neighbors and listens to them to avoid acoustic interference; his lovely repertoire may stimulate his mate to reproductive readiness; and his dialect marks him from a specific area. When I apply these adaptations to another species in the dawn chorus the complexity compounds; consider the entire chorus and it becomes overwhelming. The counterpoint in Bach's *Brandenburg Concertos* pale by comparison.

28
Trees and Caterpillars

Much of the energy passing through an Appalachian eco-system follows a single path. Arriving as sunshine, energy then flows through deciduous leaves, moth caterpillars, and fecal rain. This is why, by late summer, it is nearly impossible to find an intact leaf. A forest of holey leaves shows that caterpillars are exerting tremendous feeding pressure on broadleaved trees. Yet the struggle between trees and caterpillars would not have become a dominant act had trees served merely as passive targets. In their own subtle ways, trees fight back.

Let us first consider the larva's role in the relationship, focus-ing on the eastern tent caterpillar. Residing east of the Mississippi River from Nova Scotia to Florida, this well-known insect overwin-ters communally in egg masses on its principal host trees, cherry and apple. Deposited near branch tips the previous summer, eggs hatch as leaf buds unfurl. Because a female lays all her eggs, which contain fully formed caterpillars, in a single cluster, the "cats" that develop from one egg mass are siblings.

A few days after hatching, the caterpillars construct a tent near their tree's center, a site offering branches for support and a central position from which to forage. This permanent tent is enlarged sev-eral times a day to accommodate the growing larvae. Cats build up the tent one layer at a time and the spaces between partitions pro-vide room for up to three hundred individuals during the morning and afternoon rest periods. Small circular openings in the tent allow entry and exit.

During feeding excursions to nearby leaves, the caterpillars secrete strands of silk. Collectively, the strands form a conspicuous silk trail that provides purchase on smooth bark. When a hungry larva leaves the tent in search of food, it lays an exploratory trail chemical signal, or pheromone. Returning from a successful foraging trip, it lays a recruitment trail pheromone by brushing the tip of its abdomen on newly deposited silk trails. Following an old trail, the caterpillar elevates its abdomen, leaving no chemical. Because they are able to discern the age of a pheromone on a silk trail, cats can distinguish between trails to fresh food and paths to exhausted sites. Recruitment via pheromones leads to the efficient forwarding of caterpillars to the most productive foods, as well as the prompt abandonment of areas without young, tasty leaves. As cherry leaves age, they get tougher and drier, and provide less nutrition. As we shall see, from the tree's point of view these changes may represent an adaptive strategy to protect itself from herbivory.

Tent caterpillars create a microenvironment that allows them to be active on cool spring days. Like little greenhouses, tents admit sunshine and retain some of the converted heat within the silk layers, maintaining temperatures up to 40 degrees Fahrenheit warmer than the surrounding air. By adding more silk to the bright side of the tent, cats enlarge their greenhouse in the direction of the sun. Eventually, these sophisticated larvae turn into short-lived, plain brown moths.

Albeit social and thereby efficient, the tent caterpillar is just one of thousands of species of Appalachian moths whose larvae eat tree leaves. Damage by insect herbivores decreases tree growth, seed production, and seed viability. Trees seem so vulnerable — they are a large target, rooted to one spot, without a fly-swatting tail. Yet by hook or by crook trees persist, in part through help from birds.

Birds lend trees a little relief. At Hubbard Brook, New Hampshire ecologists used netting to exclude birds from patches of striped maple, an understory tree. After several days of protection, the densities of moth larvae were significantly greater inside the cages than outside. The researchers estimated that birds such as warblers, thrushes, and vireos removed an average of 37 percent of the caterpillars from the understory. This effect was most intense from late June to mid-July when adult birds were feeding their demanding nestlings.

Bird predation most effectively controls insect numbers when the densities of larvae lie within a normal range. At such *endemic* population levels, birds reduce and thereby regulate the densities of larval moths on forest vegetation. During *epi*demic outbreaks, though, birds may take only 0.1 to 1.0 percent of the caterpillar biomass. The situation of caterpillars going amuck describes our current gypsy moth invasion.

Trees also get some help from larval parasites, which like birds, probably make their most significant impact at normal pest levels.

Many plants have evolved non-changing, constantly expressed antipredator adaptations. Examples of these so-called constitutive defenses include the hawthorn's thorns, the rose's prickles, and the shell of a walnut.

But even with this, trees still have a defense problem. Compared to their insect pests, trees are long-lived and therefore evolve more slowly. In the tree-caterpillar arms race, insects would appear to have the edge. How do trees persist in the face of rapidly evolving pests?

We have recently discovered that trees deploy sophisticated chemical defensive weapons. For example, oaks produce tannin, an organic compound we use in the process of tanning leather. When ingested as part of mature oak leaves, tannins bind proteins into indigestible complexes that inhibit the growth of moth larvae. In Vermont, leaves of red oaks that had been defoliated by gypsy moth larvae two years in a row were drier, tougher, and had a higher concentration of tannins and phenolics, another natural insecticide, than leaves of undamaged trees. Gypsy moth larvae grow more slowly, produce smaller pupae and fewer eggs, and decline in vigor when they eat leaves of such defoliated trees. Calling it "plant conditioning," agricultural entomologists have long known that mechanical damage to the leaves of many deciduous tree species renders them less suitable as food for insects.

207

These observations suggest that trees engage their antiherbivore defenses fairly quickly. A wide variety of plants rapidly mobilize defenses in surrounding leaves and tissues after an herbivore bites. Now known in over one hundred plant species, induced changes in a plant's physical, chemical, or other features can reduce the impact of subsequent attack. Some plants are induced to synthesize toxins that poison herbivores, others produce complex compounds that interfere with the attacker's growth cycle or digestive ability. Thus, a leaf's suitability as food is not so much a function of its primary metabolites, which contribute to the growth and maintenance of the plant's cells, but of secondary metabolites, compounds synthesized specifically for defending against herbivores. There is tremendous variation of secondary compounds among plant species. (The spice, perfume, and medicine industries turn profits from this diversity of secondary chemicals.) Each plant species, even each population, produces a distinct set of secondary compounds.

Such toxic chemicals can render an otherwise suitable plant repulsive to an insect. One type of inducible defense works as follows. After a plant is attacked, it releases yet unknown substances from the wound. These chemicals disperse throughout the plant and stimulate the production of molecules that impede the breakdown of protein in the insect's gut. This turns all the leaves on that plant into poor food.

In Finland, researchers performed a series of interesting experiments on white birch, which is defoliated by the autumnal moth. Larvae that were fed undamaged leaves of shoots from which one leaf had been torn two days earlier grew more slowly and attained lower final weights than individuals that ate leaves from intact shoots. The biologists noticed that birch leaves in an area of heavy herbivory maintained an elevated concentration of phenolics for three years, while trees outside the zone maintained normal phenolic levels. The degree of resistance seemed to depend on the amount of damage.

In these studies it appeared that white birch induced two types of responses to insect predation: a resistance that was rapidly enhanced and swiftly lost in leaves of the current year, and a high resistance that persisted several years thereafter. The former tended to stabilize defoliator populations, whereas the time lag inherent in the latter may have contributed to populations that fluctuated between crashes and explosions.

Then the Finns made an astounding discovery. The growth, survival, and egg production of moths correlated positively with the distance between their food tree and the closest birch defoliated the previous year — the farther their food source was from the previously attacked birch, the more successful the moths were. Incredibly, this suggested the presence of aerial chemical communication among nearby trees. A similar phenomenon has been reported in some trees of northern Appalachia. Perhaps this is a response to airborne chemicals released by the attacked trees. As I write, the possibility of a molecular early warning system among trees is being hotly debated among forest ecologists.

In Vermont, trees inhibit gypsy moths. Gypsy moths reared on previously defoliated black oaks grew slower, produced lighter pupae, and had higher mortality than individuals that ate leaves from unaffected oaks. These changes are great enough that they could influence the course of outbreaks.

The above findings allow us to view inducible defenses at two scales, as (1) localized responses, in which herbivores are small-bodied, weak doses of the plant's defensive compounds are effective, and the response is restricted to the damaged areas; and (2) systemic responses, where herbivores move throughout the foliage, their initial damage is a cue for widespread herbivory, and the defensive response spreads throughout the plant.

An extreme case of the latter is when the induced defense spreads to an unattacked neighbor, like the case of the white birch in Finland. The "talking tree hypothesis" implies benefits for both sender and receiver. Another form of inter-plant communication is when an attacked plant emits synomones, volatile compounds that attract carnivorous insects that prey on and parasitize the plant's herbivores. The synomone may spread to nearby unattacked plants, inducing synomone production in them. Not only can predatory and

209

parasitic insects use the kinds and amounts of synomones to discriminate between herbivore- vs. mechanically-damaged plants, they can also distinguish among different herbivore species, and even among various instars of their prey.

As you may suspect, some insects have evolved anti-synomone adaptations. In Australia, several species of *Eucalyptus*-defoliating insects, including a sawfly, chew through the leaf petiole. According to the "sabotage of induced defenses hypothesis," by chewing through the leaf stem the herbivore prevents the transmission of induced defenses to other leaves, thereby minimizing the broadcast of synomones.

Currently, inducible defenses are thought to spread to undamaged leaves on the same tree, to leaves on the same tree in successive years, and even to nearby trees. Not all biologists accept these ideas, though. Some assert that these defenses may be present, but that they have negligible effects on herbivore populations. They further counter that the studies, performed in laboratories, are statistically flawed. I accept the ideas that defenses spread to other leaves within a tree and exert an influence in succeeding years in the same tree, but I question the evolutionary basis of intertree communication. Kin selection may maintain aerial communication within a group of related individuals or clones, such as aspen and beech, but kin selection is less likely to work in a randomly interbreeding population, such as oaks and hickories. Instead, perhaps the received chemical is not an adaptive signal, but is merely accidentally leaked by the damaged plant.

In the spirit of balanced reporting, since the original *Hollows* was released a competing hypothesis has been offered: The induction of resistance results from a nutrient deficiency. Whereas damaged leaves of unfertilized basket oak saplings showed high levels of anti-herbivory compounds, adding nutrients prevented the induction of these molecules within one season and among leaves within individual trees. These observations suggest that the induction of defenses may be "turned off" in well fed plants.

210

In addition to inducing defenses, a tree fights back in a totally different way — by being many individuals. To understand this idea, picture each tree as a population of buds. If a genetic mutation arises in a cell of a growing bud, the descendant cells will also carry the deviation. Mutations in buds give rise to different kinds of leaves, seeds, and defense compounds within a single plant. In essence, a tree becomes a mosaic of defense types as its buds evolve new variations.

Long life, large size, and annual regeneration of buds make it likely that variation will arise among different parts of an individual plant. Take the wildflower, spring beauty, for example: Different parts of single plants have different chromosome numbers. In one population, 68 percent of the individuals exhibited variation within themselves. Many biologists believe that this situation exists — and will be found — in trees, as well.

With two forms of within-plant variation — inducible defenses and genetic mosaics — trees present attacking insects with a complexity that normally prevents pests from overwhelming the host. Such plant complexity has several effects on herbivores. If a pest makes a poor decision as to where to settle and feed, it will grow slowly and experience low reproductive success. Further, chemical and genetic variation allow parts of individual plants to escape being eaten. If the tree concentrates pests in patches of tasty foliage, it may increase competition among and predation of the pests.

Plants also exhibit physical forms of induced defenses. Attacked by gall aphids, cottonwoods undergo premature leaf abscission. This physical change is interpreted as an adaptation that quickly reduces the pest's food supply and thereby its population, lessening its damage of the tree in the long run.

Ultimately, plant defenses catalyze the evolution of counteradaptations in some pests. For example, some insects are able to convert normally harmful substances into sources of nutrition or even use the nasty substances to defend against animals that may in turn eat them. Caterpillars of the monarch butterfly feed on milkweed leaves, which are rich in cardiac glycosides, powerful toxins that interfere

211

with basic cellular processes. The poison is retained by the adult butterflies where it provides some protection against bird predators.

Another example of an herbivore with detoxifying powers is the parsnip webworm. This moth's larvae feed on wild parsnip and other species of the carrot family, which carry high levels of the poison xanthotoxin. The webworm caterpillar maintains the biochemical machinery to detoxify this poison, but at a price — slow growth of the moth.

A lthough I have reported some controversial observations, some of which originate outside Appalachia, this essay conveys what I consider to be a likely scenario for Appalachian forests. Chemical weapons and genetic variation within individual trees provide potent defenses against voracious caterpillars that would otherwise hold an overwhelming advantage. Appalachian trees are not merely large, passive targets under attack by an efficient herbivorous army — their sophisticated adaptations make trees full equals in the plant-herbivore arms race.

Epilogue

29

The Remnant Archipelago

A s I hike the ridges and hollows of Appalachia, I am dogged by
some disturbing questions. Like cockleburs, these doubts cling
to me, tainting my Appalachian experience. I can't end this
book without trying to deal with my baggage of anxiety. What is
the fate of Appalachia? What will happen to our cove forests, lungless salamanders, dawn choruses, and, yes, even our copperheads?
Despite a sense of urgency, I freely admit that I do not have the cor-
ner on truth. Simply, I have observed some things that concern me
and have some ideas on what we might do about them.

Before Europeans arrived, an almost unbroken forest blanketed
Appalachia. Since then, the greatest change has been the disappearance of the virgin forest. In 1870, 67 percent of West Virginia was
still covered by original trees; by 1900, 33 percent remained, and
by 1910 only 13 percent stood. Today only a few hundred acres of
virgin forest remain. European colonists exploited this resource so
efficiently that by 1920 all the trees accessible by rail or river had
been logged. Except in a few small areas, forests were cut to yield the
largest possible immediate return — without the slightest reflection
on the future. After three centuries of farming, logging, and development, less than 1 percent of the virgin forest remains.

Most of today's Appalachian forest can be envisioned as an archipelago of second-growth woodlots in an ocean of pasture. Logging,
farming, road cutting, and other human activities have fragmented
the forest. This dismantling lowers the odds that native populations
will survive and therefore decreases the diversity of indigenous species. Throughout the world, habitat fragmentation is one of the most
serious causes of the present extinction crisis.

217

So what? Why should we care about biological diversity? Defined as the number of different kinds of living things and their genetic variability, biodiversity counts for several reasons. First, the number of species in a particular place indicates that ecosystem's health. Polluted streams have bullhead catfish, carp, and a few other hardy species; an untainted Appalachian run will support dozens of fishes. Second, we feel greater delight in a landscape hosting many kinds of organisms than in a species-poor place. How do you feel at dusk surrounded by fireflies, listening to the whippoorwill, and smelling trailing arbutus? Third, we don't have the slightest idea which species will serve our future needs. Scientists have explored the drug potential of only about 2 percent of the world's plant species. Who would have ever predicted that the horseshoe crab would become crucial to hematology? Would the passenger pigeon's liver have been the ideal system for studying human liver cancer? Finally, human-caused extinctions betray the attitude that other species were put on Earth for our benefit, to exploit as we see fit. We will not transcend this selfish legacy — and therefore will not be able to experience the next act in the evolutionary play — until we behave in ways that maintain biological diversity.

As a forest becomes fragmented, the average size of pieces, total habitat area, and habitat diversity decrease, while the insularity and the ratio of forest edge to forest interior increase. The first two effects require no explanation. When habitat diversity decreases, shrinking ecological islands offer fewer kinds of habitats than larger fragments. Compare the varieties of temperature, sunshine, and moisture in ridges, hollows, and streams with the relatively uniform conditions on a single mountainside. Insularity, or the effects of isolation, increases as the distances between islands increases. Geometry dictates that as an island shrinks in area, its edge overwhelms its interior area. The smaller a circle, the greater the circumference per unit of interior area — and many species need the cover, shade, humidity, echoes, and other features of interior habitat.

These consequences of fragmentation contribute to the loss of biotic diversity in three ways. Populations may be outright destroyed, severely reduced, or subdivided. Further, sources of immigrants may

218

be lost, lowering the odds that a species will reestablish itself where it has become extinct. And the environmental changes may impede immigration that normally takes place between habitat patches.

The sizes of the remnant habitat patches are important be-cause area alone strongly influences the number of species present. In cities, for example, more weed species live on large vacant lots than small ones. In Illinois, in a fairly tight increasing relationship, wood-lots of five to one thousand five hundred acres support nine to forty-three species of breeding birds, respectively. This pattern, known as the species-area relationship, has been documented for many kinds of habitats. Assuming similar habitat, large areas contain more spe-cies than small areas, in part because, compared to small areas, large areas support larger populations, which are less likely to become ex-tinct than small populations.

The degree of isolation from other habitat patches also affects the number of resident species. When animals cannot efficiently move among habitat islands, each patch comes to support an isolated population rather than one part of a large population. Inbreeding is more likely to occur in small populations than in large ones. Further, small populations may experience genetic drift, random genetic changes that deplete genetic variance. Both inbreeding and drift contribute to genetic *homozygosity*, the condition in which an or-ganism has identical genes for a given characteristic — for example, a person with two genes for blue eyes, each acquired from one parent. Compared to *homozygous* individuals, *heterozygotes* not only avoid the deleterious effects of inbreeding, such as slow growth, depressed survival, and poor reproduction, their development yields fewer con-genital defects. Homozygous individuals are more likely to develop nonidentical left and right halves than heterozygotes.

We can grasp some of the consequences of inbreeding by look-ing at the cheetah. When skin grafts are exchanged between unre-lated individuals, they are fully accepted, suggesting that all cheetahs are genetically very similar. How do we account for this completely unexpected affinity in a wild population? It is possible that a cli-matic catastrophe or hunting spree reduced the cheetah to a few individuals, wiping out a population's worth of genetic variation, and then the population rebounded from a few founders. Whatever the historical cause, genetic uniformity has the cheetah on the verge of extinction — they are susceptible to epidemics and experience high juvenile mortality.

So, how many individuals must a population have to preclude extinction? Several geneticists have estimated that the minimum number of reproductive adults needed for self-perpetuation is in the range of fifty to one hundred. Theoretical models suggest that even populations as large as five hundred may lose genetic variation faster than they gain it via mutation. Some conservation biologists use one thousand individuals as a general minimum for viable populations.

Forest fragmentation reduces effective population size by limiting each organism's ability to move among subpopulations. One remedy is to connect habitat islands, as currently advocated by the greenways movement. Effective population size may be increased by maintaining dispersal corridors among distant patches of habitat. Species subdivided into small, interconnected populations will persist when the rate of population extinction is less than or equal to the rate of population founding.

All this points to one simple idea: Rarity seems to be the best indicator of how vulnerable a species is to extinction. Before you dismiss this as self-evident, consider the power it gives us to predict the most likely candidates for extinction: top predators (golden eagle), large-bodied species (black bear), habitat specialists (Cheat Mountain salamander), and species at the outer fringes of their geographic distribution (wood turtle in the eastern panhandle of West Virginia).

In general, mammals are particularly vulnerable to extinction on habitat islands. Not only do they have low powers of dispersal, they also have high metabolic needs. Compared to wood thrushes, which can fly between woodlots, a population of waddling opossums depends more on the food and shelter of a single patch of habitat. In fact, of all vertebrate classes, mammals exhibit the fastest rates of species loss. Extreme insularity, with absolute dispersal barriers, could thoroughly extirpate mammals and other nonflying vertebrates.

Species that disperse efficiently are a bit better off. Because they can fly from patch to patch, birds maintain higher numbers of species at equilibrium than do other vertebrates. But even here fragmentation is taking its toll — breeding populations of songbirds have been dropping in small forest tracts. For bird communities in forest islands, the larger the habitat area, the greater the number of bird species; the greater the degree of isolation of forest islands, the fewer the number of species; and the greater the extent of forest fragmentation, the fewer the number of species typical of the forest interior.

It is thus mildly surprising that, with the possible exceptions of the ivory-billed woodpecker and Carolina parakeet, North American birds have not yet been pushed to extinction because of deforestation. However, the mix of species, particularly the representation of migrant songbirds, has dropped. In general, neotropical migrants, those birds that breed in North America and overwinter in Latin America, comprise up to 90 percent of the breeding pairs throughout Appalachia. In many places the diversity of our migrants has plummeted. For example, the veery, worm-eating warbler, black-and-white warbler, yellow-throated vireo, ovenbird, and American redstart, often found in large forests, are rarely seen in small woodlots.

This loss of migrants has occurred at various scales. At the local level, on a tract of virgin red spruce-northern hardwood forest on Shaver's Mountain, West Virginia, both the number of species and the population sizes of neotropical migrants dwindled between 1949 and 1983. At the continental scale, 109 species of migrants, including various species of vireos, warblers, thrushes, and flycatchers, declined during 1985-1995. Even populations of the red-eyed vireo, possibly the most common bird in Appalachia, have declined dramatically in many forest fragments.

At least two possible reasons arise for the disappearance of neotropical migrants. Because migration imposes high energy costs and short breeding seasons, neotropical migrants lay few eggs per clutch and produce only one brood per year. Compared to resident birds, they are less buffered against reproductive failure.

221

Further, neotropical migrants lay their eggs in open, cuplike nests that are vulnerable to predation and parasitism. In Illinois, the reproductive success of tufted titmice, cavity nesters, all local species, and neotropical migrants was 67, 54, 45, and 29 percent, respectively. The low fledging rate of migrants was attributed to high nest predation and cowbird parasitism allowed by their open-cup nesting habit.

Since the original version of *Hollows* was published, the forest's edge has been a focus of research. In Pennsylvania and Delaware, edge effects, in the forms of altered light, temperature, moisture, and humidity, have been detected up to 165 feet into the forest. Small mammal predators (raccoons, feral cats), egg-eating birds (crows, blue jays), competitors (starlings, English sparrows) and nest parasites (brown-headed cowbirds) are more active in the forest patches within three hundred to six hundred feet of its edge. Thus, edge effects render the functional interior area smaller than the forest patch's actual area.

A neotropical migrant that builds a domed nest, the ovenbird offers a partial, and therefore instructive, exception. In one study, ovenbirds had lower brood parasitism and higher egg survival rates than open-cup, ground-nesting birds. Although their domed nests offered some protection, the survival of ovenbirds was still lower sixty-six feet inside the edge than 660-1320 feet into the forest interior.

The cumulative effect of many impaired local patches causes broad regional impacts. In central Spain, predation rate increases in landscapes with high levels of forest fragmentation, in part because predators tend to concentrate their searching in certain forest patches. In nine landscapes of the American midwest, nest predation and parasitism increase with forest fragmentation.

Forest patches larger than 250 acres do not show the consistent loss of migrant species seen in smaller woodlots. Several findings help explain this. In the central Appalachians of Maryland, bird nests along natural forest-stream edges experience high levels of predation and parasitism. In general, whether birds live in natural

222

or human-altered landscapes, predation rates decrease as forest size increase. Predation rates soar from 2 percent in the 510,000 acres of Great Smoky Mountains National Park to 75-100 percent in wood-lots of only twenty-five acres.

The second reason for the decrease of migratory songbirds lies in the tropics — the slash-and-burn destruction of winter habitat. Tropical rain forests, where many of our birds overwinter, is being cleared at the rate of three acres per minute. Sadly, the life histories of many neotropical migrant birds may be incompatible with our fragmented forests.

Combining the effects of temperate fragmentation and tropical deforestation, it becomes intuitively obvious that the bird species most likely to be adversely affected are long-distance migrants that overwinter in the tropics and breed in the forest interiors of North America.

By deduction, some ornithologists have proposed the "nested subset hypothesis," in which the bird species of small woodlots are small subsets of the species-rich bird assemblages of large nearby con-tiguous forests. This idea has been tested in Illinois, where most, but not all, of the bird species of small woodlots are also found in larger forests. This result leaves the door open for significant randomness in local extirpations.

More generally, fragmentation may also be having subtle, in-sidious effects on Appalachian forest communities. For example, the spores of mycorrhizal fungi may disperse among habitat islands by hitchhiking on small mammals, which, as I have already said, are severely affected by insulation. Thus, the health of trees in small, isolated woodlots may depend on the minimum area and insularity requirements of small mammal populations. Here's an unexpected connection with huge implications.

So what can we do to slow or reverse the heavy toll of fragmentation? Given limited amounts of money and land, how should nature preserves be designed to minimize isolation, inbreeding, predation, and ultimately extinction?

Some conservation biologists approach this problem by applying the equilibrium theory of island biogeography. According to this idea, immigration of new species should decrease with greater isolation, and extinction should increase with smaller island size. The theory predicts that smaller and more isolated islands will have a lower number of species than larger, less isolated islands. The problem is that this theory, despite its intuitive appeal, is insufficiently validated to support its application to conservation. Some ecologists argue that one large refuge will save more species than several small refuges of equal total size; others press the contrary.

A second technical glitch is that the species-area relationship turns out to be non-linear. When you chart the frequency of occurrence of a given species as a function of fragment size, a sharp break often shows. Such incidence functions reveal that species are present in patches larger than a certain size, but occur much less frequently in smaller patches. Ignorance of this inflection point can lead to protecting habitat patches of the wrong size.

A third issue is that, unlike the dispersal routes between oceanic islands, which are thought to reduce extinction and increase recolonization, corridors within a terrestrial mosaic come with some negative effects. For example, some corridors have been found to attract and concentrate predators, which kill animals traveling between patches. Some now ask whether the conservation values of corridors have been overrated.

Until these scientific questions are settled, community ecologists will be unable to offer practical advice to county commissioners, land developers, and other people who make decisions on land uses.

I can, however, offer that the answer to each particular situation lies with the specific conservation goals. If the priority is to protect black bears, hawks, or other widely ranging animals, many

224

habitat islands with connecting corridors might work. In contrast, migrant songbirds such as the Acadian flycatcher, ovenbird, and veery would benefit from large blocks of unbroken forest. Organisms — the summer tanager, cardinal, and poison ivy, for instance — that live along habitat boundaries such as the forest edge would do better with long, skinny reserves.

Ideally, we should provide a system of habitat islands that (a) allows the development of local, genetically differentiated subpopulations and (b) does not block the flow of genes among habitat islands. Many small stepping-stone islands would link a few large and distant reserves; riparian strips would allow travel between forest lands.

Because conflicts among ecologists surface whether considering reserve area, spacing, or shape, people who attempt to preserve land and its living community are left with ambiguous scientific guidance. As irrevocable changes impact the Appalachian forest, we don't even know enough to plan the salvage operation. Even so, we must not let ignorance justify inaction. One solution is the international system of biosphere reserves.

UNESCO launched the biosphere reserve project in 1971 to conserve genetic and ecological diversity and to provide opportunities for research and education. The ideal biosphere reserve is large enough to include a complete ecosystem, including its full range of physical and biological processes. The core zone, the heart of the reserve, is strictly protected and administered as a global benchmark for studying how ecosystems function. In the United States, some wilderness areas, national parks and monuments, and wildlife sanctuaries could serve as suitable core zones. A buffer zone, designed to absorb the most severe impacts of the surrounding countryside, insulates the core.

The Southern Appalachian Biosphere Reserve cluster, with Great Smoky Mountains National Park (Tennessee and North Carolina) as the core and Oak Ridge National Laboratory (Tennessee) and Coweeta Hydrological Laboratory (North Carolina) as buffers, has served as a model for cooperative research. In northern Appalachia, Hubbard Brook Experimental Forest (New Hampshire)

225

represents a buffer for a yet-to-be determined reserve. And there is talk of establishing a biosphere reserve in central Appalachia that would include Shenandoah National Park (Virginia).

The maintenance of biosphere reserves would allow us to protect biodiversity by managing landscapes with various kinds, sizes, and shapes of patches and corridors. For example, heavily forested areas, in which breeding birds experience low predation/parasitism and high reproductive success, would export excess young to more fragmented regions. Thus, continuous core forests should be preserved as population sources for the sinks of hostile patches.

Further, as I have mentioned, the fluxes of matter, energy, and organisms across a forest-field edge are in part controlled by the kinds and amounts of fragmentation of the surrounding landscape. That is, the dynamics within a forest remnant are driven in part by forces arising outside the patch. Management of fragmented ecosystems should address both the remnants themselves and their external forces.

One benefit of mosaic management is that it allows us to focus resources on landscape connectivity. The long-term goal is to maintain a landscape of patches among which the individuals of species with varying dispersal powers can move among enough appropriate habitat patches to maintain viable populations.

Philosophically, I view biosphere reserves as another step in our ethical evolution — they affirm our commitment to the future of living diversity. From a more practical point of view, biosphere reserves represent one of the last bastions of natural Appalachian diversity, the last pockets from which broader areas will draw powers to convalesce.

Biosphere reserves are just part of the solution. The ultimate strategy must also include a form of land-use planning that maintains and increases biological diversity. When we begin to plan how to use a piece of Appalachia, we must set out from the start to save the full complement of native species. Nothing less will do.

30

Abuse, Resurrection, Hope

The depth of man's abuse of the Appalachian landscape came about 1920. Uncontrolled hunting had extirpated game, the railroad had spurred clear-cutting of the forest, and an introduced blight was decimating the elegant American chestnut. A modest reversal came with the emergence of the conservation ethic, which Aldo Leopold so forcefully expressed in *Sand County Almanac*: "In short, a land ethic changes the role of *Homo sapiens* from conqueror of the land-community to plain member and citizen of it. It implies respect for his fellow-members, and also respect for the community as such."

Since then the environmental health of Appalachia has been gradually recovering. The Lacey Act of 1900, the first federal law to protect wildlife nationwide, specifically by prohibiting its commercial exploitation and interstate shipment, was a big help. White-tailed deer now abound in some areas to the point of pestering farmers; pine, oak, and hickory reforest old eroded homesteads; and government agencies are funding the reclamation of abandoned strip mines. I savor this progress, yet see a plethora of remaining obstacles. In addition to forest fragmentation, three other big environmental stressors interfere with the successional recovery of Appalachian ecosystems: haphazard land use, acid rain, and exotic species. Even though landfills grow next to homes and surface miners dig next to schools, local governments still eschew land-use planning — not to mention the "z word." Acid rain sterilizes our streams. Ironically, emissions from high-sulfur coal torn from Appalachia's landscape and then burned in the Midwest blows back to Appalachia as a double insult. Finally, exotic species endanger native plants and animals. In the forest around my cabin, feral cats and cowbirds wreak havoc on the native warblers.

The most harmful problem, lack of land-use planning, is a crime of omission. Land-use planning allows elected officials to develop a local strategy that defines the types of changes that may be visited upon the land. A zoning ordinance codifies those desires. Many Appalachian counties have neither planner nor ordinance.

When land development proceeds without a plan, environmental impacts are usually worse than if an ordinance had been on the books. Common consequences of this omission are the building of homes in floodplains, and the digging of septic drain fields in soils that cannot assimilate the volume of sewage generated by modern households. In my area, such a policy vacuum allowed people to replace their trailers along the South Branch's riverbank after a huge flood had washed them away.

Lack of land-use planning also leads to erosion and muddy streams. Road builders expose bare soil without shielding it from erosion, developers clear subdivisions of plants that would have stabilized the topsoil, loggers clear-cut without regard to slope, and farmers plow up to the streambank. All of these practices lead to soil erosion and excess silt in streams, where it settles on living things. Sediment is particularly deadly to nonmoving, permanently attached organisms, such as aquatic plants, snails, insect larvae, and fish eggs, because it interferes with their ability to exchange gases.

A further consequence of the lack of land-use planning is the loss of biotic diversity due to haphazard forest fragmentation. We ignore the roles of reserve size, shape, and spacing in maintaining a full set of plant and animal species.

Why do governments in Appalachia lack, even resist, efforts to regulate land use? Both resident and absentee landowners seem to play roles. Highlanders are independent and skeptical of authority. A bureaucrat from the county seat telling a mountaineer what to do with his land has never "set" well. Absentee landowners also have a vested interest in resisting land-use planning. Absentee landowners, who own 72 percent of West Virginia, thwart planning through political routes. In order to institute land-use planning, both types of landowners must realize the greater potential income from planned economic development versus totally unregulated changes. Communities that passively allow aimless growth attract fly-by-night developers and toxic waste dumps.

The Appalachian Mountains, steep and covered by thin soil, cry out for controls of land development based on sound ecological principles. Without a comprehensive land-use policy, visitors will reject Appalachia; these communities will wither on the vine.

Highlanders have been slow to adopt Leopold's land ethic. The idea that God created these hills for us to use as we see fit is deeply ingrained. In my opinion, education is part of the answer. We highlanders will be more willing to change our ways when we learn that our hills are the basis of a sustainable paycheck. Scattered throughout the hills lies the blueprint: a farmer charges hunters and anglers to recreate on his land; a couple hosts tourists in a restored bed-and-breakfast; a mechanic nurtures ten acres of Christmas trees. All depend on a healthy environment.

Conservation through appreciation will not be quick or cheap, though. In many regions, it will take nothing less than a fundamental revolution of priorities.

A cid deposition, a pervasive, insidious poison produced elsewhere and imported by rain, snow, fog, sleet, and hail, is Appalachia's next environmental problem. Atmospheric acid is a contemporary example of the principle Garrett Hardin articulated in his classic essay, "Tragedy of the Commons." Hardin revealed how resources that support all of our lives, such as air, space, and water, are endangered by a few selfish individuals. First, a little technical background.

A liquid's acidity depends on its concentration of hydrogen ions, hydrogen atoms with a positive electrical charge. Acidity, measured on the pH scale, ranges from 0, the most acidic, to 14, the most alkaline; a liquid with a pH of 7 is neutral. Your stomach juices have a pH of 2, tomato juice is 4, milk 7, ammonia 11, and lye 13. As a logarithmic scale, one unit of change in pH represents a ten-fold difference in the amount of acid, e.g., a liquid with pH of 5 is one hundred times more acidic than a neutral solution.

Unpolluted rain has a pH of 5.6. This modest acidity of natural rain has three sources. First, carbonic acid forms when carbon dioxide in the atmosphere dissolves in water vapor. Second, volcanoes, geysers, and decomposing organic matter release sulfur oxides, which change to sulfuric acid in rain water. And third, electrical storms spark the formation of nitric acid in rain.

Highly acidic rain, though, is human-caused. Westerlies import sulfur-rich emissions from the major industries of the Midwest. The winds strike Appalachia and force air upward, where it cools. The condensate falls to the ground, cleaning the air of sulfur — but becoming sulfuric acid in the process.

The concentrations of hydrogen ions, sulfate, and nitrate in the precipitation of eastern North America have increased with our rising consumption of fossil-fuels. Tall smoke stacks eject their effluent high into the air, enabling the long range transport of acidic gases. In general, sulfur and nitrogen compounds are responsible for two-thirds and one-third, respectively, of the acid deposition.

The area suffering from the greatest acid impact (pH less than 4.2) is a broad oval reaching southwest from New York and New Jersey to Tennessee and Ohio. Somewhat less affected (pH less than 5.0) are the other eastern states and southeast Canada.

In Greenland, ice caps hold thousands of years worth of frozen precipitation. When the pH of this standard is compared to that of contemporary rain in the eastern United States, ours is at least thirty times more acidic. The extensive impacts of acid rain and snow, however, did not exist prior to World War II.

Two natural features — the forest canopy and the buffering capacity of rocks and soil — partially neutralize this human-caused acid. In New Hampshire, where the average pH of precipitation is 4.1, the rain falling through the northern hardwood canopies, known as throughfall, is less acidic than the direct precipitation. Neutralization of throughfall seems to be effected by the removal of hydrogen ions by deciduous leaves and the leaching of neutralizing bases from the canopy. Limestone buffers surface waters, imparting resistance to pH change because it dissolves easily and neutralizes acid. Hard, resistant bedrocks such as basalt and granite provide little buffering capacity.

Softwater lakes, which formed in areas with hard rocks such as sandstone, contain few buffers, so their pH changes rapidly when subjected to acidic precipitation. The young glacial soils of New England are naturally acidic and lack lime. Consequently, they only slightly neutralize acid deposition and allow nutrients to leach from these already poor soils. The Adirondacks are characterized by soils with little neutralizing capacity and acidified lakes. In contrast, even though they also receive acid precipitation, the Great Lakes are not acidifying because the surrounding soils buffer them well. Thus, in some areas acid deposition is overwhelming the soil's neutralizing powers.

Acid rain leaches potassium, sugars, proteins, and amino acids from tree leaves. Severely acidic rains damage the waxy coverings of leaves, which then desiccate and become susceptible to attack by fungi and bacteria. Conifers are more susceptible to damage from acid deposition than deciduous trees because their needles remain exposed year-round, and because fogs that sweep through their high-elevation habitats are often more acidic than rain at lower elevations. In conifers, initial symptoms include the loss of needles in the crown, and then over the course of several years the disease progresses downward through lower branches. Thirty years ago, dense healthy evergreen forests grew on Camels Hump in the Green Mountains of Vermont. Today, 50 percent of the red spruces are dead and firs look sick. Skeletons loom everywhere. Commercially important sugar maples are dying, too. Dead and crown-damaged trees mar the

White Mountains of New Hampshire, the central Appalachians of West Virginia, and the Great Smoky Mountains of Tennessee and North Carolina.

Compared to a pH-neutral solution, acidic precipitation dissolves higher quantities of aluminum, nickel, cadmium, manganese, zinc, lead, and copper from soils. Most of these metals are toxic at low concentrations. This synergism between acid and heavy metals is lethal to a wide variety of living things. After acid deposition intensified, roughly about 1950, the concentration of aluminum increased dramatically in the annual rings of trees. Inorganic aluminum, present in the soil, is insoluble at a pH of 5.6, but quite soluble at 4.6. Plant roots absorb soluble aluminum, which hinders their water uptake. Eventually, leaves turn brown and drop off, and the tree dies.

Excess acid also harms aquatic organisms. Below a pH of 6, fish experience various forms of reproductive failure, reducing some populations to few old, large individuals. Below a pH of 5, the fish community shifts to a few resistant species, for example from a fishery offering brook trout and smallmouth bass, to one dominated by rock bass and yellow perch.

The synergy between acid (pH) and aluminum (Al) has been well studied in the brook trout. Episodes of acidification decrease survival of early life stages. Specifically, pre-emergence and sac fry stages are hammered by low pH/high Al. In spring, adult brook trout mortality is more than 20 percent, sometimes even climbing to 100 percent, in streams with acute events of low pH/high Al. Of the two stressors, high Al is believed to cause most of the deaths.

In streams allowing some survival, brook trout moved 825-2,970 feet downstream after low pH/high Al episodes; in reference streams there was no net movement. Immigration from downstream reaches maintains brook trout populations impacted by such acute catastrophes.

Most amphibians breed in the spring, when streams and puddles receive a large input of acid from snowmelt — a winter's worth of stored pollutants. Such acid shock can wipe out an entire generation

234

of an amphibian species. Because the winters of central and southern Appalachia characteristically alternate between freezing and thawing, the most severe springtime acid shock hits northern Appalachia. The spotted salamander, which breeds in temporary pools formed by snowmelt, illustrates the effects of acid shock: egg mortality is less than 1 percent if the pH is neutral, but greater than 60 percent in springtime pools with a pH of up to 6.0.

Slowly, inexorably, Appalachia is being sterilized by this insidious cancer. What can we do about it? It might be possible to develop a strain of acid-tolerant fish. Also, adding limestone to lakes and streams works temporarily. But these measures only treat the symptoms. Because the effects of acid rain are subtle and partially hidden, it has been difficult to conclusively demonstrate their environmental significance. Focusing research solely on acid deposition has been challenging because synergistic effects are involved. Thus, some scientists have been unwilling to make a firm statement about cause and effect.

Recent studies using analytical chemistry and meteorology have located the major polluters in the north-central states between the Allegheny Mountains and the Mississippi River. Within this region, municipal power plants are the major source of sulfur dioxide. From source to deposition, pollutants travel three hundred to seven hundred miles. We can recognize the chemical signatures of regional polluters by the proportions of elements such as arsenic, antimony, selenium, and zinc in their effluent. For example, eastern utilities that burn heavy residual oil (what is left after the removal of other distillates) produce an aerosol that is distinct from that of inland coal burners. When air flows eastward, a midwestern aerosol becomes superimposed on eastern pollution.

In essence, acid precipitation is a subtle ecological change visited by humans on our Appalachian ecosystems. In the environment, it is difficult to perform controlled experiments to test acid rain's effects because of confounding variables. Because it is an interstate and international problem involving large industries, huge financial assets are at stake. The combination of scientific ambiguity and money interests account for the incomplete action by government leaders. In Europe, even though Scandinavian scientists concluded that acid rain from industrial Britain and western Europe was killing lakes, British government officials did not accept it. The Europeans' former stance of denial is analogous to the continuing foot-dragging by American officials. Our government's position that we need more scientific information before we can make correct decisions is simply an excuse for doing nothing.

Exotic species, those recent arrivals from other areas, destroy native organisms via herbivory, predation, competition, parasitism, or by being pathogens. A native species can be wiped out locally by a newcomer in a few years. Human-assisted immigrants include several honeysuckle species, kudzu, tree of heaven, English sparrow, pigs, and cats.

The American chestnut originally thrived throughout the Appalachian Mountains from southern Vermont and New Hampshire southward into northern Georgia. Attaining a height of 130 feet and occupying up to 60 percent of the canopy, American chestnut reached its largest size and greatest concentration in the Great Smoky Mountains. By 1925, an introduced blight had reached all parts of Appalachia. Chestnut blight did not eliminate the American chestnut from the forest, but it removed it from the canopy. Chestnuts continue to sprout today because the fungus does not kill the roots, but the blight kills the saplings before long.

The gypsy moth, an exotic species, is currently wreaking huge damages on Appalachian forests. In 1868, Professor Leopold Trouvelot of Medford, Massachusetts, imported several gypsy moth egg masses from southern France. He wanted to produce a better silkworm by cross-breeding gypsy and silk-worm moths. When a specimen jar fell from his window, a few moths escaped. Since then, this exotic has expanded its range an average of nine miles per year, in large part because North America does not have the natural enemies that keep the moth in check throughout Europe. It arrived in West Virginia in 1972. (By an unsettling quirk of fate, as I was researching this essay, I found the first gypsy moth egg mass along Pine Cabin Run, on the trunk of a black walnut tree.) The moth's current range includes all of the New England states, west to Michigan, and the pest continues to spread southward through West Virginia and west to Ohio. This picture will be out of date by the time you read this — most authorities see nothing to stop the moth's spread across the continent.

Gypsy moth caterpillars have strong food preferences. They readily eat oak leaves; white oaks suffer more than black oak species. They also like to eat apple, basswood, willow, and birch. Although not favored, the moths will attack American beech, black cherry, black gum, American hemlock, hickories, hornbeam, maples, pines, sassafras, and spruces. Larvae must be starving before they will defoliate the following tree species: eastern red cedar, flowering dogwood, mountain laurel, black locust, persimmon, sycamore, tulip poplar, and black walnut.

When half or more of its leaves are eaten, a hardwood tree will produce a new set of leaves by midsummer. This extra outlay decreases the tree's food reserves, weakens it, and leaves it more susceptible to drought, fungi, insects, and the stresses of winter. Weakened trees are attacked and killed by shoestring fungus and the two-lined chestnut borer. For one or two years following defoliation, the tree refoliates with small, off-color leaves, and twigs and branches die back. One heavy defoliation can cause subtle reductions in a tree's health that are detectable for a decade. A single defoliation kills some softwoods, while hardwoods die after two or more defoliations. In general, the effects of gypsy moth defoliation depend on the amount of foliage removed and the number of consecutive defoliations.

The gypsy moth's life cycle is supremely suited for converting broad leaves into caterpillar tissue. Mercifully, there is only one gypsy moth generation per year. The moths overwinter in eggs amassed on stones, walls, and logs. Eggs hatch in late April and early May. Larvae leave their egg mass and climb the tree, trailing silk threads. Reaching the top, they arch their body, drop on silken threads, and then are tugged loose by slight gusts of wind. The silk strand and the

237

caterpillar's long hairs contribute to buoyancy. After several ballooning episodes, they settle down to feed. Although most settle near the tree on which they hatched, some catch updrafts and float high above the canopy for tens or even hundreds of miles. Young caterpillars feed and rest during the day. Older individuals climb the tree at dusk, feed only at night, and descend at dawn to rest in protected sites. Larvae use silken threads to return to resting sites, such as wounds and gaps under bark.

Caterpillars mature when they are about two inches long. They enter the cocoon stage in June or early July. Adult moths emerge in ten to fourteen days and lay eggs from July through September. Adult gypsy moths do not eat.

A gypsy moth invasion proceeds through a predictable sequence. After the initial defoliation, the severity and duration of each succeeding outbreak declines. Females in stable or growing populations produce few and large egg masses — 1.5 inches long with seven hundred to one thousand eggs. In contrast, many small egg masses — 0.5 inch long, seventy-five to one hundred eggs — indicate a declining infestation.

Stretching for a positive note, there are two possible consolations balancing the acute disgust of living through a gypsy moth invasion. First, where oaks cover 60 percent of the commercial forest, as in some parts of West Virginia, repeated outbreaks may reduce the proportion of oak. This would yield tree stands of greater species diversity and resistance. Reducing the proportion of oaks, the moth's preferred food, to 15 to 25 percent of the dominant trees would give the pest less start-up momentum towards an outbreak. After the original oak-chestnut forest recovered from chestnut blight, it became the more diverse oak-hickory forest. Post-gypsy moth, we may live in an even more diverse ash-tulip poplar forest. A second potential benefit of defoliation is that it speeds nutrient cycling through larval feces and thereby increases ecosystem production.

Entomologists are studying several options, including parasites, sex attractant, and genetic defenses of trees, to control gypsy moth populations during non-outbreak periods. Further, some native ground beetles, thirty-eight species of birds including the black-capped chickadee and yellow-billed cuckoo, and several mammals such as shrews and squirrels are significant predators. So there is plenty of hope for peace after the initial invasion has waned.

In *Field Days*, essayist Roger Swain expressed his desire to get along with gypsy moths, that sooner or later biological controls will rein them in. This is fine if you are managing a forest for perpetuity, but if you are suffering through a peak year of irruption, or if your livelihood in recreation depends on healthy trees, you would be justified in cursing the things.

I have chosen to illustrate the effects of exotic species by focusing on the gypsy moth, probably because it just recently began imposing itself along Pine Cabin Run. Other imports are also changing Appalachian ecosystems. Multiflora rose, locust leaf miner, pine sawfly, rainbow trout, European starling, and the feral cat are recasting the Appalachian play right before our very eyes. And there's precious little we can do about it. Since publication of the original *Hollows*, a fifth issue has climbed in global attention. Everyone agrees that Earth's climate has been changing, and more specifically that certain regions have been warming. But opinions are mixed about its cause(s): Some argue that we are living through the warming phase of a natural long-term cycle, while others assert that increasing levels of human-produced fossil-fuel gases (e.g., carbon dioxide) are intensifying the atmosphere's greenhouse effect.

Regardless of cause, climate warming is affecting Appalachian organisms. How will a warmer climate affect the populations and distributions of our high-elevation plants, like red spruce, Table Mountain pine, and balsam fir? How will shorter winters impact the emergence of hibernating wood frogs and groundhogs, or the migratory departures of monarch butterflies and black-throated green warblers? Is bloodroot genetically programmed to emerge too late in a newly lengthened growing season to win its share of pollinators?

One of these questions has been answered for one Appalachian species, the brook trout. One researcher projected a 5 degree Fahrenheit increase in the average annual temperature in southern

Appalachia by 2100. Extrapolating across the region, he estimated that such a thermal change would elevate the brookies' lower limit by up to 2,356 feet, causing huge losses of suitable stream miles. Recalculating, a peer retorted that it will actually be worse than that!

I n this epilogue, I have considered five environmental problems facing contemporary Appalachia: forest fragmentation, lack of land-use planning, acid deposition, exotic species, and climate change — all forces that are changing our highlands forever. For the sake of Appalachia's children, including my daughter Leah, I counsel a balanced commitment to managing them all.

We have witnessed together this vast Appalachian play. From the opening act of tectonic collisions hundreds of millions of years ago, through the broad scenes of forest origins, and into the narrow vignettes of small bugs' sex lives, we have been delivered into today's environmental issues. I cannot rest knowing the joys of Appalachia may not last. The biggest things must start with a first small step. If this book helps in some small way to conserve Appalachia, possibly by fostering a deeper appreciation, then I'll be able to relax when I'm old in my rocking chair.

You are entitled to ask me what I have done, other than write a book, to help the Appalachian cause. I have committed the profit from the sales of this book to protecting local Appalachian ecosystems, especially several rivers in eastern West Virginia. My turn: What are you doing to assure continuity of the evolutionary play in Appalachia? The lament, "If I had only...," is one of life's great tragedies. I challenge you to take that next constructive step. To the extent that we rise above good intentions, roll up our sleeves, and actually do the work, the evolutionary play in Appalachia will continue.

Actors

Plants

alder - *Alnus* (birch family, Betulaceae)

alpine azalea – *Loiseleuria procumbens* (heath family, Ericaceae)

alpine bearberry – *Arctostaphylos alpina* (Ericaceae)

American basswood – *Tilia americana* (basswood family, Tiliaceae)

American beech – *Fagus grandifolia* (beech family, Fagaceae)

American chestnut – *Castanea dentata* (Fagaceae)

American hornbeam – *Carpinus caroliniana* (Betulaceae)

apple – *Malus* (rose family, Rosaceae)

balsam fir – *Abies balsamea* (pine family, Pinaceae)

balsam poplar – *Populus balsamifera* (willow family, Salicaceae)

basket oak – *Quercus prinus* (Fagaceae)

bigtooth aspen – *Populus grandidentata* (Salicaceae)

birch – *Betula* (Betulaceae)

black cherry – *Prunus serotina* (Rosaceae)

black locust – *Robinia pseudoacacia* (legume family, Leguminosae)

black oak – *Quercus velutina* (Fagaceae)

black walnut – *Juglans nigra* (walnut family, Juglandaceac)

black willow – *Salix nigra* (Salicaceae)

black tupelo – *Nyssa sylvatica* (dogwood family, Cornaceae)

bloodroot – *Sanguinaria canadensis* (poppy family, Papaveraceae)

blueberry – *Vaccinium* (Ericaceae)

242

boxelder – *Acer negundo* (maple family, Aceraceae)

bracken fern – *Pteridium aquilinum* (true fern family, Polypodiaceae)

bunchberry – *Cornus canadensis* (Cornaceae)

Carolina hemlock – *Tsuga caroliniana* (Pinaceae)

Carolina silverbell – *Halesia carolina* (snowbell family, Styracaceae)

carrot – *Daucus* (umbellifer family, Umbelliferae)

chestnut blight – *Endothia parasitica* (Fungi: class Ascomycetes)

chestnut oak – *Quercus prinus* (Fagaceae)

coltsfoot – *Tussilago farfara* (sunflower family, Asteraceae)

common persimmon – *Diospyros virginiana* (ebony family, Ebanaceae)

cottonwood – *Populus* (Salicaceae)

crested dwarf iris – *Iris cristata* (iris family, Iridaceae)

devil's walkingstick – *Aralia spinosa* (ginseng family, Araliaceae)

downy rattlesnake plaintain – *Goodyera pubescens* (orchid family, Orchidaceae)

downy serviceberry – *Amelanchier arborea* (Rosaceae)

Dutchman's breeches – *Dicentra cucullaria* (Papaveraceae)

eastern hemlock – *Tsuga canadensis* (Pinaceae)

eastern redbud – *Cercis canadensis* (Leguminosae)

eucalyptus – *Eucalyptus* (family Myrtaceae)

European white birch – *Betula pendula* (Betulaceae)

eastern red cedar – *Juniperus virginiana* (juniper family, Cupressaceae)

fir – *Abies* (Pinaceae)

fire pink – *Silene virginica* (pink family, Caryophyllaceae)

Fraser fir – *Abies fraseri* (Pinaceae)

fringetree – *Chionanthus virginicus* (olive family, Oleaceae)

flowering dogwood – *Cornus florida* (Cornaceae)

Hollows, Peepers, and Highlanders

ginseng – *Panax quinquefolium* (Araliaceae)

huckleberry – *Gaylussacia* (Ericaceae)

hickory – *Carya* (Juglandaceae)

holly – *Ilex* (holly family, Aquifoliaceae)

hepatica – *Hepatica* (buttercup family, Ranunculaceae)

Jack-in-the-pulpit – *Arisaema triphyllum* (arum family, Araceae)

jack pine – *Pinus banksiana* (Pinaceae)

Japanese honeysuckle – *Lonicera japonica* (honeysuckle family, Caprifoliaceae)

Japanese Jack-in-the-pulpit – *Arisaema japonica* (Araceae)

Japanese lady's slipper – *Cypripedium japonicum* (Orchidaceae)

kudzu – *Pueraria lobata* (pea family, Fabaceae)

Kentucky coffee-tree – *Gymnocladus dioicus* (Leguminosae)

lady's-slipper – *Cypripedium* (Orchidaceae)

maple – *Acer* (Aceraceae)

milkweed – *Asclepias* (milkweed family, Asclepiadaceae)

mountain azalea – *Rhododendron canescens* (Ericaceae)

mountain heath – *Phyllodoce caerulea* (Ericaceae)

mountain laurel – *Kalmia latifolia* (Ericaceae)

mountain oat grass – *Danthonia compressa* (grass family, Gramineae)

nodding ladies tresses – *Spiranthes cernua* (Orchidaceae)

paper birch – *Betula papyrifera* (Betulaceae)

paw paw – *Asimina triloba* (annona family, Annonaceae)

persimmon – *Diospyros* (Ebenaceae)

pignut hickory – *Carya glabra* (Juglandaceae)

pink lady's-slipper – *Cypripedium acaule* (Orchidaceae)

post oak – *Quercus stellata* (Fagaceae)

quaking aspen – *Populus tremuloides* (Salicaceae)

red oak – *Quercus rubra* (Fagaceae)

red pine – *Pinus resinosa* (Pinaceae)

red spruce – *Picea rubens* (Pinaceae)

red top – *Solidago* (composite family, Compositae)

rhododendron – *Rhododendron* (Ericaceae)

rose – *Rosa* (Rosaceae)

sassafras – *Sassafras albidum* (laurel family, Lauraceae)

scarlet oak – *Quercus coccinea* (Fagaceae)

shagbark hickory – *Carya ovata* (Juglandaceae)

showy lady's-slipper – *Cypripedium reginae* (Orchidaceae)

showy orchis – *Orchis spectabile* (Orchidaceae)

silverbell – *Halesia* (Styracaceae)

skunk cabbage – *Symplocarpus foetidus* (Araceae)

snowbells – *Styrax* (Styracaceae)

spring beauty – *Claytonia virginica* (purslane family, Portulacaceae)

spruce – *Picea* (Pinaceae)

squirrel corn – *Dicentra canadensis* (fumitory family, Fumariaceae)

star chickweed – *Stellaria pubera* (Caryophyllaceae)

stewartia – *Stewartia* (tea family, Theaceae)

striped maple – *Acer pensylvanicum* (Aceraceae)

sugar maple – *Acer saccharum* (Aceraceae)

sumac – *Rhus* (cashew family, Anacardiaceae)

sweet gum – *Liquidambar styraciflua* (witch-hazel family, Simaroubaceae)

sweetleaf – *Symplocos* (sweetleaf family, Symplocaceae)

Table Mountain pine – *Pinus pungens* (Pinaceae)

tree-of-heaven – *Ailanthus altissima* (Simaroubaceae)

trillium – *Trillium* (lily family, Liliaceae)

tulip poplar – *Liriodendron tulipifera* (magnolia family, Magnoliaceae)

violets – *Viola* (violet family, Violaceae)

white ash – *Fraxinus americana* (Oleaceae)

white oak – *Quercus alba* (Fagaceae)

white pine – *Pinus strobus* (Pinaceae)

witch-hazel – *Hamamelis virginiana* (Hamamelidaceae)

wild columbine – *Aquilegia canadensis* (Ranunculaceae)

yellow birch – *Betula alleghaniensis* (Betulaceae)

yellow lady's-slipper – *Cypripedium calceolus* (Orchidaceae)

yellowwood – *Cladrastis kentukea* (Leguminosae)

Animals

Allegheny mountain salamander – *Desmognathus ochrophaeus* (lungless salamander family, Plethodontidae)

American goldfinch – *Carduelis tristis* (finch family, Fringillidae)

American redstart – *Setophaga ruticilla* (wood warbler family, Parulidae)

ant – family Formicidae

autumnal moth – *Epirrita autumnata* (measuring worm family, Geometridae)

belted kingfisher – *Megaceryle alcyon* (kingfisher family, Alcedinidae)

black bear – *Ursus americanus* (bear family, Ursidae)

blackbanded darter – *Percina nigrofasciata* (perch family, Percidae)

black-capped chickadee – *Parus atricapillus* (titmouse family, Paridae)

blacknose dace – *Rhinichthys atratulus* (minnow family, Cyprinidae)

black-throated green warbler – *Dendroica virens* (Parulidae)

black-tipped hangingfly – *Hylobittacus apicalis* (bittacid scorpionfly family, Bittacidae)

blue jay – *Cyanocitta cristata* (crow family, Corvidae)

brook stickleback – *Culaea inconstans* (stickleback family, Gasterosteidae)

brook trout – *Salvelinus fontinalis* (trout family, Salmonidae)

brown creeper – *Certhia familiaris* (creeper family, Certhiidae)

brown-headed cowbird – *Molothrus ater* (blackbird family, Icteridae)

brown trout – *Salmo trutta* (Salmonidae)

canary – *Serinus canarius*

cardinal – *Cardinalis cardinalis* (Fringillidae)

Carolina chickadee – *Parus carolinensis* (Paridae)

Carolina parakeet – *Conuropsis carolinensis* (parrot family, Psittacidae)

Carolina wren – *Thryothorus ludovicianus* (wren family, Troglodytidae)

Cheat Mountain salamander – *Plethodon nettingi* (Plethodontidae)

cheetah – *Acinonyx jubatus* (cat family, Felidae)

chickadee – *Parus* (Paridae)

Clark's nutcracker – *Nucifraga columbiana* (Corvidae)

common garter snake – *Thamnophis sirtalis* (colubrid snake family, Colubridae)

Cope's gray tree frog – *Hyla chrysoscelis* (tree frog family, Hylidae)

copperhead – *Agkistrodon contortrix* (pit viper family, Viperidae)

cottonmouth – *Agkistrodon piscivorus* (Viperidae)

creek chub – *Semotilus atromaculatus* (Cyprinidae)

crow – *Corvus brachyrhynchos* (Corvidae)

downy woodpecker – *Picoides pubescens* (woodpecker family, Picidae)

dusky salamander – *Desmognathus fuscus* (Plethodontidae)

eastern box turtle – *Terrapene carolina* (emydid turtle family, Emydidae)

eastern gray tree frog – *Hyla versicolor* (Hylidae)

247

eastern phoebe – *Sayornis phoebe* (tyrant flycatcher family, Tyrannidae)

eastern tent caterpillar – *Malacosoma americanum* (tent caterpillar family, Lasiocampidae)

eastern timber rattlesnake – *Crotalus horridus* (Viperidae)

eastern wood peewee – *Contopus virens* (Tyrannidae)

elk – *Cervus elaphus* (deer family, Cervidae)

English sparrow – *Passer domesticus* (weaver finch family, Ploceidae)

European starling – *Sturnus vulgaris* (starling family, Sturnidae)

European minnow – *Phoxinus phoxinus* (Cyprinidae)

evening grosbeak – *Hesperiphona vespertina* (Fringillidae)

fantail darter – *Etheostoma flabellare* (Percidae)

fathead minnow – *Pimephales promelas* (Cyprinidae)

feral cat – *Felis catus* (Felidae)

field sparrow – *Spizella pusilla* (Fringillidae)

finescale dace – *Chrosomus neogaeus* (Cyprinidae)

firefly – family Lampyridae

fox squirrel – *Sciurus niger* (squirrel family, Sciuridae)

flycatcher – family Tyrannidae

gall aphid – *Pemphigus* (gall-making aphid family, Eriosomatidae)

goby – family Gobiidae

golden eagle – *Aquila chrysaetos* (hawk family, Accipitridae)

grackle – *Quiscalus* (Icteridae)

gray squirrel – *Sciurus carolinensis* (Sciuridae)

great tit – *Parus major* (Paridae)

great crested flycatcher – *Myiarchus crinitus* (Tyrannidae)

green heron – *Butorides striatus* (heron family, Ardeidae)

groundhog – *Marmota marmox* (Sciuridae)

gulf darter – *Etheostoma swaini* (Percidae)

gypsy moth – *Lymantria dispar* (tussock moth family, Liparidae)

hairy woodpecker – *Picoides villosus* (Picidae)

Hoffman's salamander – *Plethodon hoffmani* (Plethodontidae)

horseshoe crab – *Limulus polyphemus* (subphylum Chelicerata: Class Merostomata)

imitator salamander – *Desmognathus imitator* (Plethodontidae)

indigo bunting – *Passerina cyanea* (Fringillidae)

Iowa darter – *Etheostoma exile* (Percidae)

ivory-billed woodpecker – *Campephilus principalis* (Picidae)

johnny darter – *Etheostoma nigrum* (Percidae)

Jordan's salamander – *Plethodon jordani* (Plethodontidae)

least flycatcher – *Empidonax minimus* (Tyrannidae)

leopard frog – *Rana pipiens* (true frog family, Ranidae)

mink frog – *Rana septentrionalis* (Ranidae)

monarch butterfly – *Danaus plexippus* (milkweed butterfly family, Nymphalidae)

mottled sculpin – *Cottus bairdi* (sculpin family, Cottidae)

mountain lion – *Felis concolor* (Felidae)

mourning cloak butteryfly – *Nymphalis antiopa* (Nymphalidae)

mud salamander – *Pseudotriton montanus* (Plethodontidae)

naked sand darter – *Ammocrypta beani* (Percidae)

northern junco – *Junco hyemalis* (Fringillidae)

northern pike – *Esox lucius* (pike family, Esocidae)

orangebelly darter – *Etheostoma radiosum* (Percidae)

orangethroat darter – *Etheostoma spectabile* (Percidae)

ovenbird – *Seiurus aurocapillus* (Parulidae)

parsnip webworm – *Depressaria pastinacella* (moth family, Decophoridae)

Peaks of Otter salamander – *Plethodon hubrichti* (Plethodontidae)

249

Hollows, Peepers, and Highlanders

Philadelphia vireo – *Vireo philadelphicus* (vireo family, Vireonidae)

pike – *Esox lucius* (Esocidae)

purple finch – *Carpodacus purpureus* (Fringillidae)

raccoon – *Procyon lotor* (raccoon family, Procyonidae)

rainbow trout – *Salmo gairdneri* (Salmonidae)

ravine salamander – *Plethodon richmondi* (Plethodontidae)

red-backed salamander – *Plethodon cinereus* (Plethodontidae)

red-bellied woodpecker – *Melanerpes carolinus* (Picidae)

red-eyed vireo – *Vireo olivaceus* (Vireonidae)

red-headed woodpecker – *Melanerpes erythrocephalus* (Picidae)

red salamander – *Pseudotriton ruber* (Plethodontidae)

red-spotted newt – *Notophthalmus viridescens* (newt family, Salaman-
dridae)

red squirrel – *Tamiasciurus hudsonicus* (Sciuridae)

red-winged blackbird – *Agelaius phoeniceus* (Icteridae)

rufous-sided towhee – *Pipilo erythrophthalmus* (Fringillidae)

sawfly – suborder Symphyta (Hymenoptera)

sharp-shinned hawk – *Accipiter striatus* (Accipitridae)

Shenandoah salamander – *Plethodon shenandoah* (Plethodontidae)

Siberian salamander – *Hynobius keyserlingi* (Asiatic land salamander
family, Hynobiidae)

slimy salamander – *Plethodon glutinosus* (Plethodontidae)

song sparrow – *Melospiza melodia* (Fringillidae)

spotted darter – *Etheostoma maculatum* (Percidae)

spring peeper – *Hyla crucifer* (Hylidae)

spring salamander – *Gyrinophilus porphoryticus* (Plethodontidae)

stripetail darter – *Etheostoma kennicotti* (Percidae)

summer tanager – *Piranga rubra* (tanager family, Thraupidae)

swamp sparrow – *Melospiza georgiana* (Fringillidae)

termite – order Isoptera

tessellated darter – *Etheostoma olmstedi* (Percidae)

thrush – family Turdidae

tufted titmouse – *Parus bicolor* (Paridae)

two-lined salamander – *Eurycea bislineata* (Plethodontidae)

vireo – family Vireonidae

walleye – *Stizostedion vitreum* (Percidae)

warbler – Parulidae

western box turtle – *Terrapene ornata* (Emydidae)

white-breasted nuthatch – *Sitta carolinensis* (nuthatch family, Sitti-
   dae)

white-tailed deer – *Odocoileus virginianus* (Cervidae)

white-throated sparrow – *Zonotrichia albicollis* (Fringillidae)

wild turkey – *Meleagris gallopavo* (turkey family, Meleagrididae)

wolf – *Canis lupus* (dog family, Canidae)

wood frog – *Rana sylvatica* (Ranidae)

wood thrush – Hylocichla mustelina (Turdidae)

woodland buffalo – *Bison bison* (cow family, Bovidae)

worm-eating warbler – *Helmitheros vermivorus* (Parulidae)

yellow-eyed junco – *Junco phaeonotus* (Fringillidae)

zigzag salamander – *Plethodon dorsalis* (Plethodontidae)

Jargon

abdominal stove. Informal phrase for the central mass of an animal's torso that generates and retains heat.

abrasive breeding. Spawning in which a female fish is stimulated to release eggs by a male rubbing against her.

abscission layer. Zone of cells at the base of a leaf's petiole that are only weakly attached to one another and that function to jettison the leaf.

acid. Chemical compound which in solution has a sour taste; substance that when added to water increases the hydrogen ion concentration.

acid deposition. The falling of human-produced acid from the atmosphere via all forms of precipitation.

adaptation. A trait that contributes to the reproductive success of an individual organism.

adaptive radiation. The evolutionary process by which a variety of species arise from an ancestral one.

adhesion. Attraction between molecules in contact.

adipose tissue. Connective tissue in which the cells store fat droplets.

aerobic metabolism. Chemical changes in living cells that require oxygen.

aggregate. Rock composed of fragments of several different kinds of rock.

aggressive mimicry. Imitating a different animal, such as another's prey or mate, to lure prey within reach.

alarm call. Sound produced by one animal that causes others to behave defensively.

alarm signal system. The warning and defensive reactions of fish consisting of skin alarm cells, alarm substance, and alarm reaction.

allele. Alternate form of a gene; e. g., alleles for brown versus blue eyes.

allopatric speciation. Evolutionary formation of new species from geographically separated populations.

altruism. Behavior that benefits the reproductive success of others; selfless behavior.

aluminum. A lightweight (atomic number 13), abundant (8% of Earth's crust) metallic element that resists oxidation.

amino acid. Nitrogen-containing organic molecule from which protein molecules are built.

amphipod. A form of crustacean commonly called sand flea.

amplexus. The grasping of a female amphibian by a male with his forelimbs during mating.

anadromous. Fish that ascend rivers from the sea for breeding.

anaerobic metabolism. Chemical changes in living cells that are independent of oxygen.

anchor ice. Water frozen on the bottom of a stream.

anther. Part of a flower that contains pollen and is usually borne on a stalk.

anthocyanin. Blue, purple, or red pigment in plants.

anticline. An arch of stratified rock in which layers bend downward in opposite directions from the crest and form a ∩.

antifreeze. Dissolved substance that lowers the freezing point of a liquid.

antipredator adaptation. Body traits and behaviors that reduce the odds of being caught and eaten.

antiherbivory compound. Chemical that discourages animals from eating a plant.

Appalachian Plateau. Westernmost physiographic province of the Appalachian Mountains, located west of the Allegheny Front and characterized by mild deformation.

Araceae. Family of perennial herbs with tuberous roots and a pungent cell sap.

arum. Common name for plants in the family Araceae.

asexual reproduction. Producing young without the union of sperm and egg.

assemblage. The collection of species in a given area.

asthenosphere. Part of Earth's mantle below the lithosphere.

auxin. Plant hormone that, among other effects, causes cell elongation.

bald. A naturally treeless area surrounded by forest.

Batesian mimicry. Resemblance of an edible species (mimic) to a distasteful one (model). The mimic is thus protected from predators.

Beau Geste hypothesis. An idea that male birds display large repertoires to appear to be many singing males.

Beringia. The strait of land connecting Siberia and Alaska during the last glacial stage.

biogeography. The study of geographic distributions of living things.

biological diversity. The number of different kinds of living things; biodiversity.

bioluminescence. Production of light by a living thing.

biomass. The amount of living matter as measured by weight or volume.

biosphere reserve. A designated area that preserves all the functions of a natural ecosystem.

bole. The large central trunk of a tree.

boreal forest. The spruce-fir zone stretching across Canada.

Brevard Zone. The suture formed by the collision of the African and North American plates. The Brevard zone is a long fault trending northeast-southwest through Brevard, North Carolina, and connecting Atlanta, Asheville, and Roanoke.

buffer. A dissolved substance that neutralizes acid, thereby maintaining the pH of the solution.

Cambrian Period. Part of the Paleozoic Era between 590 and 505 million years ago.

cannibalism. Eating members of your own species.

canopy. The nearly continuous layer of leaves at the top of a mature forest.

canopy gap. A break in the forest canopy, usually due to one or more fallen trees.

carapace. The dorsal part of a turtle's shell.

Carboniferous Period. Part of the Paleozoic Era between 360 and 286 million years ago.

carrying capacity. The number of individuals than can be supported in a given area.

catastrophe. Sudden overwhelming stress to living things due to physical forces such as freezing, wind, fire.

cavity nester. Animal that raises its offspring in the hole of a tree.

Cenozoic Era. Part of Earth's history between 65 and 1.8 million years ago.

chance pollination. Fertilization in plants where pollen is delivered by inefficient or risky means.

character displacement. Divergence in the traits of two similar species where their ranges overlap, presumably caused by natural selection for avoiding competition.

chlorophyll. Green pigment in plants that captures the energy of sunlight.

chromosome. Long thin structure in the cell nucleus that contains DNA and bears genes.

climate change. Long-term differences in air temperature, rainfall, and other atmospheric features.

climax. The end of ecological succession; an ecological community that has reached a steady state.

cloaca. Found in some vertebrates, the common opening to the outside of the digestive, excretory, and reproductive systems.

clone. Identical asexually produced offspring, or a set of such offspring.

closed winter. A cold season in which the ground does not thaw.

club cell. Specialized cell in the skin of some fishes that synthesizes, stores, and releases alarm substance.

coadaptation. Evolution of mutually complementary adaptations in two or more species.

coastal plain. A low, flat, sediment-rich physiographic province between the Atlantic Ocean and Piedmont.

codominant species. Two or more species that equally influence what other species live in the community.

coevolution. The evolution of complementary adaptations in two or more species by mutual interactions of these traits.

cohesion. Attraction among elemental particles.

coitus. Copulation.

Collembola. Type of insect commonly called springtail.

communication. Two-way exchange of information.

community. A set of species identified by the place they live or the nature of their association.

competitive exclusion. The idea that two or more species cannot coexist indefinitely on a common scarce resource.

congenital defect. Bodily imperfection acquired during the individual's development.

conglomerate. Rock composed of round fragments held together within a cementlike matrix.

conservation ethic. Philosophy that humans should live with nature, not conquer it.

convection. Transfer of heat by movement of a fluid with nonuniform temperatures; e. g., rising hot air.

convergent evolution. Evolutionary change leading to increasing similarity.

copulation. Sexual intercourse.

copulation solicitation. A female's invitation to intercourse.

core. Central mass of an object; forest interior.

corm. Thick underground stem of a plant.

corolla. Collective term for all the petals of a flower.

corridor. Strip of habitat.

cortex. Outer layer.

cost-benefit analysis. Evaluating alternatives by comparing their ratios of monetary costs and benefits.

Cottidae. Fish family that includes sculpins.

counteradaptation. Traits of two or more species selected because of their mutual antagonism, especially in the context of competition or predation between species.

countershading. An animal's coloring in which the belly side is lighter than the top, presumably for camouflage.

courtship. Behaviors that lead to mating.

cove. Bowl-shaped valley that typically is moist and supports many plant species.

Cretaceous Period. Part of the Mesozoic Era between 144 and 65 million years ago.

Crotalidae. Family of snakes that includes pit vipers.

crown shyness gap. Small break in the canopy caused by abrasion between neighboring limbs.

crust. Outermost layer of Earth's lithosphere; it is less dense than underlying mantle.

crustal plate tectonics. The movements of Earth's lithospheric plates.

Cuculinae. Subfamily of birds that includes cuckoos.

cruising behavior. Movement by male darters searching for females among a series of nest rocks.

cryoprotectant. Chemical that protects a fluid from freezing.

crystallization. Process by which a liquid changes into a solid; or process by which a young bird's pre-song turns into the final adult song.

cultural transmission. Acquisition of behavior from other individuals.

Cyprinidae. The fish family that includes minnows.

cytoplasm. The jelly-like substance inside a cell.

darter. Common name for some bottom-dwelling species in the fish family Percidae.

dawn chorus. The collective singing by many male birds in early morning.

debris flow. Slug of solids carried by flood waters.

decibel. Unit for measuring the relative loudness of sound.

deciduous. Plant that sheds its leaves in autumn.

degree-day. A unit for measuring cumulative heat.

dendritic drainage. Pattern of watercourses characterized by randomly branching tributaries.

detoxification. Neutralizing a poison.

detritivore. Animal that eats decaying organic matter.

detritus. Loose organic material resulting from breakdown of plant and animal bodies.

Devonian Period. Part of the Paleozoic Era between 408 and 360 million years ago.

dialect. Local version of bird song.

diffusion. The random movement of particles (e.g., molecules) from an area of greater concentration to an area of lesser concentration.

digestive efficiency. Proportion of nutrients extracted from food.

disjunct distribution. Geographic pattern in which similar organisms are separated by zones devoid of those organisms.

dispersal. One-way movement of organisms, usually from an area of high density.

divergence. Evolution of different traits of related organisms in unlike environments.

domed nest. Bird nest with a side opening.

dominant behavior. Suppressing actions.

dominant species. Organisms that influence what other species coexist in an ecological community.

eastern deciduous forest. The vast hardwood, broad-leaved forest of eastern North America.

ecology. Study of interactions between organisms and their environment.

ecosystem. The set of living and nonliving things that interact in a given place.

ecotone. A zone of transition between distinctly different habitats.

ecotype. A genetically differentiated subpopulation restricted to a specific habitat.

edge detector. Sensory system that detects sharp changes between two places.

edge effect. Ecological changes in an ecotone.

emetic. A substance that induces vomiting.

endemic. Confined to a certain area.

endosperm. Nourishing tissue that surrounds the developing plant embryo in a seed.

effective population size. Size of a population, incorporating biased sex ratio, that would undergo the same amount of genetic drift as the actual population.

egg tooth. Short, horny point at the tip of the upper bill of a hatchling bird used to puncture the egg shell.

ejaculate. v., act of expelling sperm; or n., the discharged gelatinous mass containing sperm.

energy flow. Movement of energy through an ecosystem.

environmental gradient. Regular change across space in the value of an environmental variable, such as temperature or humidity.

Eocene Epoch. Part of the Paleogene Period between 58 and 37 million years ago.

ephemeral. Lasting a short time.

epidemic. Sudden rapid spread of an organism.

epiphyte. Plant that grows on another plant.

equilibrium. State of balance between opposing forces.

Etheostoma. Largest and most diverse genus of darters.

Eurycea. A genus of lungless salamander.

evolution. Genetic change in organisms from generation to generation.

exotic block. Rock formation of distant origin.

exotic species. Organism not native to an area.

extracellular ice. Water frozen in spaces between cells.

extrapair copulation. Intercourse with an individual outside the pair bond.

false alarm call. Warning shout in the absence of predators.

fatalism. Point of view in which a person feels he/she has little control over life's outcomes.

exudate. Matter that diffuses out of an organism's body.

fat body. Long, slender organs in reptiles and amphibians that store lipids.

fault. Fracture of the Earth's crust in which rock on one side of the break is displaced relative to the other.

fecal communication. Exchanging information by adding and detecting specific chemicals in feces.

fecal pellet. A solid mass voided through an anus.

fecundity. Rate at which an individual produces offspring.

fishes. Two or more species of fish.

fitness. Relative genetic contribution by an individual to the next generation.

floating male. Male animal that moves ceaselessly through his habitat because he is unable to defend a breeding territory.

flora. Set of plant species in a particular area.

flux. Movement of matter or energy across a plane.

forest edge-forest interior ratio. The amount of surrounding forest edge compared to the forest's interior core.

forest fragmentation. Process by which a continuous forest is broken into several separate woodlots.

form. Depression made by a box turtle for resting.

fragmentation of habitat. Human-caused breaks in a formerly continuous ecological community.

frass. Rain of caterpillar feces.

freeze-tolerance. Ability of an organism to survive the formation of ice inside its body.

fright reaction. Defensive behavior displayed by fish that detect alarm substance.

fry. Small fish.

Gaspe Peninsula. A finger of land north of Maine in southeast Quebec.

gene. Section of a chromosome that determines a specific trait, or section of a DNA strand that codes a specific protein molecule.

261

gene frequency. The proportion of a particular allele in the gene pool of a population.

genetic drift. Random change in gene frequencies unrelated to natural selection.

genetic variability. Differences in the hereditary makeup among individuals of a population.

genetics. Scientific study of heredity.

genotype. Genetic characteristics that determine an observable trait of an organism.

genus. Taxonomic rank between family and species that includes closely related species.

Geometridae. Family of moths commonly called inchworms or measuringworms because their caterpillars move by looping forward.

glucose. A sugar synthesized by plants during photosynthesis and broken down by animals during metabolism.

glycerol. A sweet, syrupy alcohol that functions as an antifreeze.

glycogen. Polymer of glucose that serves as the chief storage carbohydrate in animals.

glycogenesis. Interconversion of glucose and glycogen.

Gondwanaland. Southern half of Pangaea that broke away as a continent in the Triassic Period.

good genes. Genetic traits desired in mates.

gradient. Gradual change in a variable along a line.

Great Valley. Long valley between the Blue Ridge and Ridge and Valley physiographic provinces.

greenhouse effect. Warming of Earth's climate due to an increase of carbon dioxide and other atmospheric pollutants.

ground beetle. Common name for beetles of the family Carabidae.

ground cover. Short plants such as grasses, ferns, and wildflowers that form a scattered layer across the forest floor.

growth regulator. Chemical released by one individual that affects the development of another.

habitat island. A patch of a distinct habitat type.

habitat segregation. Different species occupying different habitats, presumably because of natural selection to avoid competition.

habituation. Developing tolerance to a repeated stimulus.

hangingfly. Common name for some species of the insect family Mecoptera.

hard water. Water that, because of its high levels of dissolved solids, dissolves little solute.

heath. Common name for species in the plant family Ericaceae, which are shrubby, typically evergreen plants that thrive in open, poorly drained soils.

heliotropic. Plant that turns toward the sun.

hemipenis. One of the paired copulatory organs of male snakes and lizards.

herb. A plant that does not develop overwintering woody tissue and therefore dies back to ground level in the autumn.

herbivore. Animal that eats plants.

hermaphrodite. Organism that has both male and female reproductive organs.

hibernaculum. Shelter occupied during winter by dormant animals.

hibernation. Overwintering in a state of depressed metabolism.

Holocene Epoch. Also known as the Recent Epoch, the last 11,000 years of the Neogene Period.

home range. The area over which an animal repeatedly moves in its normal activities.

homozygous. Having identical alleles at the corresponding site of homologous chromosomes.

horizon. A horizontal layer of soil with unique, distinguishable features.

humus. Organic matter in soil.

hybrid. Offspring from genetically different parents.

Hylidae. Family of frogs commonly called tree frogs.

hyphae. Threads that make up the mycelium of a fungus.

hypometabolism. Low metabolic rate.

hypothermia. Lower than normal body temperature.

hypothesis. An educated guess.

immigration. Movement of individuals into an area.

inbreeding. Reproduction by closely related individuals.

inbreeding depression. Low fitness of offspring resulting from inbreeding.

incisor. Tooth adapted to cutting.

indigenous. Living naturally in a given area.

inducible defense. A plant's ability to limit losses to herbivores by deploying anti-herbivore chemicals.

inflorescence. Flower cluster.

infrared radiation. Electromagnetic radiation beyond the red end of the visible spectrum.

injection flash. Light pulse produced by a firefly between two flashes of another individual.

in situ. In its natural place.

insularity. The degree to which a habitat patch manifests island-like features such as small size and isolation.

insulation. Material that slows the movement of heat.

interspecific competition. Use of a limited common resource by individuals of different species, causing negative consequences in individuals of one or both species.

interstadial. Period of temporary retreat by glacial ice.

intromission. Ejaculation.

invented Appalachia. The oversimplified story of Appalachian people promulgated by travel writers, journalists, and other absentee authors.

iridium. Hard, heavy metallic element of the platinum group.

island biogeography. Branch of ecology that attempts to explain the number of species on an island as an equilibrium between immigration and extinction.

isolate. Small isolated population, as in a habitat island.

Jurassic Period. Part of the Mesozoic Era between 213 and 144 million years ago.

kin recognition. Identifying genetic relatives.

kin selection. Differential reproductive success among lineages of closely related individuals because of differences in social behavior.

labellum. Middle part of an orchid's corolla.

Lampyridae. Family of insects that includes fireflies.

landscape mosaic. Pattern of various habitat patches and boundaries across a vast area.

land-use planning. The process of recommending appropriate uses of land.

larderhoarding. Storing many food items in one place.

Laurasia. The northern supercontinent made of North America, Greenland, and Eurasia during the Mesozoic Era.

Laurasian faunal element. Animal groups that arose on Laurasia after it separated from Gondwanaland.

Laurentia. Continent made of North America, Greenland, and Scotland during the Cambrian and Ordovician periods.

Laurentide Ice Sheet. Large, thick sheet of glacial ice that covered northern North America during the Pleistocene Epoch.

leachate. Liquid draining from a solid mass.

leaf-out. The time in spring when tree leaves open.

Lepidoptera. Order of insects that includes moths and butterflies.

life history. The sequence of events in an organism's life cycle.

lipid. Class of organic molecules that includes fats and waxes.

lithophyte. Plant that grows on rock.

litter. Uppermost layer of slightly decayed organic matter on the forest floor.

localized response. Effect restricted to part of a living thing.

lungless salamander. Common name for a small to medium-sized lizard-like amphibian of the family Plethodontidae.

magma. Molten rock material within the Earth.

mantle. Part of Earth's interior under the lithosphere and above the core.

marcescent leaf. Deciduous leaf that stays on its tree through winter, and is then shed next year.

mast. Nuts accumulated on the forest floor.

mast-yearing. The phenomenon of trees producing much mast only in occasional years.

mate choice. Process by which members of one sex discriminate among members of the opposite sex.

maternal factor. Non-genetic trait of an offspring acquired from its mother.

Mecoptera. Insect order that includes hangingflies.

megafauna. A community of large-bodied mammals.

meiosis. Form of cell division that produces haploid gametes.

mesic. Moderately moist.

Mesozoic Era. Part of Earth's history between 248 and 65 million years ago.

metamorphism. Compaction of rock by water, pressure, and heat.

metamorphosis. Major transformation in the body structure of an animal.

microarthropod. Minute animal with exoskeleton and jointed legs, such as daphnia.

microhabitat. The specific highly localized part of a habitat actually encountered by an individual organism.

microspermy. Production of many minute seeds.

microtopography. Variation in elevation over a small area.

mid-oceanic ridge. A long, thin raised rim on the ocean floor where plates rift apart.

migration. Two-way, round-trip movement cued by seasonal changes.

mimicry. Adaptation in which an organism looks or behaves like another kind of living thing, presumably to discourage predation.

mineralized layer. Soil horizon composed of inorganic matter that lies below the organic zone.

minnows. Common name of many fishes in the family Cyprinidae.

Miocene Epoch. Part of the Neogene Period between 24 and 5 million years ago.

mistake pollination. When a pollinating animal visits a flower that offers no reward.

mitochrondria. The cell organelle in which aerobic metabolism occurs.

mixed deciduous forest. General name for a large, complex vegetation unit dominated by deciduous trees.

mixed mesophytic forest. Subset of the mixed deciduous forest that develops on moist well-drained sites in unglaciated Appalachian plateaus.

mixed-species flock. Group of birds of several species.

monogamy. Mating system in which each individual mates with only one member of the opposite sex.

moonshine. Illegally distilled corn whiskey.

mosaic management. Controlling changes in a landscape composed of diverse habitat patches.

morph. A specific form.

mountain whites. Mountain-living descendants of original Appalachian homesteaders.

mountain love. Informal phrase for emotional bonding with the forested hills of Appalachia.

mutation. Change in genetic material that produces altered offspring.

Mullerian mimicry. Mutual likeness of two or more distasteful species to enhance repulsion of a predator.

multicellular organism. Living thing made of two or more cells.

mutualism. Association beneficial to members of two species.

mycorrhiza. Mutualistic association of a fungus and a plant root.

natural selection. Change in the frequency of genetic traits because of differential reproductive success of individuals carrying those traits.

neo-Darwinian evolution. Changes in genetic traits caused by reproductive competition among individuals.

neonate. Newborn animal.

neotropical migrant. Bird that breeds in North America and winters in Central or South America.

neuron. Nerve cell.

neurotoxin. Substance that is poisonous to nervous tissue.

neutral trait. Gene or trait that conveys no fitness consequences.

niche. Ecological role of a species in an environment, or the conditions within which an organism persists.

northern hardwood forest. Forest type located between the boreal and deciduous forests in a zone from Minnesota eastward through New England to the Atlantic Coast; dominant species include sugar maple, beech, and birch.

nucleus. Organelle that controls much of its cell's activities.

nuptial gift. Food item offered by a male animal to stimulate sexual receptivity in a female.

nutrient cycling. Recycling of elemental atoms, such as nitrogen and phosphorous, through an ecosystem.

oak-chestnut forest. Forest type found in the Ridge and Valley and Blue Ridge provinces characterized by the former dominance of American chestnut and several oak species.

open-cup nest. Bird nest in which eggs are laid in an uncovered depression.

open winter. Winters that alternate between freeze and thaw.

Orchidaceae. Plant family that includes orchids.

Ordovician Period. Part of the Paleozoic Era between 505 and 438 million years ago.

organelle. Structure in a cell with a specialized function.

orogeny. Process by which uplifting builds mountains.

osmosis. The diffusion of water through a selectively permeable membrane.

osmotic pressure. Force exerted by water during osmosis.

oviposition. Egglaying.

ovulation. Release of egg(s) from ovary.

pH. A measure of acidity or alkalinity of a solution denoted as a number on a logarithmic scale running from 0 to 14 used to express the concentration of hydrogen ions, with 7 being neutral, 0 to 7 being acidic, and above 7 being basic (alkaline).

Paleocene Epoch. Part of the Paleogene Period between 65 and 58 million years ago.

Paleogene Period. Part of the Cenozoic Era between 65 and 24 million years ago.

Paleozoic Era. Part of Earth's history between 590 and 248 million years ago.

269

Pangaea. Supercontinent that broke apart 200 million years ago, leading to today's continents.

parallel evolution. Change in a similar direction by different species over many generations.

parasitoid. Small-bodied parasite of a parasite.

parasite. Animal that lives on, eats part of, and thereby harms, a larger host animal.

parent stream. The stream yielding a tributary during stream piracy.

parental care. Acts by an adult animal that enhance the survival of an offspring.

pathogen. Disease-causing organism.

pecking order. Form of social organization in which each individual pecks others lower in the hierarchy and is pecked by those higher.

pectoralis muscle. Chief flight muscle in the breast of birds.

Percidae. Fish family that includes darters and perches.

petiole. Stem of a leaf.

phenolic. Plant-made resin with antimicrobial properties.

pheromone. Chemical used for communication between individuals.

photosynthesis. Process by which green plants capture the energy of sunlight to make carbohydrates.

physiognomy. External features of organisms such as size and shape.

physiographic province. Geographic region characterized by a distinct topography.

phytotoxin. Substance that is poisonous to plants.

Piedmont physiographic province. The gently rolling zone between coastal plain and Blue Ridge provinces.

pioneer species. Plant that establishes itself in a barren area and starts succession.

pit-and-mound relief. Ground topography characterized by earthen pits and mounds created by the decay of fallen trees; called "pillow and cradle" in New England.

plastron. Ventral part of a turtle's shell.

plate. Rigid section of Earth's lithosphere that moves over the asthenosphere.

plate tectonics. Theory that Earth's outer shell consists of several plates that interact to produce earthquakes, volcanoes, and mountains.

Pleistocene Epoch. Part of the Neogene Period between 1.8 million and 10,000 years ago.

Plethodon. Genus of woodland salamanders in the family Plethodontidae.

Plethodontidae. Family of lungless salamanders.

pollinator-limited. Plants whose reproductive rate is limited by the availability of pollinating animals.

polygyny. Mating system in which one male mates with two or more females.

polymorphism. Occurrence of several distinct forms of individuals within a population.

population. A group of individuals that interbreed, or the set of individuals of a species in a given area.

Precambrian Period. Part of Earth's history 4.6 billion to 590 million years ago.

predator swamping. Sudden increase in the numbers of a prey species, to overwhelm the predator's needs and ensure escape of at least some prey individuals; predator satiation.

proboscis. Snout, or long tubular parts of the mouth.

prokaryote. Organism whose cells contain no nucleus or other organelles.

proximate cause. Environmental cue that stimulates a response in an individual, e. g., lengthening daylight stimulates courtship.

271

pseudoaposematic coloration. False warning coloration, conspicuous patterns on palatable organisms that mimic similar colors on noxious species.

Quaternary Period. Part of the Cenozoic Era between 1.6 million years ago and the present.

recruitment. Adding new individuals to a population by processes like birth and immigration.

recruitment trail. Line of pheromone applied to a twig by one caterpillar that stimulates others to follow it, usually to fresh food.

red eft. Immature terrestrial stage of the red-spotted newt.

redd. Nest of a fish, especially trout and salmon.

reference group. Small group of people that serves as a person's psycho-social context.

reference stream. A healthy stream that serves as a model for setting restoration goals.

refuging behavior. Clustering in a protected site.

refugium. Place where species persist during long-term climatic stress.

relict. Persistent remnant of an otherwise extinct organism.

repertoire. Set of different songs vocalized by a male bird.

reproductive success. Relative to other individuals in the population, the number of an individual's offspring that reproduce.

reproductive isolation. Inability to produce fertile offspring because of geographic, genetic, or morphologic incompatibilities.

resting coil. Tightly wound shape of a snake waiting for prey.

reverberation. Repeated reflection of sound, an echo.

rhizome. Underground stem of a plant.

Ridge and Valley physiographic province. Region of the Appalachian Mountains characterized by long parallel ridges and intervening valleys.

rifting. Plates of Earth's crust moving apart.

riparian. Terrestrial ecosystem alongside a waterbody.

ritualized behavior. Sequence of actions showing little variation.

root exudate. Chemicals that leach from plant roots.

salamander. Moist-skinned, lizard-like amphibian in the order Caudata.

Salmonidae. Fish family that includes trout and salmon.

satellite male. Male animal that lingers around dominant territorial ones attempting to mate females attracted to the territory holder.

scatterhoarding. Storing a little food in each of many sites.

sculpin. Common name for fishes of the genus *Cottus* and family Cottidae.

secondary metabolite. Molecules in plants that discourage herbivory.

secondary sex characeristics. Body traits unique to one sex that play no direct role in copulation, such as red plumage of male cardinals and beard of man.

sedge. Common name for grasslike herbs of the plant family Cyperaceae, often found in wet places.

sedimentary rock. Rock formed from fragments of other rock transported from its sources, typically by water or wind, and deposited and solidified elsewhere.

seminal receptacle. Blind-ended sac in females of some animals that presumably stores sperm.

sepal. One of the green modified leaves around the outside of a flower's petals.

sequential hermaphroditism. Condition in which an organism has the ability to change sex.

sere. Series of stages of ecological succession in a particular area.

serotiny. Ability of the cones of some pines to remain closed for some time after maturity and open only after being exposed to high temperatures such as the heat of a forest fire.

serum. Watery part of an animal fluid left after coagulation.

sex. Union of sperm and egg; an individual's gender.

sex ratio. Ratio of the number of individuals of one sex to that of the other.

sexual dimorphism. Differences between the sexes in outward body characteristics.

sexual reproduction. Process by which offspring are produced by sperm fertilizing eggs.

sexual selection. Choice by one sex for specific characteristics in individuals of the opposite sex, usually exercised during courtship.

Shenandoah Valley. Name of the Great Valley as it runs through central Appalachia.

shivering. Rapid contraction and relaxation of muscles to generate heat.

shrew. Common name for small-bodied mammals of the family Soricidae, in the order Insectivora.

Silurian Period. Part of the Paleozoic Era between 438 and 408 million years ago.

size-advantage model. Hypothesis that explains fitness advantages associated with certain body sizes.

slime mold. Organism assigned to either the fungal class Myxomycetes or animal phylum Protozoa that exists as a mobile oozy mass, contains thousands of nuclei, and reproduces by spores.

soft water. Water with low levels of dissolved salts.

song overproduction. Young male bird singing a greater variety of phrases than he will eventually use as an adult.

sound power. Loudness of sound.

spadix. Floral spike with a fleshy axis.

spathe. Sheathing bract enclosing a spadix.

speciation. Process of forming new species.

species. Set of individual organisms with similar body structure that can potentially interbreed.

species-area relationship. Theory that explains the number of species as a function of habitat area.

staminate flower. A flower with stamens (male reproductive organs) but no pistils (female organs).

standing crop. Instantaneous estimate of an organism's abundance, e.g., pounds per acre.

stem flow. Water flowing down a tree trunk.

stigma. Part of the pistil (female organ) of a flower that receives pollen.

stochastic. Random; involving a random movement at each point in time.

stratification. Process of forming layers.

stream capture. Diversion of flow from one basin to another by the headward erosion of the more aggressive capturing stream; also called stream piracy.

stratum. A horizontal layer of sedimentary rock, forest leaves, or other matter.

subduction. Process by which an oceanic lithospheric plate plunges into the mantle where two plates collide.

submissive behavior. Act that communicates assent to a dominant individual.

subspecies. Taxonomic category that ranks below species; a morphologically distinguishable group whose members breed successfully with those of other groups of the same species.

succession. Replacement of species in a place through a relatively regular progression.

sunfleck. Patch of direct sunshine on the forest floor.

supercooling. Cooling a liquid below its normal freezing point without crystallization occurring.

superterritory. Area defended by a male bird that is larger than needed to supply resources for its family, presumably discouraging potential competitors from settling in the area.

surface-to-volume ratio. Ratio of surface area to internal volume of an object.

suture. Line of union.

symbiosis. Intimate, often obligatory, association of individuals of different species.

sympatry. Condition of two species occurring in the same area.

syncline. Trough of rock folded into a U shape; opposite of anticline.

synergism. Action of different agents creating a total effect greater than the sum of the two effects taken independently.

synomone. A volatile compound emitted by a plant under insect attack that attracts carnivorous insects that prey on or parasitize the plant's pests.

systemic response. An effect seen throughout an organism's body.

talus. Accumulated rock debris at the base of a cliff.

tannin. Phenolic substance in plants that deters herbivores.

taxon. A group of related living things.

tectonics. Branch of geology that focuses on structure, especially folding and faulting of rocks.

Tennessee Valley. Name of the Great Valley in southern Appalachia.

terrane. Crustal block with a geologic history distinct from that of adjoining blocks.

territory. A defended area.

Tertiary Period. Part of the Cenozoic Era between 66.4 and 1.6 million years ago.

tetrodotoxin. Poison found in pufferfish and red-spotted newts.

thermal sum. Measure of heat accumulated over a time period.

throughfall. Water falling through the forest canopy.

thrust fault. Low-angle reverse fault caused by compression of colliding plates; can result in older strata overlying younger rocks.

topographic diversity. Degree of variation in surface shape.

torpor. State of inactivity.

torso. Central trunk of an animal.

trachea. Main tube passing air to and from lungs.

tradeoff. Costs and benefits of alternative states or actions.

transepithelial ice inoculation. Quick freezing of supercooled internal body water when the animal's skin touches external ice crystals.

transpiration. Evaporation of water from the inside of a plant leaf.

transvestite. Individual that exhibits behaviors of the opposite sex.

trellised drainage. Pattern of nearly parallel streams running through valleys between folded strata.

Triassic Period. Part of the Mesozoic Era between 248 and 213 million years ago.

ultimate cause. Aspect of the environment that influences the direction of evolution.

understory. Set of plants deploying leaves at five to fifteen feet high that form a forest's middle layer.

uplifting. Landmasses elevated by the compression of colliding plates.

vacuole. Saclike organelle that stores water, food, or waste fluids.

venom. Poison secreted by an animal.

viviparity. Reproductive mode in which embryos are nurtured in the mother's body.

volatile. Readily vaporizable.

warning coloration. Conspicuous colors displayed by noxious organisms to advertise their toxicity to predators.

windthrow. Group of trees pushed over by a strong wind.

Wisconsin glacial period. Last glacial interval of the Pleistocene Epoch between 175,000 and 12,000 years ago.

woodland salamander. Common name for species in the salamander genus *Plethodon*.

woodlot. A managed patch of trees.

xanthophyll. Yellow pigments in plants.

xanthotoxin. A toxic chemical rapidly synthesized by some plants in response to damage by herbivores, presumably to reduce the impact of damaging herbivores.

xeric. Dry.

Sources

1. Prologue

Alcock, J. 1984. *Animal behavior: An evolutionary approach*, 3rd ed. Sunderland, MA: Sinauer Assoc.

———. 2001. *The triumph of sociobiology*. New York: Oxford Univ. Press.

Bake, W. A. 1977. *The Blue Ridge*. Birmingham, AL: Oxmoor House.

Brooks, M. 1965. *The Appalachians*. Grantsville, WV: Seneca Books.

———. 1967. *The life of the mountains*. New York: McGraw-Hill.

———. 1971. The southern Appalachians. In *The distributional history of the biota of the southern Appalachians, Part 3: Vertebrates, Res. Div. Mono. 4*, edited by P. C. Holt. Blacksburg, VA: Virginia Poly. Inst. and St. Univ.

Catlin, D. T. 1984. *A naturalist's Blue Ridge Parkway*. Knoxville, TN: Univ. Tennessee Press.

Clark, J. 1998. *West Virginia: The Allegheny Highlands*. Englewood, CO: Westcliffe Publishers.

Cody, M. L. 1974. Optimization in ecology. *Science* 183:1156-64.

Constantz, G. 1994. *Hollows, peepers, and highlanders: an Appalachian Mountain ecology* [1st ed.]. Missoula, MT: Mountain Press Publ. Co.

Darwin, C. R. 1859. *The origin of species by means of natural selection*. New York: Random House, The Modern Library.

Dawkins, R. 1976. *The selfish gene.* New York: Oxford Univ. Press.

Dillard, A. 1974. *Pilgrim at Tinker Creek.* New York: Bantam Books.

Doolittle, J. 1975. *The southern Appalachians.* New York: Time-Life Books.

Evans, H. E. 1966. *Life on a little-known planet.* New York: Dell.

Hutchinson, G. E. 1965. *The ecological theater and the evolutionary play.* New Haven, CT: Yale Univ. Press.

Lack, D. 1954. The evolution of reproductive rates. In *Evolution as a process,* edited by J. S. Huxley, A. C. Hardy, and E. B. Ford. London: Allen and Unwin.

Ogburn, C. 1975. *The southern Appalachians, a wilderness quest.* New York: William Morrow and Co.

Porter, E., and E. Abbey. 1973. *Appalachian wilderness, the Great Smoky Mountains.* New York: Ballantine Books.

Williams, G. C. 1966. *Adaptation and natural selection.* Princeton, NJ: Princeton Univ. Press.

Weidensaul, S. 1994. *Mountains of the heart: A natural history of the Appalachians.* Golden, CO: Fulcrum Publishing.

2. Origins

Alvarez, W., L. W. Alvarez, F. Asaro, and H. V. Michel. 1984. The end of the Cretaceous: Sharp boundary or gradual transition? *Science* 223:1183-86.

Braun, E. L. 1950. *Deciduous forests of eastern North America.* Philadelphia, PA: Blakiston.

Brooks, M. 1967. *The life of the mountains.* New York: McGraw-Hill.

_____. 1971. Cited in Chp. 1

Catlin, D. T. 1984. Cited in Chp. 1.

Cook, F. A., L. D. Brown, and J. E. Oliver. 1980. The southern Appalachians and the growth of continents. *Sci. Amer.* 243:156-68.

Cracraft, J. 1974. Continental drift and vertebrate distribution. *Ann. Rev. Ecol. Syst.* 5:215-61.

Davis, M. B. 1983. Quaternary history of deciduous forests of eastern North America and Europe. *Ann. Missouri Bot. Gard.* 70:550-63.

Delcourt, H. R., and P. A. Delcourt. 1984. Ice age haven for hardwoods. *Natural History* 9:22-28.

Fenneman, N. M. 1938. *Physiography of the eastern United States.* New York: McGraw-Hill.

Frye, K. 1986. *Roadside geology of Virginia.* Missoula, MT: Mountain Press.

Ganapathy, R. 1980. A major meteorite impact on the earth 65 million years ago: Evidence from the Cretaceous-Tertiary boundary clay. *Science* 209:921-23.

Gathright, T. M., II. 1976. Geology of the Shenandoah National Park, Virginia. *Virginia Div. Min. Res. Bull.* 86.

Gore, R. 1985. Our restless planet, Earth. *Natl. Geogr.*, August:142-81.

Hack, J. T. 1969. The area, its geology: Cenozoic development of the southern Appalachians. In *The distributional history of the biota of the southern Appalachians, Part I: Invertebrates.* Res. Div. Monogr. 1, edited by P. C. Holt. Blacksburg, VA: Virginia Poly. Inst. and St. Univ.

Hamilton, W. 1983. Cretaceous and Cenozoic history of the northern continents. *Ann. Missouri Bot. Gard.* 70:440-58.

Harris, S. L. 1990. *Agents of chaos.* Missoula, MT: Mountain Press.

Hays, J. D., J. Imbrie, and N. J. Shackleton. 1976. Variations in the earth's orbit: Pacemaker of the ice ages. *Science* 194:1121-32.

Hsu, K. J., et al. 1982. Mass mortality and its environmental consequences. *Science* 216:249-56.

Jorgensen, N. 1978. *A Sierra Club naturalist's guide to southern New England.* San Francisco, CA: Sierra Club Books.

281

McKenzie, D. P. 1983. The earth's mantle. *Sci. Amer.* 249:66-78.

McPhee, J. 1983. *In suspect terrain.* New York: Farrar, Straus, and Giroux.

Peters, P. T. 1986. Appalachian genesis. *Wonderful West Virginia* 50:10-17.

Pielou, E. C. 1991. *After the ice age: The return of life to glaciated North America.* Chicago, IL: Univ. of Chicago Press.

Shimer, J. A. 1972. *Field guide to landforms in the United States.* New York: Macmillan.

Stanley, S. M. 1986. *Earth and life through time.* New York: Freeman.

Sutton, A., and M. Sutton. 1985. *Eastern forests.* New York: Knopf.

Tilton, J. L. 1926. *Map 2, Hampshire Co., showing general and economic geology.* Morgantown, WV: West Virginia Geol. Surv.

Tapponnier, P. 1986. A tale of two continents. *Natural History* 11:56-64.

Van Diver, B. B. 1985. *Roadside geology of New York.* Missoula, MT: Mountain Press.

_____. 1990. *Roadside geology of Pennsylvania.* Missoula, MT: Mountain Press.

Watts, W. A. 1970. The full-glacial vegetation of northwestern Georgia. *Ecology* 51:17-33.

_____. 1979. Late Quaternary vegetation of central Appalachia and the New Jersey coastal plain. *Ecol. Mono.* 49:427-69.

_____. 1980. The late quaternary vegetation of the southeastern United States. *Ann. Rev. Ecol. Syst.* 11:387-409.

_____. 1983. Vegetational history of the eastern United States 25,000 to 10,000 years ago. In *Late-Quaternary environments of the United States, Vol. 1, The late Pleistocene,* edited by S. C. Porter. Minneapolis, MN: Univ. Minnesota Press.

Watts, W. A., and M. Stuiver. 1980. Late Wisconsin climate of northern Florida and the origin of species-rich deciduous forest. *Science* 210:325-27.

Weiner, J. 1986. *Planet Earth.* New York: Bantam Books.

3. Forest Design

Aber, J. D. 1979. Foliage-height profiles and succession in northern hardwood forests. *Ecology* 60:18-23.

Bazzaz, F. A. 1979. The physiological ecology of plant succession. *Ann. Rev. Ecol. Syst.* 10:351-71.

Braun, E. L. 1950. Cited in Chp. 2.

Christensen, N. L., and R. K. Peet. 1984. Convergence during secondary forest succession. *J. Ecol.* 72:25-36.

Core, E. L. 1966. *Vegetation of West Virginia.* Parsons, WV: McClain.

Good, N. F. 1968. A study of the natural replacement of chestnut in six stands in the highlands of New Jersey. *Bull. Torrey Bot. Club* 95:240-53.

Henry, J. D., and J. M. A. Swan. 1974. Reconstructing forest history from live and dead plant material: An approach to the study of forest succession in southwest New Hampshire. *Ecology* 55:772-83.

Horn, H. S. 1971. *The adaptive geometry of trees.* Princeton, NJ: Princeton Univ. Press.

Keever, C. 1950. Causes of succession on old fields of the piedmont, North Carolina. *Ecol. Mono.* 20:229-50.

Krefting, L. W. and C. E. Ahlgren. 1974. Small mammals and vegetation changes after fire in a mixed conifer-hardwood forest. *Ecology* 55:1391-98.

McIntosh, R. P. 1970. Community, competition, and adaptation. *Quart. Rev. Biol.* 45:259-80.

Moore, J. C., T. V. St. John, and D. C. Coleman. 1985. Ingestion of vesicular-arbuscular mycorrhizal hyphae and spores by soil microarthropods. *Ecology* 66:1979-81.

Newell, S. J., and E. J. Tramer. 1978. Reproductive strategies in herbaceous plant communities during succession. *Ecology* 59:228-34.

Nicholson, S. A., J. T. Scott, and A. R. Breisch. 1979. Structure and succession in the tree stratum at Lake George, New York. *Ecology* 60:1240-54.

Niering, W. A., and R. H. Goodwin. 1974. Creation of relatively stable shrubland with herbicides: Arresting "succession" on rights-of-way and pastureland. *Ecology* 55:784-95.

Odum, E. P. 1969. The strategy of ecosystem development. *Science* 164:262-70.

Pickett, S.T.A. 1976. Succession: An evolutionary interpretation. *Am. Nat.* 110:107-19.

Smith, A. P. 1973. Stratification of temperate and tropical forests. *Am. Nat.* 107:671-83.

Strausbaugh, P. D., and E. L. Core. n.d. *Flora of West Virginia*. Grantsville, WV: Seneca Books.

Sutton, A., and M. Sutton. 1985. *Eastern forests*. New York: Knopf.

Terborgh, J. 1985. The vertical component of plant species diversity in temperate and tropical forests. *Am. Nat.* 126:760-76.

Tinker, P. B., and A. Gildon. 1982. Mycorrhizal fungi and ion uptake. In *Metals and micronutrients, uptake and utilization by plants*, edited by D. A. Robb and W. S. Pierpoint. Phytochemical Soc. Europe Symp. Ser. No. 21. San Diego, CA: Academic Press.

White, P. S. 1979. Pattern, process, and natural disturbance in vegetation. *Bot. Rev.* 45:229-99.

Whittaker, R. H. 1956. Vegetation of the Great Smoky Mountains. *Ecol. Mono.* 26:1-80.

4. Creating Diversity

Braun, E. L. 1950. Cited Chp. 2.

Brooks, M. 1948. Notes on the Cheat Mountain salamander. *Copeia.* 1948:240-44.

____. 1955. An isolated population of the Virginia varying hare. *J. Wildl. Mngmt.* 19:54-61.

Deeney, E. S., Jr. 1976. Time-worn highlands and coastal plain. In

Our continent: A natural history of North America. Washington, DC: National Geographic Society.

Echelle, A. A., A. F. Echelle, M. H. Smith, and L. G., Hill. 1975. Analysis of genic continuity in a headwater fish, *Etheostoma radiosum* (Percidae). *Copeia* 1975:197-204.

Echelle, A. A., A. F. Echelle, and B. A. Taber. 1976. Biochemical evidence for congeneric competition as a factor restricting gene flow between populations of a darter (Percidae: *Etheostoma*). *Copeia* 1976:228-35.

Green, N. B., and T. K. Pauley. 1987. *Amphibians and reptiles in West Virginia.* Pittsburgh, PA: Univ. of Pittsburgh Press.

Hocutt, C. H. 1979. Drainage evolution and fish dispersal in the central Appalachians. *Geol. Soc. Am. Bull., Part II* 90:197-234.

Hocutt, C. H., R. F. Denoncourt, and J. R. Stauffer, Jr. 1978. Fishes of the Greenbrier River, West Virginia, with drainage history of the central Appalachians. *J. Biogeogr.* 5:59-80.

Jenkins, R. E., E. A. Lachner, and F. J. Schwartz. 1971. Fishes of the central Appalachian drainage: Their distribution and dispersal. In *The distributional history of the biota of the southern Appalachians, Part III: Vertebrates, Res. Div. Monogr. 4,* edited by P. C. Holt. Blacksburg, VA: Virginia Poly. Inst. and St. Univ.

Jopson, H. G. M. 1971. The origin of the reptile fauna of the southern Appalachinas. In *The distributional history of the biota of the southern Appalachians, Part III: Vertebrates, Res. Div. Mono. 4,* edited by P. C. Holt. Blacksburg, VA: Virginia Poly. Inst. and St. Univ.

Kendeigh, S. C. 1974. *Ecology, with special reference to animals and man.* Englewood Cliffs, NJ: Prentice-Hall.

Knight, R. L., and M. W. Call. 1980. The common raven. *Tech. Note 344.* U.S. Dept. Interior, Bur. Land Mngmt.

Little, E. L. Jr. 1971. Endemic, disjunct and northern trees in the southern Appalachians. In *The distributional history of the biota of the southern Appalachians, Part II: Flora. Res. Div. Monogr.*

2, edited by P. C. Holt. Blacksburg, VA: Virginia Poly. Inst. and St. Univ.

Mathews, R. C., Jr., and A. C. Echternacht. 1984. Herpetofauna of the spruce-fir ecosystem in the southern Appalachian mountain regions, with emphasis on the Great Smoky Mountains National Park. In *The southern Appalachian spruce-fir ecosystem: Its biology and threats*, edited by P. S. White. Research/Resources Mngmt. Report SER-71. Washington, DC: U.S. Dept. Interior, Natl. Park Serv.

Matthews, W. J., R. E. Jenkins, and J. T. Styron Jr. 1982. Systematics of two forms of blacknose dace, *Rhinichthys atratulus* (Pisces: Cyprinidae) in a zone of syntopy, with a review of the species group. *Copeia* 1982:902-20.

Mohlenbrock, R. H. 1985. Alpine Garden, New Hampshire. *Natural History* 7:22-27.

Oosting, H. J., and W. D. Billings. 1951. A comparison of virgin spruce-fir forest in the northern and southern Appalachian system. *Evolution* 32:84-103.

Page, L. M. 1983. *Handbook of darters*. Neptune City, NJ: TFH Publications.

Rabenold, K. N. 1978. Foraging strategies, diversity, and seasonality in bird communities of Appalachian spruce-fir forests. *Ecol. Mono.* 48:397-424.

Sharp, A. J. 1971. Epilogue. In *The distributional history of the biota of the southern Appalachians, Part II: Flora*. Res. Div. Mono. 2, edited by P. C. Holt. Blacksburg, VA: Virginia Poly. Inst. and St. Univ.

Stauffer, J. R. Jr., C. II. Hocutt, and D. S. Lee. 1978. The zoogeography of the freshwater fishes of the Potomac River basin. In *The freshwater Potomac: Aquatic communities and environmental stresses*, edited by K. C. Flynn and W. T. Mason. Rockville, MD: Interstate Comm. Potomac R. Basin.

Stauffer, J. R. Jr., B. M. Burr, C. H. Hocutt, and R. E. Jenkins. 1982. Checklist of the fishes of the central and northern Appalachian Mountains. *Proc. Biol. Soc. Washington* 95:27-47.

Tilley, S. G., and P. M. Schmerdtteger. 1981. Electrophoretic variation in Appalachian populations of the *Desmognathus fuscus* complex (Amphibia: Plethodontidae). *Copeia* 1981:109-19.

Wake, D. B., and J. F. Lynch. 1976. *The distribution, ecology, and evolutionary history of plethodontid salamanders in tropical America.* Sci. Bull. 25. Los Angeles, CA: Natural History Museum.

White, P. S. 1984. The southern Appalachian spruce-fir ecosystem, an introduction. In *The southern Appalachian spruce-fir ecosystem: Its biology and threats*, edited by P.S. White. *Research/Resources Mngmt. Report SER-71*. Washington, DC: U.S. Dept. Interior, Natl. Park Serv.

Woods, F. W., and R. E. Shanks. 1959. Natural replacement of chestnut by other species in the Great Smoky Mountains National Park. *Ecology* 40:349-61.

Zobel, D. B. 1969. Factors affecting the distribution of *Pinus pungens*, an Appalachian endemic. *Ecol. Mono.* 39:271-301.

5. Catastrophe and the Appalachian Quilt

Barden, L. S. 1979. Serotiny and seed viability of *Pinus pungens* in the southern Appalachians. *Castanea* 44:44-47.

_____. 1979. Tree replacement in small canopy gaps of a *Tsuga canadensis* forest in the southern Appalachians, Tennessee. *Oecologia* 44:141-42.

_____. 1980. Tree replacement in a cove hardwood forest of the southern Appalachians. *Oikos* 35:16-19.

_____. 1981. Forest development in canopy gaps of a diverse hardwood forest of the southern Appalachian Mountains. *Oikos* 37:205-09.

_____. 1983. Size, age, and growth rate of trees in canopy gaps of a cove hardwood forest in the southern Appalachians. *Castanea* 48:19-23.

Beatty, S. W. 1984. Influence of microtopography and canopy species on spatial patterns of forest understory plants. *Ecology* 65:1406-19.

Bormann, F. H., and G. E. Likens. 1979. Catastrophic disturbance and the steady state in northern hardwood forests. *Am. Sci.* 67:660-69.

Bratton, S. P. 1976. Resource division in an understory herb community: Responses to temporal and microtopographic gradients. *Am. Nat.* 110:679-93.

Canham, C. D., and O. L. Loucks. 1984. Catastrophic windthrow in the presettlement forests of Wisconsin. *Ecology* 65:803-09.

Davis, M. B., ed. 1996. *Eastern old-growth forests: Prospects for rediscovery and recovery.* Washington DC: Island Press.

Day, F. P. Jr., and C. D. Monk. 1974. Vegetation patterns on a southern Appalachian watershed. *Ecology* 55:1064-74.

Fox, J. F. 1977. Alternation and coexistence of tree species. *Am. Nat.* 111:69-89.

Gant, R. E., and E. E. C. Clebsch. 1975. The allelopathic influences of *Sassafras albidum* in old-field succession in Tennessee. *Ecology* 56:604-15.

Gemborys, S. R. 1974. The structure of hardwood forest ecosystems of Prince Edward County, Virginia. *Ecology* 55:614-21.

Gleick, J. *Chaos: Making a new science.* New York: Viking.

Harmon, M. E. 1984. Survival of trees after low-intensity surface fires in Great Smoky Mountains National Park. *Ecology* 65:796-802.

Harmon, M. E., S. P. Bratton, and P. S. White. 1983. Disturbance and vegetation response in relation to environmental gradients in the Great Smoky Mountains. *Vegetatio* 55:129-39.

Jones, E. W. 1945. The structure and reproduction of the virgin forest of the north temperate zone. *New Phytol.* 44:130-48.

Leak, W. B. 1975. Age distribution in virgin red spruce and northern hardwoods. *Ecology* 56:1451-54.

Lorimer, C. G. 1977. The presettlement forest and natural disturbance cycle of northeastern Maine. *Ecology* 50.139-48.

_____. 1980. Age structure and disturbance history of a southern Ap-
palachian virgin forest. *Ecology* 61:1169-84.

McCormick, J. F., and R. B. Platt. 1980. Recovery of an Appalachian
forest following the chestnut blight, or Catherine Keever —
you were right! *Am. Midl. Nat.* 104:264-73.

McEvoy, T. J., T. L. Sharik, and D. W. Smith. 1980. Vegetative structure of an Appalachian oak forest in southwestern Virginia.
Am. Midl. Nat. 103:96-105.

Muller, C. H. 1966. The role of chemical inhibition (allelopathy) in
vegetation composition. *Bull. Torrey Bot. Club* 93:332-51.

_____. 1970. The role of allelopathy in the evolution of vegetation.
In *Biochemical coevolution: Proc. 29th Ann. Biol. Coll., 1968,*
edited by K. L. Chambers. Corvallis, OR: Oregon St. Univ.
Press.

Oliver, C. D., and E. P. Stephens. 1977. Reconstruction of a mixed-
species forest in central New England. *Ecology* 58:562-72.

Putz, F. E., G. G. Parker, and R. M. Archibald. 1984. Mechanical
abrasion and intercrown spacing. *Am. Midl. Nat.* 112:24-28.

Racine, C. H. 1971. Reproduction of three species of oak in relation
to vegetational and environmental gradients in the southern
Blue Ridge. *Bull. Torrey Bot. Club* 98:297-310.

Reiners, W. A., and G. E. Lang. 1979. Vegetational patterns and processes in the balsam fir zone, White Mountains, New Hampshire. *Ecology* 60:403-17.

Rogers, R. S. 1980. Hemlock stands from Wisconsin to Nova Scotia:
Transitions in understory composition along a floristic gradient. *Ecology* 61: 178-93.

_____. 1983. Small-area coexistence of vernal forest herbs: Does func-
tional similarity of plants matter? *Am. Nat.* 121:835-50.

_____. 1985. Local coexistence of deciduous-forest groundlayer spe-
cies growing in different seasons. *Ecology* 66:701-07.

289

Schemske, D. W., M. F. Willson, M. N. Melampy, L. J. Miller, L. Verner, K. M. Schemske, and L. D. Best. 1978. Flowering ecology of some spring woodland herbs. *Ecology* 59:351-66.

Sousa, W. P. 1984. The role of disturbance in natural communities. *Ann. Rev. Ecol. Syst.* 15:353-91.

Turner, B. H., and E. Quarterman. 1975. Allelochemic effects of *Petalostemon gattingeri* on the distribution of *Arenaria patula* in cedar glades. *Ecology* 56:924-32.

VanVoris, P., R. V. O'Neill, W. R. Emanuel, and H. H. Shugart. 1980. Functional complexity and ecosystem stability. *Ecology* 61:1352-60.

White, P. S., M. D. MacKenzie, and R. T. Busing. 1985. Natural disturbance and gap phase dynamics in southern Appalachian spruce-fir forests. *Canad. J. For. Res.* 15:233-40.

Whitney, G. G. 1984. Fifty years of change in the arboreal vegetation of Hart's Content, an old-growth hemlock-white pine-northern hardwood stand. *Ecology* 65:403-08.

Whittaker, R. H., and P. P. Feeny. 1971. Allelochemics: Chemical interactions between species. *Science* 171:757-70.

Williamson, G. B. 1975. Pattern and seral composition in an old-growth beech-maple forest. *Ecology* 56:727-31.

6. Balds

Barden, L. S. 1978. Regrowth of shrubs in grassy balds of the southern Appalachians after prescribed burning. *Castanea* 43:238-46.

Billings, W .D., and A. F. Mark. 1957. Factors involved in the persistence of montane treeless balds. *Ecology* 38:140-42.

Braun, E. L. 1950. Cited in Chp. 2.

Camp, W. H. 1931. The grass balds of the Great Smoky Mountains of Tennessee and North Carolina. *Ohio J. Sci.* 31:157-164.

Catlin, D. T. 1984. Cited in Chp. 1.

Johnson, R. 1992. Will "mountain goats" help save the southern balds? *Appalachia* 25 (2):16-21.

Knoepp, J. D., L. L. Tieszen, and G.G. Fredlund. 1998. Assessing the vegetation history of three southern Appalachian balds through soul organic matter analysis. *USDA Forest Service Res. Paper SRS-13*. Ashville, NC: USDA, Southern Research Station.

Lindsay, M. M., and S. P. Bratton. 1979. Grassy balds of the Great Smoky Mountains: their history and flora in relation to potential management. *Envtl. Mgt*. 3:417-30.

Mark, A. F. 1958. The ecology of the southern Appalachian grass balds. *Ecol. Mono*. 28:293-336.

Rentch, J. S., and R. H. Fortney. 1997. The vegetation of West Virginia grass bald communities. *Castanea* 62:147-60.

Saunders, P. R., ed. 1981. *Status and management of southern Appalachian Mountain balds*. Cullowhee NC: Western Carolina Univ.

Sullivan, J. H., and J. D. Pittillo. 1988. Succession of woody plants into a high elevation grassy bald of the Balsam Mountains. *Castanea* 53:245-51.

Wells, B. W. 1937. Southern Appalachian grass balds. *Elisha Mitchell Sci. Soc. J*. 53:1-26.

Whittaker, R. H. 1956. Cited in Chp. 2.

7. The Asian Connection

Boufford, D. E., and S. A. Sponberg. 1983. Eastern Asian-eastern North American phytogeographical relationships: A history from the time of Linnaeus to the twentieth century. *Ann. Missouri Bot. Gard*. 70:423-39.

Braun, E. L. 1950. Cited in Chp. 2.

Cheng, Z. 1983. A comparative study of the vegetation in Hubei Province, China, and in the Carolinas of the United States. *Ann. Missouri Bot. Gard*. 70:571-75.

Davis, M. B. 1983. Quaternary history of deciduous forests of eastern North America and Europe. *Ann. Missouri Bot. Gard*. 70:550-63.

Hamilton, W. 1983. Cretaceous and Cenozoic history of the northern continents. *Ann. Missouri Bot. Gard.* 70:440-58.

Hsu, J. 1983. Late Cretaceous and Cenozoic vegetation in China, emphasizing their connections with North America. *Ann. Missouri Bot. Gard.* 70:490-508.

Kato, M., and K. Iwatsuki. 1983. Phytogeographic relationships of pteridophytes between temperate North America and Japan. *Ann. Missouri Bot. Gard.* 70:724-33.

Little, E. L. Jr. 1983. North American trees with relationships in eastern Asia. *Ann. Missouri Bot. Gard.* 70:605-15.

Parks, C. R., N. G. Miller, J. F. Wendel, and K. M. McDougal. 1983. Genetic divergence within the genus *Liriodendron* (Magnoliaceae). *Ann. Missouri Bot. Gard.* 70:658-66.

Sing-chi, C. 1983. A comparison of orchid floras of temperate North America and eastern Asia. *Ann. Missouri Bot. Gard.* 70:713-23.

White, P. S. 1983. Eastern Asian-eastern North American floristic relations: The plant community level. *Ann. Missouri Bot. Gard.* 70:734-47.

Ying, T. 1983. The floristic relationships of the temperate forest regions of China and the United States. *Ann. Missouri Bot. Gard.* 70:597-604.

Zhengyi, W. 1983. On the significance of the Pacific intercontinental discontinuity. *Ann. Missouri Bot. Gard.* 70:577-90.

8. The Improbable Lady's-slipper

Dafni, A. 1984. Mimicry and deception in pollination. *Ann. Rev. Ecol. Syst.* 15:259-78.

Dodson, C. H. 1966. Studies in orchid pollination — *Cypripedium, Phragmipedium* and allied genera. *Am. Orchid Soc. Bull.* 35:125-28.

Dressler, R. L. 1981. *The orchids: Natural history and classification.* Cambridge, MA: Harvard Univ. Press.

Hugo, N. 1990. Lady's slippers. *Virginia Wildlife*, June: 34.

Luer, C. A. 1975. *The native orchids of the United States and Canada excluding Florida*. New York: New York Bot. Gard.

Primack, R. B., and P. Hall. 1990. Costs of reproduction in the pink lady's slipper orchid: a four-year experimental study. *Am. Nat.* 136:638-56.

Stoutamire, W. P. 1964. Seeds and seedlings of native orchids. *The Michigan Botanist* 3:107-19.

_____. 1967. Flower biology of the lady's-slippers. *The Michigan Botanist* 6:159-75.

_____. 1971. Pollination in temperate American orchids. In *Proc. 6th World Orchid Conf., Sydney, Australia, 1969*, edited by M. J. Corrigan. Sydney, Australia: Halstead Press.

_____. 1974. Relationships of the purple-fringed orchids *Platanthera psycodes* and *P. grandiflora*. *Brittonia* 26:42-58.

_____. 1978. Pollination of *Tipularia discolor*, an orchid with modified symmetry. *Am. Orchid Soc. Bull.* 47:413-15.

_____. 1983. Early growth in North American terrestrial orchid seedlings. In *Proc. Symp. II and Lectures, North American Terrestrial Orchids*, edited by E. H. Plaxton. Southfield, MI: Michigan Orchid Society.

Waters, V. H., and C. C. Waters. 1973. *A survey of the slipper orchids*. Shelby, NC: Carolina Press.

9. Sexual Decisions of Jack-in-the-pulpit

Bierzychudek, P. 1981. Pollinator limitation of plant reproductive effort. *Am. Nat.* 117:838-40.

_____. 1982. The demography of Jack-in-the-pulpit, a forest perennial that changes sex. *Ecol. Mono.* 52:335-51.

_____. 1984. Assessing "optimal" life histories in a fluctuating environment: The evolution of sex-changing by Jack-in-the-pulpit. *Am. Nat.* 123:829-40.

_____. 1984. Determinants of gender in Jack-in-the-pulpit: The influence of plant size and reproductive history. *Oecologia* 65:14-18.

Charnov, E. L. 1982. *The theory of sex allocation*. Princeton, NJ: Princeton Univ. Press.

Ghiselin, M. T. 1969. The evolution of hermaphroditism among animals. *Quart. Rev. Biol.* 44:189-208.

Gould, S. J. 1985. *The flamingo's smile*. New York: Norton.

Lovett Doust, J., and P. B. Cavers. 1982. Sex and gender dynamics in Jack-in-the-pulpit, *Arisaema triphyllum* (L.) Schott (Araceae). *Ecology* 63:797-808.

Maekawa, T. 1924. On the phenomena of sex transition in *Arisema japonica. Hokkaido Imp. Univ. J. Coll. Agr.* 13:217-305.

Parker, M. A. 1987. Pathogen impact on sexual vs. asexual reproductive success in *Arisaema triphyllum. Am. J. Bot.* 74:1758-63.

Policansky, D. 1981. Sex choice and the size advantage model in Jack-in-the-pulpit *(Arisaema triphyllum). Proc. Natl. Acad. Sci.* 78:1306-08.

_____. 1982. Sex change in plants and animals. *Ann. Rev. Ecol. Syst.* 13:471-95.

_____. 1987. Evolution, sex, and sex allocation. *BioScience* 37:466-68.

_____. 1987. Sex choice and reproductive costs in Jack-in-the-pulpit. *BioScience* 37:476-81.

Schaffner, J. H. 1922. Control of sexual state in *Arisaema triphyllum* and *A. dracontium. Am. J. Bot.* 9:72-78.

10. Nuptial Gift of the Hangingfly

Thornhill, R. 1976. Sexual selection and nuptial feeding behavior in *Bittacus apicalis* (Insecta: Mecoptera). *Am. Nat.* 110:529-48.

_____. 1977. The comparative predatory and sexual behavior of hangingflies (Mecoptera: Bittacidae). *Occ. Pap. Mus. Zool. Univ. Michigan*, No. 677.

_____. 1979. Adaptive female-mimicking behavior in a scorpionfly. *Science* 205:412 14.

_____. 1980. Mate choice in *Hylobittacus apicalis* (Insecta: Mecoptera) and its relation to some models of female choice. *Evolution* 34:519-38.

_____. 1980. Sexual selection in the black-tipped hangingfly. *Sci. Am.* 242 (6):162-72.

_____. 1984. Alternative female choice tactics in the scorpionfly *Hylobittacus apicalis* (Mecoptera) and their implications. *Am. Zool.* 24:367-83.

11. *Femmes Fatales of Twilight*

Buck, J., and E. Buck. 1978. Toward a functional interpretation of synchronous flashing by fireflies. *Am. Nat.* 112:471-92.

Carlson, A. D., and J. Copeland. 1978. Behavioral plasticity in the flash communication systems of fireflies. *Amer. Sci.* 66:340-46.

Copeland. J., and A. Moiseff. 1995. The occurrence of synchrony in the North American firefly *Photinus carolinus* (Coleoptera: Lampyridae). *J. Insect Behav.* 8:381-94.

Lall, A. B., H. II. Seliger, W. H. Biggley, and J. E. Lloyd. 1980. Ecology of colors of firefly bioluminescence. *Science* 210:560-62.

Lloyd, J. E. 1980. Male *Photuris* fireflies mimic sexual signals of their females' prey. *Science* 210:669-71.

_____. 1981. Mimicry in the sexual signals of fireflies. *Sci. Am.* 245 (1):138-45.

_____. 1981. Firefly mate-rivals mimic their predators and vice versa. *Nature* 290:498-500.

_____. 1983. Bioluminescence and communication in insects. *Ann. Rev. Entomol.* 28:131-60.

_____. 1984. On deception, a way of all flesh, and firefly signalling and systematics. *Oxford Surv. Evol. Biol.* 1: 48-84.

_____. 1984. Occurrence of aggressive mimicry in fireflies. *Florida Entomologist* 67:368-76.

_____. 1990. Firefly semiosystematics and predation: A history. *Florida Entomologist* 73:51-66.

Lloyd, J. E., and S. R. Wing. 1983. Nocturnal aerial predation of fireflies by light-seeking fireflies. *Science* 222:634-35.

McElroy, W. D., and H. H. Seliger. 1962. Biological luminescence. In *The living cell, readings from Scientific American.* San Francisco: W. H. Freeman.

Moiseff, A., and J. Copeland. 1995. Mechanisms of synchrony in the North American firefly *Photinus carolinus* (Coleoptera: Lampyridae). *J. Insect Behav.* 8:395-407.

Thornhill, R., and J. Alcock. 1983. *The evolution of insect mating systems.* Cambridge, MA: Harvard Univ. Press.

Zimmer, C. 1994. Fireflies in lockstep. *Discover,* June: 30-31.

12. Small Fishes in Shallow Headwaters

Angermeier, P. L. 1982. Resource seasonality and fish diets in an Illinois stream. *Env. Biol. Fish.* 7:251-64.

Beauchamp, G. K., K. Yamazaki, and E. A. Boyse. 1985. The chemosensory recognition of genetic individuality. *Sci. Am.* 253:86-92.

Brown, G. E., D. P. Chivers, and R. J. F. Smith. 1995. Localized defecation by pike: A response to labeling by cyprinid alarm pheromone? *Behav. Ecol. Sociobiol.* 36:105-10.

Cerri, R. D. 1983. The effect of light intensity on predator and prey behaviour in a cyprinid fish: Factors that influence prey risk. *Anim. Behav.* 31:736-42.

Cerri, R. D., and D. F. Fraser. 1983. Predation and risk in foraging minnows: Balancing conflicting demands. *Am. Nat.* 121:552-61.

Chivers, D. P., and R. J. F. Smith. 1994. Intra- and interspecific avoidance of areas marked with skin extract from brook sticklebacks (*Culaea inconstans*) in a natural habitat. *J. Chem. Ecol.* 20:1517-24.

_____. 1994. Fathead minnows, *Pimephales promelas*, acquire predator recognition when alarm substance is associated with the sight of unfamiliar fish. *Anim. Behav.* 48:597-605.

_____. 1995. Chemical recognition of risky habitats is culturally transmitted among fathead minnows, *Pimephales promelas* (Osteichthyes, Cyprinidae). *Ethology* 99:286-96.

Cooper, J. C., and A. D. Hasler. 1976. Electrophysiological studies of morpholine-imprinted coho salmon (*Oncorhynchus kisutch*) and rainbow trout (*Salmo gairdneri*). *J. Fish. Res. Bd. Canada* 33:688-94.

Fraser, D. F. 1983. An experimental investigation of refuging behaviour in a minnow. *Can. J. Zool.* 61:666-72.

Fraser, D. F., and R. D. Cerri. 1982. Experimental evaluation of predator-prey relationships in a patchy environment: Consequences for habitat use patterns in minnows. *Ecology* 63:307-13.

Fraser, D. F., and E. E. Emmons. 1984. Behavioral response of juvenile blacknose dace (*Rhinichthys atratulus*) to varying densities of predatory creek chub (*Semotilus atromaculatus*). *Can. J. Fish. Aquat. Sci.* 41:364-70.

Fraser, D. F., and T. E. Sise. 1980. Observations on stream minnows in a patchy environment: A test of a theory of habitat distribution. *Ecology* 61:790-97.

Gee, J. H. 1974. Behavioral and developmental plasticity of buoyancy in the longnose, *Rhinichthys cataractae*, and blacknose, *R. atratulus* (Cyprinidae) dace. *J. Fish. Res. Bd. Can.* 31:35-41.

Gerking, S. D. 1950. Stability of a stream fish population. *J. Wildl. Mngmt.* 14:193-202.

_____. 1953. Evidence for the concepts of home range and territory in stream fishes. *Ecology* 34:347-65.

_____. 1959. The restricted movement of fish populations. *Biol. Rev.* 34:221-42.

Hasler, A. D. 1966. *Underwater guideposts*. Cambridge, MA: Univ. of Wisconsin Press.

Lawrence, B. J., and R. J. F. Smith. 1989. Behavioral response of solitary fathead minnows, *Pimephales promelas*, to alarm substance. *J. Chem. Ecol.* 15:209-19.

Liley, N. R. 1982. Chemical communication by fish. *Can. J. Fish. Aquat. Sci.* 39:22-35.

Magurran, A. E. 1989. Acquired recognition of predator odour in the European minnow (*Phoxinus phoxinus*). *Ethology* 82:216-23.

Mathis, A., and R. J. F. Smith. 1992. Avoidance of areas marked with a chemical alarm substance by fathead minnows (*Pimephales promelas*) in a natural habitat. *Can. J. Zool.* 70:1473-76.

_____. 1993. Chemical labeling of northern pike (*Esox lucius*) by the alarm pheromone of flathead minnows. *J. Chem. Ecol.* 19:1967-79.

_____. 1993. Fathead minnows, *Pimephales promelas*, learn to recognize northern pike, *Esox Lucius*, as predators on the basis of chemical stimuli from minnows in the pike's diet. Anim. Behav. 46:645-56.

Page, L. M. 1983. Cited in Chp 4.

Reed, R. J. 1968. Mark and recapture studies of eight species of darters (Pisces: Percidae) in three streams of northwestern Pennsylvania. *Copeia* 1968:172-75.

Schlosser, I. J. 1982. Fish community structure and function along two habitat gradients in a headwater stream. *Ecol. Mono.* 52:395-414.

Scholz, A. T., R. M. Horrall, J. C. Cooper, and A. D. Hasler. 1976. Imprinting to chemical cues: The basis for home stream selection in salmon. *Science* 192:1247-49.

Smith, R. J. F. 1973. Testosterone eliminates alarm substance in male fathead minnows. *Can. J. Zool.* 51:875-76.

_____. 1977. Chemical communication as adaptation: Alarm substance of fish. In *Chemical signals in vertebrates*, edited by D.

Muller-Schwarze and M. M. Mozell. New York: Plenum.

_____. 1979. Alarm reaction of Iowa and johnny darters (*Etheostoma,* Percidae, Pisces) to chemicals from injured conspecifics. *Can. J. Zool.* 57:1278-82.

_____. 1982. Reaction of *Percina nigrofasciata, Ammocrypta beani,* and *Etheostoma beani* (Percidae, Pisces) to conspecific and intergeneric skin extracts. *Can. J. Zool.* 60:1067-72.

_____. The response of *Asterropteryx semipunctatus* and *Gnatholepis anjerensis* (Pisces, Gobiidae) to chemical stimuli from injured conspecifics, an alarm response in gobies. *Ethology* 81:279-90.

Smith, R. J. F., and B. J. Lawrence. 1992. The response of a bumblebee goby, *Brachygobius sabanus,* to chemical stimuli from injured conspecifics. *Envtl. Biol. Fishes* 34:103-08.

Smith, R. J. F., and J. D. Smith. 1983. Seasonal loss of alarm substance cells in *Chrosomus neogaetus, Notropis venustus,* and *N. whipplei. Copeia* 1983:822-26.

Thunberg, B. E. 1971. Olfaction in parent stream selection by the alewife *(Alosa pseudoharengus). Anim. Behav.* 19:217-25.

Wisenden, B. D., D. P. Chivers, and R. J. F. Smith. 1994. Risk-sensitive habitat use by brook stickleback (*Culaea inconstans*) in areas associated with minnow alarm pheromone. *J. Chem. Ecol.* 20:2975-83.

13. Darter Daddies

Atz, J. W. 1940. Reproductive behavior in the eastern johnny darter, *Boleosoma nigrum olmstedi. Copeia* 1940:100-06.

Brown, L. 1981. Patterns of female choice in mottled sculpins (Cottidae, Teleostei). *Anim. Behav.* 29:375-82.

Brown, L., and J. F. Downhower. 1982. Polygamy in the mottled sculpins *(Cottus bairdi)* of southwestern Montana (Pisces: Cottidae). *Can. J. Zool.* 60:1973-80.

Constantz, G. D. 1979. Social dynamics and parental care in the tessellated darter. *Proc. Acad. Nat. Sci. Phila.* 131:131-38.

_____. 1985. Allopaternal care in the tessellated darter (Pisces: Percidae). *Env. Biol. Fish.* 14:175-83.

DeWoody, J. A., D. E. Fletcher, S. D. Wilkins, and J. C. Avise. 2000. Parentage and nest guarding in the tessellated darter (*Etheostoma olmstedi*) assayed by microsattelite markers (*Perciformes: Percidae*). *Copeia* 2000:740-47.

Downhower, J. F., and L. Brown. 1979. Seasonal changes in the social structure of a mottled sculpin *(Cottus bairdi)* population. *Anim. Behav.* 27:451-58.

_____. 1980. Mate preferences of female mottled sculpins, *Cottus bairdi. Anim. Behav.* 28:728-34.

_____. 1981. The timing of reproduction and its behavioral consequences for mottled sculpins, *Cottus bairdi.* In *Natural selection and social behavior,* edited by R. D. Alexander and D. W. Tinkle. New York: Chiron Press.

Downhower, J. F., L. Brown, R. Pederson, and G. Staples. 1983. Sexual selection and sexual dimorphism in mottled sculpins. *Evolution* 37:96-103.

Kuehne, R. A., and R. W. Barbour. 1983. *The American darters.* Lexington: Univ. Press of Kentucky.

Page, L. M. 1983. *Handbook of darters.* Neptune City, NJ: TFH Publications.

Thomas, L. 1980. Altruism. In *Late night thoughts on listening to Mahler's ninth symphony.* New York: Viking Press.

14. To the Brook Trout, with Esteem

Cooper, E. L. 1967. Growth and longevity of brook trout (*Salvelinus fontinalis*) in populations subjected to light exploitation. *Trans. Am. Fish. Soc.* 96:383-86.

_____. 1983. *Fishes of Pennsylvania and the northeastern United States.* University Park, PA: Penn. St. Univ. Press.

Cooper, E. L., and R. C. Scherer. 1967. Annual production of brook trout *(Salvelinus fontinalis)* in fertile and infertile streams of Pennsylvania. *Proc. Pa. Acad. Sci.* 41:65-70

Gradall, K. S., and W. A. Swenson. 1982. Responses of brook trout and creek chubs to turbidity. *Trans. Am. Fish. Soc.* 111:392-95.

Hanson, D. L., and T. F. Waters. 1974. Recovery of standing crop and production rate of a brook trout population in a flood-damaged stream. *Trans. Am. Fish. Soc.* 103:431-39.

Hutchings, J. A. 1991. Fitness consequences of variation in egg size and food abundance in brook trout *Salvelinus fontinalis. Evolution* 45:1162-68.

_____. 1994. Age- and size-specific costs of reproduction within populations of brook trout, *Salvelinus fontinalis. Oikos* 70:12-20.

Lennon, R. E. 1967. Brook trout of Great Smoky Mountains National Park. *U.S. Bur. Sport Fish and Wildl., Tech. Paper 15.* Washington, DC.

McCormick, S. D., and R. J. Naiman. 1984. Osmoregulation in the brook trout, *Salvelinus fontinalis* — II. Effects of size, age and photoperiod on seawater survival and ionic regulation. *Comp. Biochem. Physiol.* 79A:17-28.

McNicol, R. E., and D. L. G. Noakes. 1981. Territories and territorial defense in juvenile brook charr, *Salvelinus fontinalis* (Pisces: Salmonidae). *Can. J. Zool.* 59:22-28.

_____. 1984. Environmental influences on territoriality of juvenile brook charr, *Salvelinus fontinalis*, in a stream environment. *Env. Biol. Fish.* 10:29-42.

Menendez, R. 1976. Chronic effects of reduced pH on brook trout. *J. Fish. Res. Bd. Canada* 33:118-23.

Naiman, R. J., S. D. McCormick, W. L. Montgomery, and R. Morin. Unpubl. ms. Anadromous brook trout, *Salvelinus fontinalis: Opportunities and constraints for population enhancement.*

Neves, R. J., and G. B. Pardue. 1983. Abundance and production of fishes in a small Appalachian stream. *Trans. Am. Fish. Soc.*

112:21-26.

Power, G. 1980. The brook charr, *Salvelinus fontinalis*. In *Charrs: Salmonid fishes of the genus* Salvelinus, edited by E.K. Balon. The Hague: Dr. W. Junk Publ.

Smith, P. P., and J. B. Atkinson. 1999. Flood and debris-flow effects on Virginia brook trout populations. *Proc. Ann. Conf. SE Assn. Fish & Wildl. Agencies* 53:91-99

Waters, T. F. 1982. Annual production of a stream brook charr population and by its principal invertebrate food. *Env. Biol. Fish.* 7:165-70.

_____. 1983. Replacement of brook trout by brown trout over 15 years in a Minnesota stream: Production and abundance. *Trans. Am. Fish. Soc.* 112:137-46.

Webster, D. A., and G. Eiriksdottir. 1976. Upwelling water as a factor influencing choice of spawning sites by brook trout (*Salvelinus fontinalis*). *Trans. Am. Fish. Soc.* 105:416-21.

Whitworth, W. E., and R. J. Strange. 1983. Growth and production of sympatric brook and rainbow trout in an Appalachian stream. *Trans. Am. Fish. Soc.* 112:469-75.

Wydoski, R. S., and E. L. Cooper. 1966. Maturation and fecundity of brook trout from infertile streams. *J. Fish. Res. Bd. Can.* 23:623-49.

15-17. A Lungless Salamander Trilogy

Brodie, E. D. Jr., and R. R. Howard. 1973. Experimental study of Batesian mimicry in the salamanders *Plethodon jordani* and *Desmognathus ochrophaeus*. *Am. Midl. Nat.* 90:38-46.

Bruce, R. C. 1980. A model of the larval period of the spring salamander, *Gyrinophilus porphyriticus*, based on size-frequency distributions. *Herpetologica* 36:78-86.

_____. 1982. Larval periods and metamorphosis in two species of salamanders of the genus *Eurycea*. *Copeia* 1982:117-27.

_____. 1982. Egg-laying, larval periods, and metamorphosis of *Eurycea bislineata* and *E. junaluska* at Santeetlah Creek, North Carolina. *Copeia* 1982:755-62.

_____. 1985. Larval periods, population structure and the effects of stream drift in larvae of the salamanders *Desmognathus quadramaculatus* and *Leurognathus marmoratus* in a southern Appalachian stream. *Copeia* 1985:847-54.

_____. 1985. Larval period and metamorphosis in the salamander *Eurycea bislineata*. *Herpetologica* 41:19-28.

Danstedt, R. T., Jr. 1975. Local geographic variation in demographic parameters and body size of *Desmognathus fuscus* (Amphibia: Plethodontidae). *Ecology* 56:1054-67.

David, R. S., and R. G. Jaeger. 1981. Prey location through chemical cues by a terrestrial salamander. *Copeia* 1981:435-40.

Dunn, E. R. 1927. A new mountain race of *Desmognathus*. *Copeia* 1927:84-86.

Feder, M. E. 1983. Integrating the ecology and physiology of plethodontid salamanders. *Herpetologica* 39:291-310.

Forester, D. C. 1979. The adaptiveness of parental care in *Desmognathus ochrophaeus* (Urodela: Plethodontidae). *Copeia* 1979: 332-41.

_____. 1981. Parental care in the salamander *Desmognathus ochrophaeus*: Female activity pattern and trophic behavior. *J. Herpetol.* 15:29-34.

Fraser, D. F. 1976. Coexistence of salamanders in the genus *Plethodon*: A variation of the Santa Rosalia theme. *Ecology* 57:238-51.

_____. 1976. Empirical evaluation of the hypothesis of food competition in salamanders of the genus *Plethodon*. *Ecology* 57:459-71.

Gabor, C. R., and R. G. Jaeger. 1995. Resource quality affects the agonistic behaviour of territorial salamanders. *Anim. Behav.* 49:71-79.

Grobman, A. B. 1944. The distribution of salamanders of the genus

Plethodon in eastern United States and Canada. *Ann. New York Acad. Sci.* 45:261-316.

Hairston, N. G. 1980. The experimental test of an analysis of field distributions: Competition in terrestrial salamanders. *Ecology* 61:817-26.

_____. 1980. Species packing in the salamander genus *Desmognathus*: What are the interspecific interactions involved? *Am. Nat.* 115:354-66.

_____. 1981. An experimental test of a guild: Salamander competition. *Ecology* 62:65-72.

_____. 1983. Alpha selection in competing salamanders: Experimental verification of an *a priori* hypothesis. *Am. Nat.* 122: 105-13.

Hairston, N. G. Sr. 1986. Species packing in *Desmognathus* salamanders: Experimental demonstration of predation and competition. *Am. Nat.* 127:266-91.

Highton, R. 1962. Geographic variation in the life history of the slimy salamander. *Copeia* 1962:597-613.

_____. 1972. Distributional interactions among eastern North American salamanders of the genus *Plethodon*. In *The distributional history of the biota of the southern Appalachians, Part III: Vertebrates. Research Division Monograph 4*, edited by P.C. Holt. Blacksburg, VA: Virginia Poly. Inst. and St. Univ.

Highton, R., and R. D. Worthington. 1967. A new salamander of the genus *Plethodon* from Virginia. *Copeia* 1967:617-26.

Hom, C. L., N. H. Willits, and C. W. Clark. 1990. Fitness consequences of nest defense in plethodontid salamanders: Predictions of a dynamic optimization model. *Herpetologica* 46:304-19.

Horne, E. A. 1988. Aggressive behavior of female red-backed salamanders. *Herpetologica* 44:203-09.

Jaeger, R. G. 1970. Potential extinction through competition between two species of terrestrial salamanders. *Evolution* 24:632-42.

_____. 1971. Moisture as a factor influencing the distributions of two species of terrestrial salamanders. *Oecologia* 6:191-207.

_____. 1971. Competitive exclusion as a factor influencing the distributions of two species of terrestrial salamanders. *Ecology* 52:632-37.

_____. 1972. Food as a limited resource in competition between two species of terrestrial salamanders. *Ecology* 53:535-46.

_____. 1978. Plant climbing by salamanders: Periodic availability of plant-dwelling prey. *Copeia* 1978:686-91.

_____. 1979. Seasonal spatial distributions of the terrestrial salamander *Plethodon cinereus*. *Herpetologica* 35:90-93.

_____. 1980. Microhabitats of a terrestrial forest salamander. *Copeia* 1980:265-68.

_____. 1980. Density-dependent and density-independent causes of extinction of a salamander population. *Evolution* 34:617-21.

_____. 1980. Fluctuations in prey availability and food limitation for a terrestrial salamander. *Oecologia* 44:335-41.

_____. 1981. Dear enemy recognition and the costs of aggression between salamanders. *Am. Nat.* 117:962-74.

_____. 1981. Birds as inefficient predators on terrestrial salamanders. *Am. Nat.* 117:835-37.

_____. 1984. Agonistic behavior of the red-backed salamander. *Copeia* 1984:309-14.

Jaeger, R. G., and W. F. Gergits. 1979. Intra- and interspecific communication in salamanders through chemical signals on the substrate. *Anim. Behav.* 27:150-56.

Jaeger, R. G., and J. K. Schwarz. 1991. Gradational threat postures by the red-backed salamander. *J. Herpetol.* 25:112-14.

Jaeger, R. G., and S. E. Wise. 1991. A reexamination of the male salamander "sexy faeces hypothesis." *J. Herpetol.* 25:370-73.

Jaeger, R. G., D. E. Barnard, and R. G. Joseph. 1982. Foraging tactics of a terrestrial salamander: Assessing prey density. *Am. Nat.* 119:885-90.

Jaeger, R. G., J. M. Goy, M. Tarver, and C. E. Marquez. 1986. Salamander territoriality: Pheromonal markers as advertisement by males. *Anim. Behav.* 34:860-64.

Jaeger, R. G., D. Kalvarsky, and N. Shimizu. 1982. Territorial behaviour of the red-backed salamander: Expulsion of intruders. *Anim. Behav.* 30:490-96.

Jaeger, R. G., J. Schwarz, and S. E. Wise. 1995. Territorial male salamanders have foraging tactics attractive to gravid females. *Anim. Behav.* 49:633-39.

Jaeger, R. G., J. A. Wicknick, M. R. Griffis, and C. D. Anthony. 1995. Socioecology of a terrestrial salamander: juveniles enter adult territories during stressful foraging periods. *Ecology* 76:533-43.

Kaplan, R. H., and M. L. Crump. 1978. The non-cost of brooding in *Ambystoma opacum*. *Copeia* 1978:99-103.

Keen, W. H. 1982. Habitat selection and interspecific competition in two species of plethodontid salamanders. *Ecology* 63:94-102.

_____. 1984. Influence of moisture on the activity of a plethodontid salamander. *Copeia* 1984:684-88.

Keen, W. H., and S. Sharp. 1984. Responses of a plethodontid salamander to conspecific and congeneric intruders. *Anim. Behav.* 32:58-65.

Kleeberger, S. R. 1984. A test of competition in two sympatric populations of desmognathine salamanders. *Ecology* 65:1846-56.

Labanick, G. M., and R. A. Brandon. 1981. An experimental study of Batesian mimicry between the salamanders *Plethodon jordani* and *Desmognathus ochrophaeus*. *J. Herpetol.* 15:275-81.

Mathis, A. 1989. Do seasonal spatial distributions in a terrestrial salamander reflect reproductive behavior or territoriality? *Copeia* 1989:788-91.

_____. 1990. Territorial salamanders assess sexual and competitive information using chemical signals. *Anim. Behav.* 40:953-62.

_____. 1990. Territoriality in a terrestrial salamander: The influence of resource quality and body size. *Behaviour* 112:162-75.

_____. 1991. Large male advantage for access to females: Evidence of male-male competition and female discrimination in a territorial salamander. *Behav. Ecol. Sociobiol.* 29:133-38.

_____. 1991. Territories of male and female terrestrial salamanders: Costs, benefits, and intersexual spatial associates. *Oecologia* 86:433-40.

Mathis, A., R. G. Jaeger, W. H. Kean, P. K. Ducey, S. C. Walls, and B. W. Buchanan. 1995. Aggression and territoriality by salamanders and a comparison with the territorial behavior of frogs. In: *Social behavior,* Vol. 2 of *Amphibian biology,* edited by H. Heatwole and B. K. Sullivan. Chipping Norton, NSW, Australia: Surrey Beatty & Sons.

Nussbaum, R. A. 1985. The evolution of parental care in salamanders. *Misc. Publ. Mus. Zool. Univ. Michigan* 169:1-50.

Simon, G. S., and D. M. Madison. 1984. Individual recognition in salamanders: Cloacal odours. *Anim. Behav.* 32:1017-20.

Simons, R. R., and B. E. Felgenhauer. 1992. Identifying areas of chemical signal production in the red-backed salamander, *Plethodon cinereus. Copeia* 1992:776-81.

Simons, R. R., R. G. Jaeger, and B. E. Felgenhauer. 1995. Juvenile terrestrial salamanders have active cloacal glands. *Copeia* 1995:481-83.

Simons, R. R., R. G. Jaeger, and B. E. Felgenhauer. 1997. Competitor assessment and area defense by territorial salamanders. *Copeia* 1997:70-76.

Southerland, M. T. 1986. Coexistence of three congeneric salamanders: The importance of habitat and body size. *Ecology* 67:721-28.

Thomas, J. S., R. G. Jaeger, and E. A. Horne. 1989. Are all females welcome? Agonistic behavior of male red-backed salamanders. *Copeia* 1989:915-20.

Tilley, S. G. 1972. Aspects of parental care and embryonic development in *Desmognathus ochrophaeus. Copeia* 1972:532-40.

_____. 1974. Structures and dynamics of populations of the salamander *Desmognathus ochrophaeus* cope in different habitats. *Ecology* 55:808-17.

307

Tilley, S. G., B. L. Lundrigan, and L. P. Brower. 1982. Erythrism and mimicry in the salamander *Plethodon cinereus. Herpetologica* 38:409-17.

Walls, S. C., A. Mathis, R. G. Jaeger, and W. F. Gergits. 1989. Male salamanders with high-quality diets have faeces attractive to females. *Anim. Behav.* 38:546-48.

Wells, K. D. 1980. Spatial associations among individuals in a population of slimy salamanders *(Plethodon glutinosus). Herpetologica* 36:271-75.

Wilbur, H. M. 1972. Competition, predation, and the structure of the *Ambystoma-Rana sylvatica* community. *Ecology* 53:3-21.

_____. 1977. Propagule size, number, and dispersion pattern in *Ambystoma* and *Ascelpias. Am. Nat.* 111:43-68.

Wrobel, D. J., W. F. Gergits, and R. G. Jaeger. 1980. An experimental study of interference competition among terrestrial salamanders. *Ecology* 61:1034-39.

18. Love Among the Frogs

Berven, K. A. 1981. Mate choice in the wood frog, *Rana sylvatica. Evolution* 35:707-22.

Berven, K. A., and T. A. Grudzien. 1990. Dispersal in the wood frog *(Rana sylvatica)*: Implications for genetic population structure. *Evolution* 44:2047-56.

Cornell, T. J., K. A. Berven, G. J. Gamboa. 1989. Kin recognition by tadpoles and froglets of the wood frog *Rana sylvatica. Oecologia* 78:312-16.

Costanzo, J. P., and R. E. Lee, Jr. 1991. Freeze-thaw injury in erythrocytes of the freeze-tolerant wood frog, *Rana sylvatica. Am. J. Physiol.* 261:R1346-50.

Davis, M. S., and G. W. Folkerts. 1986. Life history of the wood frog, *Rana sylvatica* LeConte (Amphibia: Ranidae) in Alabama. *Brimleyana* 12:29-50.

Dillard, A. 1974. *Pilgrim at Tinker Creek*. New York: Bantam Books.

Fellers, G. M. 1975. Behavioral interactions in North American treefrogs (Hylidae). *Chesapeake Sci.* 16:218-19.

_____. 1979. Aggression, territoriality, and mating behaviour in North American tree frogs. *Anim. Behav.* 27:107-19.

_____. 1979. Mate selection in the gray tree frog, *Hyla versicolor. Copeia* 1979:286-90.

Fishwild, T. G., R. A. Schemidt, K. M. Jankens, K. A. Berven, G. J. Gamboa, and C. M. Richards. 1990. Sibling recognition by larval frogs (*Rana pipiens, R. sylvatica,* and *Pseudacris crucifer*). *J. Herpetol.* 24:40-44.

Forester, D. C., and D. V. Lykens. 1988. The ability of wood frog eggs to withstand prolonged terrestrial stranding: An empirical study. *Can. J. Zool.* 66:1733-35.

Gamboa, G. J., K. A. Berven, R. A. Schemidt, T. G. Fishwild, and K. M. Jankens. 1991. Kin recognition by larval wood frogs (*Rana sylvatica*): Effects of diet and prior exposure to conspecifics. *Oecologia* 86:319-24.

Gatz, A. J. Jr. 1981. Size selective mating in *Hyla versicolor* and *Hyla crucifer. J. Herpetology* 15:114-16.

Gerhardt, H. C. 1978. Temperature coupling in the vocal communication system of the gray tree frog, *Hyla versicolor. Science* 199:992-94.

_____. 1982. Sound pattern recognition in some North American treefrogs (Anura: Hylidae): Implications for mate choice. *Amer. Zool.* 22:581-95.

_____. 1983. Acoustic communication in treefrogs. *Verh. Dtsch. Zool. Ges.* 1983:25-35.

Gerhardt, H. C., and G. M. Klump. 1988. Masking of acoustic signals by the chorus background noise in the green tree frog: A limitation on mate choice. *Anim Behav.* 36:1247-49.

Green, D. M., and J. Carson. 1988. The adhesion of treefrog toepads to glass: Cryogenic examination of a capillary adhesion system. *J. Natl. Hist.* 22:131-35.

Hopey, M. E., and J. W. Petranka. 1994. Restriction of wood frogs to fish-free habitats: How important is adult choice? *Copeia* 1994:1023-25.

Howard, R. D. 1980. Mating behaviour and mating success in wood frogs, *Rana sylvatica*. *Anim. Behav.* 28:705-16.

_____. Reproductive success in two species of anurans. *In: Reproductive success,* edited by T. Clutton-Brock. Chicago: Univ. of Chicago Press.

Howard, R. D., and A. G. Kluge. 1985. Proximate mechanisms of sexual selection in wood frogs. *Evolution* 39:260-77.

King, R. B., and B. King. 1991. Sexual differences in color and color change in wood frogs. *Can. J. Zool.* 69:1963-68.

Klump, G. M., and H. C. Gerhardt. 1987. Use of non-arbitrary acoustic criteria in mate choice by female gray tree frogs. *Nature* 326:286-88.

Morris, M. R. 1989. Female choice of large males in the treefrog *Hyla chrysoscelis*: The importance of identifying the scale of choice. *Behav. Ecol. Sociobiol.* 25:275-81.

Orians, G. H. 1969. On the evolution of mating systems in birds and mammals. *Am. Nat.* 103:589-603.

Perrill, S. A. 1984. Male mating behavior in *Hyla regilla*. *Copeia* 1984:727-32.

Perrill, S. A., H. C. Gerhardt, and R. Daniel. 1978. Sexual parasitism in the green tree frog (*Hyla cinerea*). *Science* 200:1179-80.

_____. 1982. Mating strategy shifts in male green treefrogs (*Hyla cinerea*): An experimental study. *Anim. Behav.* 30:43-48.

Petranka, J. W., and D. A. G. Thomas. 1995. Explosive breeding reduces egg and tadpole cannibalism in the wood frog, *Rana sylvatica*. *Anim. Behav.* 50:731-39.

Rautio, S. A., E. A. Bura, K. A. Berven, and G. J. Gamboa. 1991. Kin recognition in wood frog tadpoles (*Rana sylvatica*): Factors affecting spatial proximity to siblings. *Can. J. Zool.* 69:2569-71.

Ritke, M. E., and J. G. Babb. 1991. Behavior of the gray treefrog

(*Hyla chrysoscelis*) during the non-breeding season. *Herp. Rev.* 22:5-7.

Ritke, M. E., and R. D. Semlitsch. 1991. Mating behavior and determinants of male mating success in the gray treefrog, *Hyla chrysoscelis*. *Can. J. Zool.* 69:246-50.

Roble, S. M. 1985. Observations on satellite males in *Hyla chrysoscelis, Hyla picta*, and *Pseudacris triseriata*. *J. Herpetol.* 19:432-36.

Sullivan, B. K., and S. H. Hinshaw. 1992. Female choice and selection on male calling behaviour in the gray treefrog *Hyla versicolor*. *Anim. Behav.* 44:733-44.

Waldman, B. 1982. Adaptive significance of communal oviposition in wood frogs, *Rana sylvatica*. *Behav. Ecol. Sociobiol.* 10:169-74.

Waldman, B., and M. J. Ryan. 1983. Thermal advantages of communal egg mass deposition in wood frogs (*Rana sylvatica*). *J. Herpetol.* 17:70-72.

Welch, A. M., R. D. Semlitsch, and H. C. Gerhardt. 1998. Call duration as an indicator of genetic quality in male gray tree frogs. *Science* 280:1928-30.

Wells, K. D. 1977. The social behaviour of anuran amphibians. *Anim. Behav.* 25:666-93.

Woolbright, L. L., E. J. Greene, and G. C. Rapp. 1990. Density-dependent mate searching strategies of male woodfrogs. *Anim. Behav.* 40:135-42.

19. Box Turtle's Independence

Adams, N. A., D. C. Claussen, and J. Skillings. 1989. Effects of temperature on voluntary locomotion of the eastern box turtle, *Terrapene carolina carolina*. *Copeia* 1989:905-15.

Braun, J., and G. R. Brooks, Jr. 1987. Box turtles (*Terrapene carolina*) as potential agents for seed dispersal. *Am. Midl. Nat.* 117:312-18.

Claussen, D. L., P. M. Daniel, S. Jiang, and N. A. Adams. 1991. Hibernation in the eastern box turtle, *Terrapene c. carolina*. *J. Herpetol.* 25:334-41.

Congdon, J. D., and J. W. Gibbons. 1990. The evolution of turtle life histories. In *Life history and ecology of the slider turtle*, edited by J. W. Gibbons. Washington DC: Smithsonian Inst. Press.

Congdon, J. D., R. E. Gatten, Jr., and S. J. Morreale. 1989. Overwintering activity of box turtles (*Terrapene carolina*) in South Carolina. *J. Herpetol.* 23:179-81.

Costanzo, J. P., and D. L. Claussen. 1990. Natural freeze tolerance in the terrestrial turtle, *Terrapene carolina. J. Exptl. Zool.* 254:228-32.

Dolbeer, R. A. 1969. *A study of population density, seasonal movements and weight changes, and winter behavior of the eastern box turtle,* Terrapene c. carolina L., *in eastern Tennessee.* Master's thesis, University of Tennessee.

____. 1971. Winter behavior of the eastern box turtle, *Terrapene c. carolina*, in eastern Tennessee. *Copeia* 1971:758-60.

Gibbons, J. W. 1987. Why do turtles live so long? *BioScience* 37: 262-69.

Nichols, J. T. 1939. Data on size, growth, and age in the box turtle, *Terrapene carolina. Copeia* 1939:14-20.

Obbard, M. E., and R. J. Brooks. 1981. A radio-telemetry and mark-recapture study of activity in the common snapping turtle, *Chelydra serpentina. Copeia* 1981:630-37.

Schwartz, C. W., and E. R. Schwartz. 1974. The three-toed box turtle in central Missouri: Its population, home range, and movements. *Terrestrial Ser. No. 5.* Jefferson City, MO: Missouri Dept. Conserv.

Schwartz, E. R., and C. W. Schwartz. 1991. A quarter-century study of survivorship in a population of three-toed box turtles in Missouri. *Copeia* 1991:1120-23.

Schwartz, E. R., C. W. Schwartz, and A. R. Kiester. 1984. The three-toed box turtle in central Missouri, Part II: A nineteen-year study of home range, movements and population. *Terrestrial Ser. No. 12.* Jefferson City, MO: Missouri Dept. Conserv.

Stickel, L. F. 1950. Populations and home range relationships of the box turtle, *Terrapene c. carolina* (Linnaeus). *Ecol. Mono.* 20:351-78.

Strass, P. K., K. J. Miles, B. S. McDonald, and I. L. Brisbin. 1982. An assessment of factors associated with the daytime use of resting forms by eastern box turtles *(Terrapene carolina carolina)*. *J. Herpetol.* 16:320-22.

Stuart, M. D., and G. C. Miller. 1987. The eastern box turtle, *Terrapene c. carolina* (Testudines: Emydidae) in North Carolina. *Brimleyana* 13:123-31.

Wiens, J. A. 1977. On competition and variable environments. *Am. Sci.* 65:590-97.

Williams, E. C. Jr. 1961. A study of the box turtle, *Terrapene carolina carolina* (L.), population in Allee Memorial Woods. *Proc. Indiana Acad. Sci.* 71:399-406.

20. Copperhead's Year

Brown, W.S. 1982. Overwintering body temperatures of timber rattlesnakes *(Crotalus horridus)* in northeastern New York. *J. Herpetol.* 16:145-50.

Duvall, D., G. W. Schuett, and S. J. Arnold. 1993. Ecology and evolution of snake mating systems. In *Snakes — ecology and behavior*, edited by R. A. Seigel and J. T. Collins. New York: McGraw-Hill.

Fitch, H. S. 1960. Autecology of the copperhead. *Univ. Kansas Publ. Mus. Nat. History* 13:85-288.

Greene, H. W. 1997. *Snakes: The evolution of mystery in nature.* Berkeley, CA: Univ. of California Press.

Hubbell, S. 1986. *A country year: Living the questions.* New York: Random House.

Jackson, J. F., W. Ingram III, and H. W. Campbell. 1976. The dorsal pigmentation pattern of snakes as an antipredator strategy: A multivariate approach. *Am. Nat.* 110:1029-53.

Linzey, D. W., and M. J. Clifford. 1981. *Snakes of Virginia*. Charlottesville, VA: Univ. Press of Virginia.

Macartney, J. M., P. T. Gregory, and K. W. Larsen. 1988. A tabular survey of data on movements and home ranges of snakes. *J. Herpetol.* 22:61-73.

Mitchell, J. C. 1994. *The reptiles of Virginia*. Washington, DC: Smithsonian Inst. Press.

Reinert, H. K. 1984. Habitat separation between sympatric snake populations. *Ecology* 65:478-86.

____. 1984. Habitat variation within sympatric snake populations. *Ecology* 65:1673-82.

Schuett, G. W., and J. C. Gillingham. 1986. Sperm storage and multiple paternity in the copperhead, *Agkistrodon contortrix*. *Copeia* 1986:807-11.

____. 1988. Courtship and mating of the copperhead, *Agkistrodon contortrix*. *Copeia* 1988:374-81.

Schwenk, K. 1994. Why snakes have forked tongues. *Science* 263:1573-77.

Seigel, R. A., and H. S. Fitch. 1985. Annual variation in reproduction in snakes in a fluctuating environment. *J. Anim. Ecol.* 54:497-505.

Shine, R. 1978. Sexual size dimorphism and male combat in snakes. *Oecologia* 33:269-77.

Shine, R., and J. J. Bull. 1977. Skewed sex ratios in snakes. *Copeia* 1977:228-34.

____. 1979. The evolution of live-bearing in lizards and snakes. *Am. Nat.* 113:905-23.

Shively, S. H., and J. C. Mitchell. 1994. Male combat in copperheads (*Agkistrodon contortrix*) from northern Virginia. *Banisteria* 3:29-30.

Smith, R. L., ed. 1985. *Sperm competition and the evolution of animal mating systems*. New York: Academic Press.

Weinstein, S. A., P. J. Lafaye, and L. A. Smith. 1991. Observations on a venom neutralizing fraction isolated from serum of the

314

northern copperhead, *Agkistrodon contortrix mokasen*. *Copeia* 1991:777-86.

21. Oaks and Squirrels

Allen, D. L. 1942. Populations and habits of the fox squirrel in Allegan County, Michigan. *Am. Midl. Nat.* 27:338-79.

Allen, D. S. and W. P. Aspey. 1986. Determinants of social dominance in eastern gray squirrels (*Sciurus carolinensis*): A quantitative assessment. *Anim. Behav.* 34:81-89.

Baker, R. H. 1944. An ecological study of tree squirrels in eastern Texas. *J. Mammal.* 25:8-24.

Brown, L. G., and L. E. Yaeger. 1945. Fox and gray squirrels in Illinois. *Ill. Nat. Hist. Surv.* 23:449-532.

Cahalane, V. H. 1942. Caching and recovery of food by the western fox squirrel. *J. Wildl. Mngmt.* 6:338-52.

Fitzwater, W. D., and W. J. Frank. 1944. Leaf nests of gray squirrels in Connecticut. *J. Mammal.* 25:160-70.

Gorman, O. T., and R. R. Roth. 1989. Consequences of a temporarily and spatially variable food supply for an unexploited gray squirrel (*Sciurus carolinensis*) population. *Am. Midl. Nat.* 121:41-60.

Heinrich, B. 1997. *The trees in my forest*. New York, NY: HarperCollins.

Jacobs, L. 1989. Cache economy of the gray squirrel. *Natural History* 10:41-46.

____. 1992. The effect of handling time on the decision to cache by gray squirrels. *Anim. Behav.* 43:522-24.

Janzen, D. H. 1971. Seed predation by animals. *Ann. Rev. Ecol. Syst.* 2:465-92.

Koprowski, J. L. 1992. Do estrous female gray squirrels, *Sciurus carolinensis*, advertise their receptivity? *Canad. Fld-Nat.* 106:392-94.

____. 1992. Removal of copulatory plugs by female tree squirrels. *J. Mammal.* 73:572-76.

_____. 1993. Alternative reproductive tactics in male eastern gray squirrels: "Making the best of a bad job." *Behav. Ecol.* 4:165-71.

_____. 1993. The role of kinship in field interactions among juvenile gray squirrels (*Sciurus carolinensis*). *Can. J. Zool.* 71:224-26.

Lewis, A. R. 1980. Patch use by gray squirrels and optimal foraging. *Ecology* 61:1371-79.

Lishak, R. S. 1982. Gray squirrel mating calls: A spectrographic and ontogenic analysis. *J. Mammal.* 63:661-63.

_____. 1984. Alarm vocalizations of adult gray squirrels. *J. Mammal.* 65:681-84.

Moller, H. 1983. Foods and foraging behavior of red (*Sciurus vulgaris*) and grey (*Sciurus carolinensis*) squirrels. *Mammal Rev.* 13:81-98.

Newman, J. A., and T. Caraco. 1987. Foraging, predation hazard and patch use in grey squirrels. *Anim. Behav.* 35:1804-13.

Newman, J. A., G. M. Recer, S. M. Zwicker, and T. Caraco. 1988. Effects of predation hazard on foraging "constraints": Patch-use strategies in gray squirrels. *Oikos* 53:93-97.

Nixon, C. M., M. W. McClain, and R. W. Donohoe. 1975. Effects of hunting and mast crops on a squirrel population. *J. Wildl. Mngmt.* 39:1-25.

Palmer, W. L. 1998. Acorn production in a mixed-oak stand in central Pennsylvania: Twenty-seven years of data. Final Report for Project 06210, Job 21004, Pennsylvania Game Comm., Harrisburg, PA.

Pasitschniak-Arts, M., and J. F. Bendell. 1990. Behavioural differences between locally recruiting and dispersing gray squirrels, *Sciurus carolinensis. Can. J. Zool.* 68:935-41.

Peattie, D. C. 1948. *A natural history of trees of eastern and central North America.* Boston, MA: Houghton Mifflin.

Sharp, W. M., and V. G. Sprague. 1967. Flowering and fruiting in the white oaks: Pistillate flowering, acorn development, weather, and yields. *Ecology* 48:243-51.

Shettleworth, S. J. 1983. Memory in food-hoarding birds. *Sci. Am.* 248 (3):102-10.

Smallwood, P. D., and W. D. Peters. 1986. Gray squirrel food preferences: The effects of tannin and fat concentration. *Ecology* 67:168-74.

Sork, V. L., J. Bramble, and O. Sexton. 1993. Ecology of mast fruiting in three species of North American deciduous oaks. *Ecology* 74: 528-41.

Stapanian, M. A., and C. C. Smith. 1978. A model for seed scatterhoarding: Coevolution of fox squirrels and black walnuts. *Ecology* 59:884-96.

_____. 1984. Density-dependent survival of scatterhoarded nuts: An experimental approach. *Ecology* 65:1387-96.

Thompson, D. C. 1978. Regulation of a northern grey squirrel (*Sciurus carolinensis*) population. *Ecology* 59:708-15.

Uhlig, H. G. 1956. *The gray squirrel: Its life hostory, ecology, and population characteristics in West Virginia*. Pittman-Robertson Project 31-R. Charleston, WV: Conservation Commission of West Virginia.

Weckerly, F. W., K. E. Nicholson, and R. D. Semlitsch. 1989. Experimental test of discrimination by squirrels for insect-infested and noninfested acorns. *Am. Midl. Nat.* 122:412-15.

Weigl, P. D., and E. V. Hanson. 1980. Observational learning and the feeding behavior of the red squirrel *Tamiasciurus hudsonicus*: The ontogeny of optimization. *Ecology* 61:213-18.

22. Highlanders

Adams, N. 2001. *Far Appalachia: following the New River north*. New York: Delacorte Press.

Adovasio, J. M., and J. Page. 2002. *The first Americans: in pursuit of archaeology's greatest mystery*. New York: The Modern Library.

Barlow, C. 2000. *The ghosts of evolution: nonsensical fruit, missing partners, and other ecological anachronisms*. New York: Basic Books.

Catlin, D. T. 1984. Cited in Chp. 1.

Caudill, H. M. 1962. *Night comes to the Cumberlands*. Boston: Little, Brown.

Cunningham, R. 1987. *Apples on the flood: Minority discourse and Appalachia*. Knoxville, TN: Univ. of Tennessee Press.

Day, G. M. 1953. The Indian as an ecological factor in the northeastern forest. *Ecology* 34:329-46.

Diamond, J. M. 1987. Who were the first Americans? *Nature* 329:580-81.

Dillard, A. 1974. *Pilgrim at Tinker Creek*. New York: Bantam Books.

Dykeman, W., and J. Stokely. 1995. The people and the land. *Appalachia* 28(1&2):1-11.

Frazier, C. 1997. *Cold Mountain*. New York: Atlantic Monthly Press.

Gaventa, J. 1980. *Power and powerlessness: Quiescence and rebellion in an Appalachian Valley*. Urbana, IL: Univ. of Illinois Press.

Giardina, D. 1989. *Storming Heaven*. New York: Ivy Books.

Kephart, H. 1976. *Our southern highlanders*. Knoxville, TN: Univ. of Tennessee Press.

Krech, S., III. 1999. *The ecological Indian: Myth and history*. New York: Norton.

Lewis, R. L. 1998. *Transforming the Appalachian countryside: Railroads, deforestation, and social change in West Virginia 1880-1920*. Chapel Hill, NC: Univ. of North Carolina Press.

MacNeil, M. 1975. A Shenandoah Story: A song and narrative on the record album *Shenandoah Spring*. Westview Music, BMI. Available from Skyline Records, Rt. 1, Box 57, Swoope, VA 24479.

McMichael, E. V. 1968. *Introduction to West Virginia archeology*. Morgantown, WV: West Virginia Geol. and Econ. Surv.

McPhee, J. 1983. *In suspect terrain*. New York: Farrar, Straus, and Giroux.

Miles, E. B. [1905] 1975. *The spirit of the mountains*. Knoxville, TN: Univ. of Tennessee Press.

Moize, E. A. 1985. Daniel Boone, first hero of the frontier. *Natl. Geogr.* 168 (6):812-41.

Moore, J. A. 1985. Science as a way of knowing II — Human ecology. *Amer. Zool.* 25:483-637.

O'Brien, J. 2001. *At home in the heart of Appalachia.* New York: Knopf.

Parton, D. 1994. *Dolly: My life and other unfinished business.* New York: HarperCollins.

Pudup, M. B., D. B. Billings, and A. L. Waller, eds. 1995. *Appalachia in the making: The mountain south in the nineteenth century.* Chapel Hill, NC: Univ. of North Carolina Press.

Pyne, S. J. 1983. Indian fires. *Natural History* 92 (2):6-11.

Scherman, T. 1985. A man who mined musical gold in the southern hills. *Smithsonian* 16 (1):173-96.

Shapiro, H. D. 1978. *Appalachia on our mind: The southern mountains and mountaineers in the American consciousness, 1870-1920.* Chapel Hill, NC: Univ. of North Carolina Press.

Smith, B. D. 1989. Origins of agriculture in eastern North America. *Science* 246:1566-71.

Thornborough, L. 1937. *The Great Smoky Mountains.* New York: Thomas Y. Crowell.

Weller, J. E. 1965. *Yesterday's people: Life in contemporary Appalachia.* Lexington, KY: Univ. Press of Kentucky.

Williams, J. A. 2002. *Appalachia: A history.* Chapel Hill, NC: Univ. of North Carolina Press.

Wigginton, E. 1972. *The foxfire book.* Garden City, NY: Anchor Press-Doubleday.

____. 1975. *Foxfire 3.* Garden City, NY: Anchor Press-Doubleday.

Wolfram, W. and N. Schilling-Estes. 1998. *American English: Dialects and variation.* Malden, MA: Blackwell.

23. Autumn Leaves

Escudero, A., and J. M. del Arco. 1987. Ecological significance of the phenology of leaf abscission. *Oikos* 49:11-14.

Fluchel, R. W. 1988. Tell autumn trees by color. *Missouri Conservationist*, October: 10-15.

Hendry, G. 1988. Where does all the green go? *New Scientist* 120(November 5):38-42.

Jacobs, W. P. 1955. What makes leaves fall? *Sci. Am.*, November: 3-7.

Kimball, J. W. 1983. *Biology*, 5th ed. Menlo Park, CA: Benjamin/Cummings.

Niklas, K. J. 1992. *Plant biomechanics: an engineering approach to plant form and function*. Chicago, IL: Univ. of Chicago Press.

_____. 1997. *The evolutionary biology of plants*. Chicago IL: Univ. of Chicago Press.

Northington, D. K., and J. R. Goodin. 1984. *The botanical world*. St. Louis, MO: Times Mirror/Mosby College.

Patit, C. W. 2002. Autumn's crimson tide. *US News & World Report*, October 14, 70.

Raven, P. H., and H. Curtis. 1970. *Biology of plants*. New York: Worth.

Smith, T. 1991. Nature's procrastinators. *Missouri Conservationist*, November: 22-23.

USDA FS. 1977. *Autumn colors* (poster). USDA Forest Service, Southern Region. Distributed by Div. Forestry, WV Dept. Natural Resources.

24. Window on Bird Politics

Alcock, J. 1984. Cited in Chp. 1.

Baker, C. M., C. S. Belcher, L. G. Deutsch, G. L. Sherman, and D. B. Thompson. 1981. Foraging success in *Junco* flocks and the effects of social hierarchy. *Anim. Behav.* 29:137-42.

Baker, M. C., and S. F. Fox. 1978. Dominance, survival and enzyme polymorphism in dark-eyed juncos, *Junco hyemalis*. *Evolution* 32:697-711.

Balph, M. H. 1977. Winter social behaviour of dark-eyed juncos: Communication, social organization and ecological implications. *Anim. Behav.* 25:859-84.

Balph, M. H., D. F. Balph, and H. C. Romesburg. 1979. Social status signaling in winter flocking bird: An examination of current hypothesis. *Auk* 96:78-93.

Barash, D. P. 1974. An advantage of winter flocking in the black-capped chickadee, *Parus atricapillus*. *Ecology* 55:674-76.

Berner, T. O., and T. C. Grubb, Jr. 1985. An experimental analysis of mixed-species flocking in birds of deciduous woodland. *Ecology* 66:1229-36.

Brawn, J. D., and F. B. Samson. 1983. Winter behavior of tufted titmice. *Wilson Bull.* 95:222-32.

Caraco, T. 1982. Flock size and the organization of behavioral sequences in juncos. *Condor* 84:101-05.

Caraco, T., and S. L. Lima. 1985. Foraging juncos: Interaction of reward mean and variability. *Anim. Behav.* 33:216-24.

Caraco, T., S. Martindale, and H. R. Pulliam. 1980. Avian flocking in the presence of a predator. *Nature* 285:400-01.

Charnov, E. L., and J. R. Krebs. 1975. The evolution of alarm calls: altruism or manipulation? *Am. Nat.* 109:107-12.

Cimprich, D. A., and T. C. Grubb, J. 1994. Consequences for Carolina chickadees of foraging with tufted titmice in winter. *Ecology* 75:1615-25.

Czikeli, H. 1983. Agonistic interactions within a winter flock of slate-coloured juncos (*Junco hyemalis*): Evidence for the dominants' strategy. *Z. Tierpsychol.* 61:61-66.

Dugatkin, L. A. 1997. *Cooperation among animals: An evolutionary perspective*. New York: Oxford Univ. Press.

Fretwell, S. 1969. Dominance behaviour and winter habitat distribution in juncos (*Junco hyemalis*). *Bird-banding* 40:1-25.

Gill, F. B. 1990. *Ornithology*. New York: Freeman.

Glase, T. C. 1973. Ecology of social organization in the black-capped chickadee. *Living Bird* 12:235-67.

Gluck, E. 1986. Flock size and habitat-dependent food and energy intake of foraging goldfinches. *Oecologia* 71:149-55.

Hamilton, W. D. 1971. Geometry for the selfish herd. *J. Theor. Biol.* 31:295-311.

Hartzler, J. E. 1970. Winter dominance relationships in black-capped chickadees. *Wilson Bull.* 82:427-34.

Hill, G. E. 1986. The function of distress calls given by tufted titmice (*Parus bicolor*): An experimental approach. *Anim. Behav.* 34:590-98.

Hutto, R. L. 1988. Foraging behavior patterns suggest a possible cost associated with participation in mixed-species bird flocks. *Oikos* 51:79-83.

Ketterson, E. D. 1979. Aggressive behavior in wintering dark-eyed juncos: Determinants of dominance and their possible relation to geographic variation in the sex-ratio. *Wilson Bull.* 91:371-83.

_____. 1979. Status signalling in dark-eyed juncos. *Auk* 96:94-99.

Lima, S. L. 1984. Downy woodpecker foraging behavior: Efficient sampling in simple stochastic environments. *Ecology* 65:166-74.

Loery, G., and J. D. Nichols. 1985. Dynamics of a black-capped chickadee population, 1958-1983. *Ecology* 66:1195-1203.

Moller, A. P. 1988. False alarm calls as a means of resource usurpation in the great tit *Parus major*. *Ethology* 79:25-30.

Morse, D. H. 1970. Ecological aspects of some mixed-species foraging flocks of birds. *Ecol. Mono.* 40:130-68.

_____. 1980. *Behavioral mechanisms in ecology*. Cambridge, MA: Harvard Univ. Press.

Piper, W. H. 1990. Exposure to predators and access to food in wintering white-throated sparrows *Zonotrichia albicollis*. *Behav.* 112:284-98.

_____. 1990. Site tenacity and dominance in wintering white-throated sparrows *Zonotrichia albicollis*. (Passeriformes: Emberizidae). *Ethology* 85:114-22.

Piper, W. H., and R. H. Wiley. 1990. The relationship between social dominance, subcutaneous fat, and annual survival in wintering white-throated sparrows (*Zonotrichia albicollis*). *Behav. Ecol. Sociobiol.* 26:201-08

Popp, J. W. 1988. Scanning behavior of finches in the mixed-species groups. *Condor* 90:510-12.

Roberts, R. C. 1979. The evolution of avian food-storing behavior. *Am. Nat.* 114:418-38.

Rowher, S., and P. W. Ewald. 1981. The cost of dominance and advantages of subordination in a badge signaling system. *Evolution* 35:441-54.

Schneider, K. J. 1984. Dominance, predation, and optimal foraging in white-throated sparrows. *Ecology* 65:1820-27.

Smith, S. M. 1984. Flock switching in chickadees: Why be a winter floater? *Am. Nat.* 123:81-98.

_____. 1985. The tiniest established permanent floater crap game in the northeast. *Natural History* 3:43-47.

Sullivan, K. 1985. Selective alarm calling by downy woodpeckers in mixed-species flocks. *Auk* 102:184-87.

Waite, T. A., 1987. Vigilance in the white-breasted nuthatch: Effects of dominance and sociality. *Auk* 104:429-34.

Waite, T. A., and T. C. Grubb, Jr. 1988. Copying of foraging locations in mixed-species flocks of temperate-deciduous woodland birds: An experimental study. *Condor* 90:132-40.

Watt, D. J., C. J. Ralph, and C. T. Atkinson. 1984. The role of plumage polymorphism in dominance relationships of the white-throated sparrow. *Auk* 101:110-20.

25. Thwarting Swords of Ice

Carey, C., and R.L. Marsh. 1981. Shivering finches. *Natural History* 90:58-63.

Costanzo, J. P., and R. E. Lee, Jr. 1991. Freeze-thaw injury in erythrocytes of the freeze-tolerant wood frog, *Rana sylvatica*. *Am. J. Physiol.* 261:R1346-50.

Costanzo, J. P., R. E. Lee, Jr., and M. F. Wright. 1991. Effect of cooling rate on the survival of frozen wood frogs, *Rana sylvatica*. *J. Comp. Physiol.* B:225-29.

_____. 1991. Glucose loading prevents freezing injury in rapidly cooled wood frogs. *Am. J. Physiol.* 261:R1549-53.

_____. 1992. Cooling rate influences cryoprotectant distribution and organ dehydration in freezing wood frogs. *J. Exptl. Zool.* 261:373-78.

Dethier, V. G. 1980. *The world of the tent-makers: A natural history of the eastern tent caterpillar*. Amherst, MA: Univ. of Massachusetts Press.

Emery, A. R., A. H. Berst, and K. Kodaira. 1972. Under-ice observations of wintering sites of lepoard frogs. *Copeia* 1972:123-26.

Fitzpatrick, L. C. 1976. Life history patterns of storage and utilization of lipids for energy in amphibians. *Amer. Zool.* 16:725-32.

George, M. F., S. G. Hong, and M. J. Burke. 1977. Cold hardiness and deep supercooling of hardwoods: Its occurrence in provenance collections of red oak, yellow birch, black walnut, and black cherry. *Ecology* 58:674-80.

Hamilton, W. J., Jr. 1934. The life history of the rufescent woodchuck, *Marmota monax rufescens* Howell. *Ann. Carnegie Museum* 23:85-178.

Heinrich, B., and T. P. Mommsen. 1985. Flight of winter moths near 0° C. *Science* 228:177-79.

Heinrich, B. 2003. *Winter world: the ingenuity of animal survival*. New York: HarperCollins.

Layne, J. R., Jr., and R. E. Lee, Jr. 1987. Freeze tolerance and the dynamics of ice formation in wood frogs (*Rana sylvatica*) from southern Ohio. *Can .J. Zool.* 65:2062-65.

Layne, J. R., Jr., R. E. Lee, Jr., and T. L. Heil. 1989. Freezing-induced changes in the heart rate of wood frogs (*Rana sylvatica*). *Am. J. Physiol.* 257:R1046-49.

Layne, J. R., Jr., R. E. Lee, Jr., and J. L. Huang. 1990. Inoculation triggers freezing at high subzero temperatures in a freeze-tolerant frog (*Rana sylvatica*) and insect (*Eurosta solidaginis*). *Can. J. Zool.* 68:506-10.

Marchand, P. J. 1987. *Life in the cold.* Hanover, NH: University Press of New England.

Moen, A. N. 1968. Energy exchange of white-tailed deer, western Minnesota. *Ecology* 49:676-82.

_____. 1976. Energy conservation by white-tailed deer in the winter. *Ecology* 57:192-98.

Moen, A. N., and C. W. Severinghaus. 1984. Hair depths of the winter coat of white-tailed deer. *J. Mammal.* 65:497-99.

Schmid, W. D. 1982. Survival of frogs in low temperature. *Science* 215:697-98.

Schmidt-Nielsen, K. 1981. Countercurrent systems in animals. *Sci. Amer.* 244:118-28.

Sutton, A., and M. Sutton. 1985. Cited in Chp. 2.

Thorkelson, J., and R. K. Maxwell. 1974. Design and testing of a heat transfer model of a raccoon (*Procyon lotor*) in a closed tree den. *Ecology* 55:29-39.

Ultsch, G. R., R. W. Hanley, and T. R. Bauman. 1985. Responses to anoxia during simulated hibernation in northern and southern painted turtles. *Ecology* 66:388-95.

Walker, J. 1986. The amateur scientist: Exotic patterns appear in water when it is freezing or melting. *Sci. Am.* 255 (1):114-19.

26. Spring Tensions

Bonta, M. 1991. *Appalachian spring*. Pittsburgh, PA: Univ. of Pittsburgh Press.

Catlin, D. T. 1984. Cited in Chp. 1.

Schemske, D. W., M. F. Willson, M. N. Melampy, L. J. Miller, L. Verner, K. M. Schemske, and L. D. Best. 1978. Flowering ecology of some spring woodland herbs. *Ecology* 59:351-66.

27. Dawn Chorus

Baker, M. C., and M. A. Cunningham. 1985. The biology of birdsong dialects. *Behav. and Brain Sci.* 8:85-133.

Baker, M. C., T. K. Bjerke, H. Lampe, and Y. Espmark. 1986. Sexual Response of female great tits to variation in size of male's song repertoires. *Am. Nat.* 128:491-98.

Baptista, L. F., and L. Petrinovich. 1984. Social interaction, sensitive phases and the song template hypothesis in the white-crowned sparrow. *Anim. Behav.* 32:172-81.

Beletsky, L. D. 1989. Communication and the cadence of birdsong. *Am. Midl. Nat.* 122:298-306.

Best, L. B. 1977. Territory quality and mating success in the field sparrow (*Spizella pusilla*). *Condor* 79:192-204.

Brooks, R. J., and J. B. Falls. 1975. Individual recognition in white-throated sparrows. I. Discrimination of songs of neighbors and strangers. *Can. J. Zool.* 53:879-88.

_____. 1975. Individual recognition by song in white-throated sparrows. III. Song features used in individual recognition. *Can. J. Zool.* 53:1749-61.

Brown, J. H., and G. H. Orians. 1970. Spacing patterns in mobile animals. *Ann. Rev. Ecol. Syst.* 1:239-62.

Brown, J. L. 1964. The evolution of diversity in avian territorial systems. *Wilson Bull.* 76:160-69.

_____. 1969. Territorial behavior and population regulation in birds. *Wilson Bull.* 81:293-329.

Burger, J. 1981. Super territories: A comment. *Am. Nat.* 118:578-80.

Calder, W. A., III. 1990. The scaling of sound output and territory size: are they matched? *Ecology* 71:1810-16.

Carey, M., and V. Nolan, Jr. 1975. Polygyny in indigo buntings. *Science* 190:1296-97.

Catchpole, C. K. 1987. Birdsong, sexual selection and female choice. *TREE* 2:94-97.

Date, E. M., and R. E. Lemon. 1993. Sound transmission: A basis for dialects in birdsong? *Behaviour* 124:291-312.

Emlen, S. T. 1971. The role of song in individual recognition in the indigo bunting. *Z. Tierpsychol.* 28:241-46.

Falls, J. B., and R. J. Brooks. 1975. Individual recognition by song in white-throated sparrows. II. Effects of location. *Can. J. Zool.* 53:1412-20.

Fergus, C. 1984. *The wingless crow.* Harrisburg, PA.: Penn. Game Comm.

Ficken, M. S. 1981. What is the song of the black-capped chickadee? *Condor* 83:384-86.

Ficken, M. S., and C. M. Weise. 1984. A complex call of the black-capped chickadee (*Parus atricapillus*). I. Microgeographic variation. *Auk* 101:349-60.

Ficken, M. S., R. W. Ficken, and K. M. Apel. 1985. Dialects in a call associated with pair interactions in the black-capped chickadee. *Auk* 102:145-51.

Ficken, R. W., M. S. Ficken, and J. P. Hailman. 1974. Temporal pattern shifts to avoid acoustic interference in singing birds. *Science* 183:762-63.

Ficken, R. W., J. W. Popp, and P. E. Matthiae. 1985. Avoidance of acoustic interference by ovenbirds. *Wilson Bull.* 97:569-71.

Greenlaw, J. S. 1978. The relation of breeding schedule and clutch size to food supply in the rufous-sided towhee. *Condor*

80:24-33.

Henwood, K., and A. Fabrick. 1979. A quantitative analysis of the dawn chorus: Temporal selection for communicatory optimization. *Am. Nat.* 114:260-74.

Hogstedt, G. 1980. Evolution of clutch size in birds: Adaptive variation in relation to territory quality. *Science* 210:1148-50.

Kiester, E., Jr., and W. Kiester. 2002. Birdbrain breakthrough. *Smithsonian* 33(3):36-38.

Kroodsma, D. E. 1976. Reproductive development in a female songbird: Differential stimulation by quality of male song. *Science* 192:574-75.

_____. 1977. Correlates of song organization among North American wrens. *Am. Nat.* 111:995-1008.

_____. 1985. Development and use of two song forms by the eastern phoebe. *Wilson Bull.* 97:21-29.

Kroodsma, D. E., and B. E. Byers. 1991. The function(s) of bird song. *Amer. Zool.* 31:318-328.

Lambrechts, M., and A. A. Dhondt. 1988. The anti-exhaustion hypothesis: A new hypothesis to explain song performance and song switching in the great tit. *Anim. Behav.* 36:327-34.

Mace, R. 1986. Importance of female behaviour in the dawn chorus. *Anim. Behav.* 34:621-22.

Marler, P., and S. Peters. 1982. Long-term storage of learned birdsongs prior to production. *Anim. Behav.* 30:479-82.

Marler, P., and R. Pickert. 1984. Species-universal microstructure in the learned song of the swamp sparrow (*Melospiza georgiana*). *Anim. Behav.* 32:673-89.

Marler, P., and V. Sherman. 1985. Innate differences in singing behaviour of sparrows reared in isolation from adult conspecific song. *Anim. Behav.* 33:57-71.

McGregor, P. K., J. R. Krebs, and C. M. Perrins. 1981. Song repertoires and lifetime reproductive success in the great tit (*Parus major*). *Am. Nat.* 118:149-59.

Morton, E. S. 1975. Ecological sources of selection on avian sounds. *Am. Nat.* 109:17-34.

Murray, B. G. Jr. 1971. The ecological consequences of interspecific territorial behavior in birds. *Ecology* 52:414-23.

Nottebohm, F. 1989. From bird song to neurogenesis. *Sci. Am.* 260 (Feb):74-79.

Orians, G. H., and M. F. Willson. 1964. Interspecific territories of birds. *Ecology* 45:736-45.

Payne, R. B. 1981. Population structure and social behavior: models for testing the ecological significance of song dialects in birds. In *Natural selection and social behavior,* edited by R. D. Alexander and D.W. Tinkle. New York: Chiron Press.

_____. 1982. Ecological consequences of song matching: Breeding success and intraspecific mimicry in indigo buntings. *Ecology* 63: 401-11.

_____. 1983. The social context of song mimicry: Song-matching dialects in indigo buntings *(Passerina cyanea). Anim. Behav.* 31: 788-805.

Petrinovich, L., and L. F. Baptista. 1984. Song dialects, mate selection, and breeding success in white-crowned sparrows. *Anim. Behav.* 32:1078-88.

Petrinovich, L., and T. L. Patterson. 1981. The responses of white-crowned sparrows to songs of different dialects and subspecies. *Z. Tierpsychol.* 57:1-14.

Popp, J. W., R. W. Ficken, and J. A. Reinartz. 1985. Short-term avoidance of interspecific acoustic interference among forest birds. *Auk* 102: 744-48.

Rice, J. 1978. Ecological relationships of two interspecifically territorial vireos. *Ecology* 59: 526-38.

Richards, G. D., and R. H. Wiley. 1980. Reverberations and amplitude fluctuations in the propagation of sound in a forest: Implications for animal communication. *Am. Nat.* 115:381-99.

Ritchison, G. 1988. Responses of yellow-breasted chats to the songs of neighboring and non-neighboring conspecifics. *J. Field Ornithol.* 59:37-42.

Ryan, M. J., and E. A. Brenowitz. 1985. The role of body size, phylogeny, and ambient noise in the evolution of bird song. *Am. Nat.* 126:87-100.

Schoener, T. W. 1968. Sizes of feeding territories among birds. *Ecology* 49:123-41.

Searcy, W. A. 1984. Song repertoire size and female preferences in song sparrows. *Behav. Ecol. Sociobiol.* 14:281-86.

_____. 1992. Song repertoire and mate choice in birds. *Amer. Zool.* 32:71-80.

Searcy, W. A., and P. Marler. 1984. Interspecific differences in the response of female birds to song repertoires. *Z. Tierpsychol.* 66:128-42.

Searcy, W. A., and M. Andersson. 1986. Sexual selection and the evolution of song. *Ann. Rev. Ecol. Syst.* 17:507-33.

Searcy, W. A., P. D. McArthur, and K. Yasukawa. 1985. Song repertoire size and male quality in song sparrows. *Condor* 87:222-28.

Simpson, B. S. 1985. Effects of location in territory and distance from neighbours on the use of song repertoires by Carolina wrens. *Anim. Behav.* 33:793-804.

Slater, P. J. B. 1986. The cultural transmission of bird song. *TREE* 1:94-97.

_____. 1989. Bird song learning: causes and consequences. *Ethol. Ecol. & Evol.* 1:19-46.

Smith, W. J. 1977. *The behavior of communicating: An ethological approach.* Cambridge, MA: Harvard Univ. Press.

Trainer, J. M. 1983. Changes in song dialect distributions and microgeographic variation in song of white-crowned sparrows (*Zonotrichia leucophrys nuttalli*). *Auk* 100:568-82.

Verner, J. 1977. On the adaptive significance of territoriality. *Am.*

Nat. 111:769-75.

Weary, D. M., K. J. Norris, and J. B. Falls. 1990. Song features birds use to identify individuals. *Auk* 107:623-25.

Weary, D. M., R. E. Lemon, and S. Perreault. 1992. Song repertoires do not hinder neighbor-strange discrimination. *Behav. Ecol. Sociobiol.* 31:441-47.

Weeden, J. S., and J. B. Falls. 1959. Differential responses of male ovenbirds to recorded songs of neighboring and more distant individuals. *Auk* 76:343-51.

Whitney, C. L. 1991. Avoidance of song matching in the wood thrush: a field experiment. *Wilson Bull.* 103:96-101.

Yasukawa, K., and W. A. Searcy. 1985. Song repertoires and density assessment in red-winged blackbirds: Further tests of the Beau Geste hypothesis. *Behav. Ecol. Sociobiol.* 16:171-75.

28. Trees and Caterpillars

Adler, F. R., and C. D. Harvell. 1990. Inducible defenses, phenotypic variability and biotic environments. *TREE* 5:407-10.

Baldwin, I. T., and J. C. Schultz. 1983. Rapid changes in tree leaf chemistry induced by damage: evidence for communication between plants. *Science* 221:277-79.

Belsky, A. J. 1986. Does herbivory benefit plants? A review of the evidence. *Am. Nat.* 127:870-92.

Berenbaum, M. R., and A. R. Zangerl. 1994. Costs of inducible defense: Protein limitation, growth, and detoxification in parsnip webworms. *Ecology* 75:2311-17.

Dethier, V. G. 1980. *The world of the tent-makers: A natural history of the eastern tent caterpillar.* Amherst, MA: Univ. of Massachusetts Press.

Edwards, P. B., and W. J. Wanjura. 1989. Eucalypt-feeding insects bite off more than they can chew: Sabotage of induced defences? *Oikos* 54:246-48.

Edwards, P. J., and S. D. Wratten. 1982. Wound-induced changes in palatability in birch *(Betula pubescens* Ehrh. ssp. *pubescens). Am. Nat.* 120:816-18.

Fitzgerald, T. D. 1983. Caterpillar on a silken thread. *Natural History* 92:56-63.

Fowler, S. V., and J. H. Lawton. 1985. Rapidly induced defenses and talking trees: The devil's advocate position. *Am. Nat.* 126:181-95.

Freeland, W. J., and D. H. Janzen. 1974. Strategies in herbivory by mammals: The role of plant secondary compounds. *Am. Nat.* 108:269-89.

Harvell, C. D. 1990. The ecology and evolution of inducible defenses. *Quart. Rev. Biol.* 65:323-40.

Haukioja, E. 1980. On the role of plant defences in the fluctuation of herbivore populations. *Oikos* 35:202-13.

Haukioja, E., and S. Neuvonen. 1985. Induced long-term resistance of birch foliage against defoliators: Defensive or incidental? *Ecology* 66:1303-08.

Haukioja, E., and P. Niemela. 1977. Retarded growth of a geometrid larva after mechanical damage to leaves of its host tree. *Ann. Zool. Fennici* 14:48-52.

_____. 1979. Birch leaves as a resource for herbivores: Seasonal occurrence of increased resistance in foliage after mechanical damage of adjacent leaves. *Oecologia* 39:151-59.

Haukioja, E., J. Suomela, and S. Neuvonen. 1985. Long-term inducible resistance in birch foliage: Triggering cues and efficacy on a defoliator. *Oecologia* 65:363-69.

Heichel, G. H., and N. C. Turner. 1984. Branch growth and leaf numbers of red maple *(Acer rubrum* L.) and red oak *(Quercus rubra* L.): Response to defoliation. *Oecologia* 62:1-6.

Holmes, R. T., J. C. Schultz, and P. Nothnagle. 1979. Bird predation on forest insects: An exclosure experiment. *Science* 206:462-63.

Hunter, M. D., and J. C. Schultz. 1995. Fertilization mitigates chemical induction and herbivore responses within damaged oak trees. *Ecology* 76:1226-32.

Karban, R., and I. T. Baldwin. 1997. *Induced responses to herbivory.* Chicago, IL: Univ. of Chicago Press.

Karban, R., and J. H. Myers. 1989. Induced plant responses to herbivory. *Ann. Rev. Ecol. & Syst.* 20:331-48.

Lewis, W. H., R .L. Oliver, and T. K. Luikart. 1971. Multiple genotypes in individuals of *Claytonia virginiana. Science* 172:564-65.

Morse, D. H. 1971. The insectivorous bird as an adaptive strategy. *Ann. Rev. Ecol. Syst.* 2:177-200.

Neuvonen, S., and K. Danell. 1987. Does browsing modify the quality of birch foliage for *Epirrita autumnata* larvae? *Oikos* 49:156-60.

Neuvonen, S., and E. Haukioja. 1984. Low nutritive quality as defence against herbivores: Induced responses in birch. *Oecologia* 63:71-74.

Rosenthal, G. A. 1986. The chemical defenses of higher plants. *Sci. Am.* 254:94-99.

Schultz, J. C. 1988. Plant responses induced by herbivores. *TREE* 3:45-49.

Schultz, J. C., and I. T. Baldwin. 1982. Oak leaf quality declines in response to defoliation by gypsy moth larvae. *Science* 217:149-50.

Sork, V. 1983. Mast-fruiting in hickories and availability of nuts. *Am. Midl. Nat.* 109:81-88.

Tollrian, R., and C. D. Harvell, eds. 1999. *The ecology and evolution of inducible defenses.* Princeton, NJ: Princeton Univ. Press.

Weinstein, P. 1990. Leaf petiole chewing and the sabotage of induced defences. *Oikos* 58:231-33.

White, J. 1979. The plant as a metapopulation. *Ann. Rev. Ecol. Syst.* 10:109-45.

Whitham, T. G., A. G. Williams, and A. M. Robinson. 1984. The variation principle: Individual plants as temporal and spatial mosaics of resistance to rapidly evolving pests. In *A new ecology: Novel approaches to interactive systems*, edited by P. W. Price, C. N. Slobodchikoff, and W. S. Gaud. New York: Wiley.

Whittaker, R. H., and P. P. Feeny. 1971. Allelochemics: Chemical interactions between species. *Science* 171:757-70.

Williams, A. G., and T. G. Whitham. 1986. Premature leaf abscission: an induced plant defense against gall aphids. *Ecology* 67:1619-27.

29. The Remnant Archipelago

Askins, R. A. 1995. Hostile landscapes and the decline of migratory songbirds. *Science* 267:1956-57.

Blake, J. G. 1991. Nested subsets and the distribution of birds on isolated woodlots. *Conserv. Biol.* 5:58-66.

Blake, J. G., and J. R. Karr. 1987. Breeding birds of isolated woodlots: Area and habitat relationships. *Ecology* 68:1724-34.

Bolgiano, C. 1998. *The Appalachian forest: a search for roots and renewal.* Mechanicsburg, PA: Stackpole Books.

Bollinger, E. K., and E. T. Linder. 1994. Reproductive success of neotropical migrants in a fragmented Illinois forest. *Wilson Bull.* 106:46-54.

Bollinger, E. K., and R. G. Park. 1995. Depredation of artificial avian nests: A comparison of forest-field and forest-lake edges. *Am. Midl. Nat.* 134:200-03.

Connor, E. F., and E. D. McCoy. 1979. The statistics and biology of the species-area relationship. *Am. Nat.* 113:791-833.

Crowe, T. M. 1979. Lots of weeds: Insular phytogeography of vacant urban lots. *J. Biogeogr.* 6:169-81.

Diamond, J. M. 1975. The island dilemma: Lessons of modern biogeographic studies for the design of nature reserves. *Biol. Conserv.* 7:129-46.

_____. 1976. Island biogeography and conservation: Strategy and limitations. *Science* 193:1027-29.

Diffendorfer, J. E., M. S. Gaines, and R. D. Holt. 1995. Habitat fragmentation and movements of three small mammals (*Sigmodon, Microtus,* and *Peromyscus*). Ecology 76:827-39.

Engel, J. R. 1985. Renewing the bond of mankind and nature: Biosphere reserves as sacred space. *Orion* 4:52-59.

Franklin, I. R. 1980. Evolutionary change in small populations. In *Conservation biology,* edited by M. E. Soule and B. A. Wilcox. Sunderland, MA: Sinauer Assoc.

Franklin, J. F. 1977. The biosphere reserve program in the United States. *Science* 195:262-67.

Fraver, S. 1994. Vegetation responses along edge-to-interior gradients in the mixed hardwood forests of the Roanoke River basin, North Carolina. *Conserv. Biol.* 8:822-32.

Fuller, D. O. 2001. Forest fragmentation in Loudoun County, Virginia, USA evaluated with multitemporal Landsat imagery. *Landscape Ecol.* 16:627-42.

Gates, J. E., and N. R. Giffen. 1991. Neotropical migrant birds and edge effects at a forest-stream ecotone. *Wilson Bull.* 103:204-17.

Gregg, W. P., Jr. 1983. MAB and its biosphere reserves project: A new dimension in global conservation. *Papers from the 1982 Strategy Conference.* The George Wright Forum.

Hall, G. A., 1984. Population decline of neotropical migrants in an Appalachian forest. *Amer. Birds* 38:14-18.

Harris, L. D. 1984. *The fragmented forest.* Chicago, IL: Univ. of Chicago Press.

Howe, R. W. 1984. Local dynamics of bird assemblages in small forest habitat islands in Australia and North America. *Ecology* 65:1585-1601.

IUCN Conservation Monitoring Centre. 1983. *MAB information system biosphere reserves, compilation 3.* September.

Kindlmann, P. 1983. Do archipelagos really preserve fewer species than one island of the same total area? *Oecologia* 59:141-44.

Kroodsma, R. L. 1984. Ecological factors associated with degree of edge effect in breeding birds. *J. Wildl. Mngmt.* 48:418-25.

———. 1984. Effect of edge on breeding forest bird species. *Wilson Bull.* 96:426-36.

Lande, R. 1988. Genetics and demography in biological conservation. *Science* 241:1455-60.

MacArthur, R. H., and E. O. Wilson. 1967. *The theory of island biogeography*. Princeton, NJ: Princeton Univ. Press.

Margules, C., A. J. Higgs, and R. W. Rafe. 1982. Modern biogeographic theory: Are there any lessons for nature reserve design? *Biol. Conserv.* 24:115-28.

Matlack, G. R. 1993. Microenvironment variation within and among forest edge sites in the eastern United States. *Biol. Conserv.* 66:185-94.

McIntyre, N. E. 1995. Effects of forest patch size on avian diversity. *Landscape Ecol.* 10:85-99.

Morse, D. H. 1989. *American warblers*. Cambridge, NJ: Harvard Univ. Press.

Murcia, C. 1995. Edge effects in fragmented forests: Implications for conservation. *TREE* 10:58-62.

Niering, W. A., and R. H. Goodwin. 1974. Creation of relatively stable shrublands with herbicides: Arresting "succession" on rights-of-way and pastureland. *Ecology* 55:784-95.

O'Brien, S. J., D. E. Wildt, and M. Bush. 1986. The cheetah in genetic peril. *Sci. Am.* 254 (5):84-92.

O'Brien, S. J., et al. 1985. Genetic basis for species vulnerability in the cheetah. *Science* 227:1428-34.

Paton, P. W. C. 1994. The effect of edge on avian nest success: how strong is the evidence? *Conserv. Biol.* 8:17-26.

Quammen, D. 1996. *The song of the dodo: Island biogeography in an age of extinctions*. New York: Touchstone.

Rappole, J. H. 1995. *The ecology of migrant birds: A neotropical perspective*. Washington, DC: Smithsonian Inst. Press.

Riebesell, J. F. 1982. Arctic-alpine plants on mountaintops: Agreement with island biogeography theory. *Am. Nat.* 119:657-74.

Robinson, S. K., F. R. Thompson III, T. M. Donovan, D. R. Whitehead, and J. Faaborg. 1995. Regional forest fragmentation and the nesting success of migratory birds. *Science* 267:1987-90.

Saunders, D. A., R. J. Hobbs, and C. R. Margules. 1991. Biological consequences of ecosystem fragmentation: A review. *Conserv. Biol.* 5:18-32.

Shaffer, M. L. 1981. Minimum population sizes for species conservation. *BioScience* 31:131-34.

Shure, D. J., and D. L. Phillips. 1991. Patch size of forest openings and arthropod populations. *Oecologia* 86:325-44.

Simberloff, D. S., and L. G. Abele. 1976. Island biogeography theory and conservation practice. *Science* 191:285-86.

_____. 1982. Refuge design and island biogeographic theory: Effects of fragmentation. *Am. Nat.* 120:41-50.

Soule, M. E. 1980. Thresholds for survival: maintaining fitness and evolutionary potential. In *Conservation biology*, edited by M. E. Soule and B. A. Wilcox. Sunderland, MA: Sinauer Assoc.

_____. ed. 1987. *Viable populations for conservation*. New York: Cambridge Univ. Press.

Tallamy, D. W. 1983. Equilibrium biogeography and its application to insect host-parasite systems. *Am. Nat.* 121:244-54.

Telleria, J. L., and T. Santos. 1992. Spatiotemporal patterns of egg predation in forest islands: An experimental approach. *Biol. Conserv.* 62:29-33.

Terborgh, J. 1989. *Where have all the birds gone?* Princeton: Princeton Univ. Press.

_____. 1992. Why American songbirds are vanishing. *Sci. Am.* 266:98-104.

Terborgh, J., and B. Winter. 1980. Some causes of extinction. In *Conservation biology*, edited by M. E. Soule and B. A. Wilcox. Sunderland, MA: Sinauer Assoc.

Washburn, J. O. 1984. The gypsy moth and its parasites in North America: A community in equilibrium? *Am. Nat.* 124:288-92.

Wauer, R. H. n.d. *Resource management in biosphere reserves.*

Wiens, J. A. 1994. Habitat fragmentation: Island vs. landscape perspectives on bird conservation. *Ibis* 137:S97-S104.

Wilcove, D. S. 1985. Nest predation in forest tracts and the decline of migratory songbirds. *Ecology* 66:1211-14.

Wilcove, D. S., and R. F. Whitcomb. 1983. Gone with the trees. *Natural History*, September: 82-91.

Wilcox, B. A. 1980. Insular ecology and conservation. In *Conservation biology*, edited by M. E. Soule and B. A. Wilcox. Sunderland, MA: Sinauer Assoc.

Wilcox, B. A., and D. D. Murphy. 1985. Conservation strategy: The effects of fragmentation on extinction. *Am. Nat.* 125:879-87.

Wilson, E. O., and E. O. Willis. 1975. Applied biogeography: The design of nature preserves. In *Ecology and evolution of communities*, edited by M. L. Cody and J.M. Diamond. Cambridge, MA: Belknap Press.

_____. n.d. *Parks, bioreserves, and recreation.* Unpubl. ms.

Yahner, R. H. 1992. Dynamics of a small mammal community in a fragmented forest. *Am. Midl. Nat.* 127:381-391.

Yahner, R. H., and D. P. Scott. 1988. Effects of forest fragmentation on depredation of artificial nests. *J. Wildl. Mngmt.* 52:158-161.Unpubl. ms.

30. Abuse, Resurrection, Hope

Baes, C. F., III, and S. B. McLaughlin. 1984. Trace elements in tree rings: Evidence of recent and historical air pollution. *Science*

224:494-97.

Boring, L. R., C. D. Monk, and W. T. Swank. 1981. Early regeneration of a clear-cut southern Appalachian forest. *Ecology* 62:1244-53.

Bratton, S. P. 1975. The effect of the European wild boar, *Sus scrofa*, on gray beech forest in the Great Smoky Mountains. *Ecology* 56:1356-66.

Campbell, R. W. 1979. Gypsy moth: Forest influence. *Agric. Info. Bull. No. 423*. Washington, DC: USDA, Forest Service.

Carline, R. F., C. J. Gagen, and W. E. Sharpe. 1994. Brook trout (*Salvelinus fontinalis*) population dynamics and mottled sculpin (*Cottus bairdi*) occurrence in relation to acidic episodes in streams. *Ecol. Freshwater Fish* 3:107-15.

Carrick, T. R. 1979. The effect of acid water on the hatching of salmonid eggs. *J. Fish Biol.* 14:165-72.

Clarkson, R. B. 1964. *Tumult on the mountains: Lumbering in West Virginia-1770-1920*. Parsons, WV: McClain.

Cronan, C. S., and W. A. Reiners. 1983. Canopy processing of acidic precipitation by coniferous and hardwood forests in New England. *Oecologia* 59:216-23.

Fiss, F. C., and R. F. Carline. 1993. Survival of brook trout embryos in three episodically acidified streams. *Trans. Am. Fish. Soc.* 122:268-78.

Flannery, T. 2001. *The eternal frontier: An ecological history of North America and its peoples*. New York: Atlantic Monthly Press.

Flebbe, P. A. 1993. Comment on Meisner (1990). *Can. J. Fish. Aq. Sci.* 50:883-84.

Fritz, E. S. 1980. *Potential impacts of low pH on fish and fish populations*. Washington, DC: U.S. Dept. Interior, Fish and Wildl. Serv.

Fromm, P. O. 1980. A review of some physiological and toxicological responses of freshwater fish to acid stress. *Env. Biol. Fish.* 5:79-93.

Gagen, C. J., W. E. Sharpe, and R. F. Carline. 1993. Mortality of brook trout, mottled sculpins, and slimy sculpins during acidic episodes. *Trans. Am. Fish. Soc.* 122:616-28.

_____. 1994. Downstream movement and mortality of brook trout (*Salvelinus fontinalis*) exposed to acidic episodes in streams. *Can. J. Fish. Aq. Sci.* 51:1620-28.

Galloway, J. N., G. E. Likens, and M. E. Hawley. 1984. Acid precipitation: Natural versus anthropogenic components. *Science* 226:829-30.

Gaventa, J. 1980. Cited in Chp. 22.

Giardina, D. 1987. Cited in Chp. 22.

Glenn, L. C. 1911. Denudation and erosion in the southern Appalachian region and the Monongahela basin. *U.S. Geol. Surv. Prof. Paper 72.* Washington, DC: U.S. Dept. Interior.

Gorham, E., F. B. Martin, and J. T. Litzau. 1984. Acid rain: Ionic correlations in the eastern United States, 1980-1981. *Science* 225:407-09.

Haines, B., M. Stefani, and F. Hendrix. 1980. Acid rain: Threshold of leaf damage in eight plant species from a southern Appalachian forest succession. *Water, Air, and Soil Pollution* 14:403-07.

Haines, T. A. 1981. Acidic precipitation and its consequences for aquatic ecosystems: A review. *Trans. Am. Fish. Soc.* 110:669-707.

Johnson, A. H., T. G. Siccama, R. S. Turner, and D. G. Lord. 1984. Assessing the possibility of a link between acid precipitation and decreased growth rates of trees in the northeastern United States. In *Direct and indirect effects of acidic deposition on vegetation*, edited by R. A. Linthurst. Boston, MA: Butterworth.

Johnson, N. M., G. E. Likens, M. C. Feller, and C. T. Driscoll. 1984. Acid rain and soil chemistry. *Science* 225:1424-25.

LaBastille, A. 1987. *Beyond Black Bear Lake*. New York: Norton.

Leonard, D. E. 1981. Bioecology of the gypsy moth. In *The gypsy moth: Research toward integrated pest management*, edited by C.

C. Doane and M. L. McManus. USDA, *Forest Service Tech. Bull. 1584.* Washington, DC: GPO.

Leopold, A. 1966. *A Sand County almanac.* New York: Ballantine Books.

Lewis, R. L. 1998. Cited in Chp. 22.

Likens, G. E., R. F. Wright, J. N. Galloway, and T. J. Butler. 1979. Acid rain. *Sci. Am.* 241 (4):43-51.

Mason, C. J., and M. L. McManus. 1981. Larval dispersal of the gypsy moth. In The gypsy moth: Research toward integrated pest management, edited by C. C. Doane and M. L. McManus. U.S. Dept. Agric., *Forest Service Tech. Bull. 1584.* Washington, DC: GPO.

Meisner, J. D. 1990. Effect of climatic warming on the southern margins of the native range of brook trout, *Salvelinus fontinalis. Can. J. Fish. & Aq. Sci.* 47:1065-70.

Pierce, B. A., and J. M. Harvey. 1987. Geographic variation in acid tolerance of Connecticut wood frogs. *Copeia* 1987:94-103.

Pierce, B. A., J. B. Hoskins, and E. Epstein. 1984. Acid tolerance in Connecticut wood frogs (*Rana sylvatica*). *J. Herpetol.* 18:159-67.

Pough, F. H. 1976. Acid precipitation and embryonic mortality of spotted salamanders, *Ambystoma maculatum. Science* 192:68-70.

Rahn, K. A., and D. H. Lowenthal. 1986. The acid rain whodunit. *Natural History,* July: 62-65.

Schofield, C. L. 1976. Acid precipitation: Effects on fish. *Ambio* 5:228-30.

Sharpe, W. E., and J. R. Drohan, eds. 1999. *The effects of acidic deposition on Pennsylvania's forest.* University Park, PA: Envtl. Resources Research Inst., Penn. St. Univ.

Smith, C. W. G. 1986. What's killing the sugar maples? *Country Journal,* March: 46-49.

341

Smith, H. R., and R. A. Lautenschlager. 1981. Gypsy moth predators. In *The gypsy moth: Research toward integrated pest management*, edited by C. C. Doane and M. L. McManus. USDA, *Forest Service Tech. Bull. 1584*. Washington, DC: GPO.

Swain, R. B. 1983. *Field days*. New York: Charles Scribner's Sons.

Index

abdominal cavity, 185

abdominal stove, 180, 183, 186-7

abrasive spawning, 83-4

abscission layer, 167-8; premature, 211

absentee landowners, 159, 230-1, 159-60

acid: deposition, 231-5, 240; rain, 96, 99, 229,232-3, 235-6; rain, in Europe, 236; shock, 234-5

acorn, 37, 143-9; dispersal, 146; germination, 146; yields, 144

adaptation, 2-3, 14, 28, 35, 54, 75, 83-5, 106, 122, 129, 131, 136, 145, 156, 165, 167, 180, 182, 186-7, 192, 200-1

adaptive radiation, 26, 117

adaptively neutral trait, 165-6, 192

Adirondacks, 233

Admiralty Island, 29

adrenal glands, of birds, 173

aerobic metabolism, 184-5

aggressive behavior, 75-6, 97, 103-5, 110, 174, 176, 195, 200

Africa, 10-11, 46, 48, 51-2, 152

African Americans, 160

Alabama, 9, 24

alarm call, of birds, 172-7; false ventriloquism, 172

alarm pheromone, of tadpoles, 121

alarm substance, emitted by fish, 83-6

alarm system, of fish, 83

Alaska, 26, 47, 152

alder, 41

algae, 20-1, 96

alligator, 46

Allegheny Mountains, 235

allopatric speciation, 25, 28, 31

Alps, 10, 12

altruism, 90, 93, 172

aluminum, 234

amphibians, response to acid shock, 234-5

amphipod, 98

anadromy, of brook char, 98

anaerobic metabolism, 184-5

anchor ice, 97

Andes, 10, 12

ant, 104

anther, 53, 60

anthocyanin, 166-7

antifreeze, in tissues, 183, 187

antiherbivore defenses, 208

antiherbivory compounds, 210

antimonotony hypothesis, 200

antipredator adaptation, 207

antipredator behavior, 85, 121

antiquity, of Appalachia, 1, 12, 26

aphid, 211

Appalachee Indians, 151

Appalachian Mountains, definition of, 7; naming of, 151

Appalachian Plateau, 7, 10

apple, 205, 237

Araceae, 59

Arkansas, 13

arthropods, 67, 69, 71

arum, 59

asexual reproduction, 52, 59

ash, 19, 34, 238

Asheville, N.C., 11, 152

Asia, 26, 45, 48

Asians, 152

aspen, 210; bigtooth, 34; quaking, 29, 34

Australia, 210

autumn, 1-2, 60, 81, 128, 134, 147, 165-8, 185-6, 202

auxin, 167

azalea, 41

Bach, 203

backyard biology, 2

balds, 41-3, 156; alder, 41; grass, 41-2; heath, 41-3; meadow, 41

Balsam Mountains, N.C., 110

banjo, 157

barrens, 41

basswood, 19, 34, 237

bats, 186

bear, 187, 220, 224

Beau Geste hypothesis, 199

beech, 34, 42, 148, 210, 237; American, 18-19, 237

beetles, ground, 239; larvae, 147

Beringia, 26, 46, 152

Big Run, W.Va., 95

biological diversity, 12, 26, 33, 36-8, 218, 226

biosphere reserves, 225; buffer zone, 225; core zone, 225

birch, 13, 209; gray, 29; paper, 34; white, 208-9; yellow, 18

bird nests, 222

birds, 25-6, 33, 36, 82-3, 115-17, 225-6, 239

birdsong, 195-203; dialect, 200-1; interference, 198; refraction, 197; repertoire, 198; reverberation, 197; ventriloquism, 197; volume, 197

bison, 43

blackbird, 199

bloodroot, 156, 190, 192, 239

bloom sequence, 191

blueberry, 41

Blue Ridge, 41, 99, 110-12, 151, 153, 155, 161

Blue Ridge Parkway, 52

Boone, Daniel, 155

boreal forest, 13, 29-30, 34-6, 52, 103, 109

borer, two-lined chestnut, 237

Borland, Hal, 183

brain disease, 202

Brevard Zone, 10

bristle, 60, 143

Britain, 157, 236

Brooks, Maurice, 3

buckeye, 42; yellow, 30, 34

buds, tree as a population of, 211

buffering capacity, 233

bullfrog, 122

bull-tongue, 156

bunchberry, 29

bunting, indigo, 200-1

burn, 19, 35-7, 41-2

bushmaster, 136

butterfly: monarch, 211; mourning cloak, 183; tiger swallowtail, 1

butternut, 148
calcium oxalate, 60
Camels Hump, Vt., 233
camouflage, 52, 82-3, 139, 197
Canada, 28, 34, 98, 174, 232
canary, 202
cannibalism, 85, 91, 121-2
canopy, 19-20,33-4, 36-9, 59, 64, 145, 190, 192, 195, 233, 236, 238
canopy gap, 18, 33, 37, 39, 127, 156
carbon dioxide, 102, 232, 239
carbonic acid, 232
Carboniferous, 11
cardinal, 171, 225
Carolinas, 46
carotene, 165
carrot, 212
catastrophes, 18, 219, 234
caterpillar, eastern tent, 182, 205-12; exploratory trail, 206; hatching, 205; recruitment trail, 206; tent structure, 206
catfishes, 12, 30, 83, 218
cats, 236; feral, 222-230
cattle, 42-3
caudal luring, 137
cavity nester, 197, 222
cedar, 22, 237
cells, 21, 83, 166-7, 179, 202, 208, 211
central Appalachia, 4, 7, 17, 34, 41, 155, 183, 222, 226, 234
char, brook, 98
cheetahs, genetic uniformity of, 219
chemical gradient, 138
chemical signals, 105, 206

chemical signature, of polluting aerosols, 202
Cherokee Indians, 41, 151-2, 155
cherry, 205-6; black, 34, 37, 191, 237
chestnut, 34, 37, 143, 238; American, 13, 19, 36-7, 229, 236
chestnut blight, 36, 236, 238
chickadee, black-capped, 171-2, 174, 197, 200, 239; breeding territory, 174; Carolina, 176; communal territory, 175; "fee bee" call, 198; floater, 174-5; flock regular, 175; "gargle" call, 198, 200; insertion, 175; monogamous pairs, 174; nocturnal hypothermia in, 181-2; peck order, 175
chickweed, 191
China, 46, 59
chipmunk, 148, 186
chlorophyll, 165, 166-7
chorus frog, 122
chub, 51, 82; creek, 83, 86, 97, 189
circumpolar distribution, 52
circumpolar plant community, 46
Civil War, 160
clear-cutting, 229
clethra, 30
climate change, 42, 111, 240
climax, 17-18, 36
cloaca, 104-5, 135, 139
clones, tree, 210
club cells, 83, 85-6
clutch size, of birds, 196, 221
coadaptation 122
coal, 99, 159-60, 229, 235
coalfields, 160

coastal plain, 7, 13, 52

coevolution, 14

coffee-tree, 45

coitus. 135

columbine, 191

communication, aerial chemical, 138, 209

competition: interspecific, 21, 110-12, 196; intraspecific, 196

competitive exclusion, 111

conglomerate, 8

connectivity, 226

conservation ethic, 226

convergence, 162

Copland, Aaron, 189

copperhead, 46, 217, 133-40; basking, 133; combat 135-6; courtship, 134-5; egg tooth, 136-7; emergence, 136; facial pit, 137; feeding, 136; fertilization, 136; fetal membrane, 137; hemipenis, 135; hibernaculum, 134; home range, 133; poison fang, 137-8; resting coil, 137; shedding, 139-40; sperm competition, 134; tail vibration, 137; venom, 139; viviparity, 136

copulation, 68-70, 76-7

copulation solicitation, 199

cork cells, 167

corm, 59-61

corridor, 153, 220, 224-6

cost-benefit, of leaf-out timing, 38, 189, 191

cost of reproduction, 97

cottonwood, 211

counteradaptations, in insect pests, 75, 211

counter-current heat exchanger, 181

countershading, 82, 86

courtship, 67, 89, 103-4, 134-5, 197

cove hardwood forest, 34, 39

cover object, 103, 105

cowbirds, 222, 230

Coweeta, N.C., 225

creeper, brown, 171

Cretaceous, 47-51

crown: shyness gaps, 63; suppression, 144

cryoprotectant, 184

cuckoo, 239

Cuculinae, 183

cultural tradition, 147

Cumberland Gap, 155

Cumberland River, 31

Cumberland Valley, 8

Cypripedioideae, 52

dace, 83, 86; blacknose, 82; finescale, 84

daddy longlegs, 67

darter, 29-30, 81, 89-93, 137-8; *Etheostoma*, 26-8

darter, tessellated, 89-90, 92; courtship, 89; cruising males, 91; egg cleaning, 90-1; egg membrane, 91; floating male, 90-1; nest rock, 90-1; promiscuity of, 91; territorial male, 90

Darwin, Charles, 2, 90

day length, 191

"dear enemy" recognition, 104, 200

debris flow, 99

deer, 36-7, 85, 145, 147-8, 151, 154, 181, 229

defense: chemical, 211-12; by trees

against herbivores, 208-10

defense types, tree as a mosaic of, 211

defoliation, 237-8

deforestation, 221, 223

degree-days, 119

dehydration, 186

Delaware, 222

Delaware Indians, 153

Denmark, 172

desert plants, 167

Dethier, Vincent, 179

detoxification, 208

Devonian shale, 11, 96

dialect, of highlanders, 156; of birds, 200

diet quality, 147, 152, 159

digestive efficiency, 67, 104-5, 208

Dillard, Annie, 4, 120, 161

Diptera, 67

diseases, of young trees, 36, 38, 233

disjunction, 45-6

dispersal, 55,146; corridors, 153, 155, 220

dispersing humans, 151-2, 154-5

disturbance, 35-7, 42, 186

disturbance-adapted species, 18

dogwood, 19, 29, 45, 165; flowering, 19, 191, 237

domed nest, 222

dominance, 34, 135, 174, 176

drainage: dendritic, 10; trellised, 10

drought, 42, 81, 103, 110-11, 131, 167, 237

Dutchman's breeches, 190-1

eagle, golden, 220

eastern deciduous forest, 4, 19, 30, 43, 53, 154

ecological release, 111

edge detector, 138

edge effect, 222

education, its derision by highlanders, 160

eft, red, 115, 117

egg jelly, 121

egg predator, 90, 92

electric power plants, 99

elk, 154

endemic species, 26, 28,29,30,46, 207

endemic population levels, 207

endosperm, 54

energy flow, through the forest, 63,166

envenomate, 138

Eocene, 47

ephemeral plants, 190

epidemic outbreaks, 207

erosion, 1, 8, 10, 12, 21, 96, 154, 230

Eucalyptus, 210

European settlers, 8, 41, 151, 153-4, 157

Evans, Howard Ensign, 4

evolution: convergence, 167; divergence, 28; natural selection, 53, 70, 74, 81, 90, 93, 116, 125, 146, 172, 192, 195-6; parallelism, 47

evolutionary arms race, 77

exotic species, 35-6, 229-30, 236, 239-40

explosive breeding, 120, 122, 125

extinction, 30, 96, 111-12, 117, 217-221, 224

extracellular ice, 184

extrapair copulation, 199

fall color, 4, 166

fat stores, 97, 180; in birds, 173; in groundhog, 186

fatalism, of highlanders, 78, 158, 160

fecal communication, 104

fecal pellets, 104, 105

fecal rain, 205

fecal recognition, 84

feces, 84, 104-5, 121, 190, 238

fer-de-lance, 136

Fergis, Charles, 195

ferns, 1, 17, 20, 22, 25, 38-9, 46; bracken, 43

fertilization, low rate of, 54, 191

fiddle player, 157

finch, purple, 171,174

Finland, 208-9

fir, 13, 29, 42; *Abies intermedia*, 29; balsam, 29-30, 34, 239; Fraser, 30, 42

fire, 1, 8, 20, 35-6, 42, 96, 151, 153

fire-dependent plants, 35

firefly, 2, 73-8, 218; aerial predation, 76; aggressive mimicry, 76-7; alternate mating strategy, 76; injection flash, 76-7

fire-return interval, 35

fish, 10, 26, 30, 81-6; aggregation, 82; migration, 81; reproductive failure, 234; schools, 81, 83-4

flash floods, 81

flocks, bird, 154; balancing feeding efficiency and predation risk, 174; chase-offs within, 173; dominance relationships,

174; mixed-species, 171-2, 174, 176; role in food-finding, 173; single-species, 171; size, 173-4

flood plains, 156

floods, 81, 98

Florida, 151, 181, 205; Keys, 181

flowering plants, 13, 51, 61

flux, 102, 226

flycatcher, 221: Acadian, 225; great crested, 198; least, 198

Folded Appalachians, 8

folklife, 160

food preference, 147, 237

forest: core decline, 154; fragmentation, 217-18, 220-3; horizontal layering, 19; patches, 19, 37-8, 222 ; structure, 3, 17-22; virgin, 39, 154-5

forest edge, 218, 225; ratio to interior, 218

fossil fuel, 232, 239

fossil record, 47

fox, 37

fracture, rock, 45

freeze tolerance, 18, 42, 129, 184, 186

fright reaction, 83

frog: chorus, 2, 119, 122; cricket, 122; leopard, 184; pickerel, 122

frog, gray tree, 122-3; dominant males, 124; call, 124; mating, 123; overwintering, 119; satellite males, 124

frog, wood, 184-6; chorus, 119; eggs, 120-1; emergence, 119; mating, 120; metamorphosis, 120; solar heating of eggs, 120

Frost, Robert, 73, 183

frost line, 128
fruit, 54, 60, 131, 143, 190
fry, 97-8, 234
fungi, 20-1, 38, 55, 223, 233
fungus gnat, 60
fungus, 59, 236-7
Gaspé Peninsula, 7
gene flow, 27, 123
genetic: analyses, 92; defenses, 238; drift, 28, 219; heterozygosity, 219; homozygosity, 219; isolation, 27; mosaic, tree as a, 211; quality, 123, 136; variation, 211
geographic barriers, 102
Geometridae, 183
Georgia, 7, 8, 41, 75, 96, 236
germination, of orchids, 54
ginger, 156
ginseng, 156
glaciation, 12-13, 26, 30-1, 47; Wisconsin, 12
glucose, 184-6
glycerol, 183-4
glycogen, 123, 184-5
glycoside, cardiac, 211
goldfinch, 171, 174
Gondwanaland, 12, 51
good genes hypothesis, 123
gradient: disturbance, 33-37; environmental, 33-4, 37, 47
grass, 151; mountain oat, 41, 43
grazing animals, role in maintaining balds, 43
Great Lakes, 95, 233
Great Smoky Mountains, 7-8, 25, 27, 29, 35, 78, 109-10, 115, 152, 223, 225, 234, 236
Great Valley, 8, 153

Greenbrier River, W.Va., 31
Greene County, Tenn., 157
greenhouse effect, 239
Greenland, 232
Green Mountains, Vt., 233
greenways, 220
grosbeak, 171
ground cover, 19, 20, 22, 38, 46, 63, 67, 102, 127, 190
groundhog, 186
growth regulator, 121
growth suppression, 38
Gulf Coast, 13
gum, 237
habitat: diversity, 36; fragmentation, 36, 217; islands, 27-8, 109; patches, 219; selection, 111; size, 219
habituation, 199-200
Hampshire County, W.Va., 133
hangingfly, 67-71; copulation, 68-70; nuptial gift, 70; transvestites, 69
Hardin, Garrett, 231
hare, 231
hard-water stream, 96
hawk, 139, 172, 224; broad-winged, 51; sharp-shinned, 172
Hawksbill Mountain, Va., 110-12
hawthorn, 207
headwaters, 27, 81-6
heat loss, in winter, 181
head production, by plants, 180-1
heart failure, 185-6
hellbender, 46
hemlock, 95; Carolina, 30, 45; eastern, 19
hepatica, 190; round-lobed, 190
herb, 38-9, 43, 47, 59-60, 63

Hercules-club, 45
heron, 81
hibernation, 128-9, 134, 186
hickory, 13, 37, 45, 189, 229, 238;
    nuts 146; pignut, 37; shagbark,
    37, 182
highlanders, 151-61, 230-231
Himalayas, 12
holly, 45
home range, 127
homesteaders, 153
honeybee, 183
honeysuckle, 236
hornbeam, 237
houseflies, 67
Hubei, China, 46
Hubbard Brook, N.H., 206, 225
Hubbell, Sue, 140
huckleberry, 41
Hudson River, 7
humidity, 105, 222
hunting, by man, 183-5, 229
hunting-gathering economy, 152
Hutchinson, G. Evelyn, 1
hyphae, 20
hypometabolism, 131, 186
hypothermia, nocturnal, 182
ice, 13, 27,29-30, 42, 120-1, 168,
    179-87
ice age, 29, 151-2, 156
Ice Mountain, W.Va., 29
illegitimate birth, 159
Illinois, 219, 222-3
immunity, 21, 139
imprint, 82
inbreeding: by highlanders, 156;
    reduced by transients, 129; its
    reduction in reserves, 224; in
    small populations, 96, 219

incidence function, 224
incisor, 146
independence, of highlanders,
    158, 230
indigenous Americans, 151
individual recognition, 104
individual reproductive success,
    106, 145, 166, 192, 195-6
inducible defenses, in trees, 181-
    83
infant mortality, of highlanders,
    158
insect herbivore, 206
insularity, 218, 220, 233
insulation, 134, 180-3, 187, 223
interglacials, 30
Interior Plateau, 8
interstadials, 12
intromission, 135
invention of Appalachia, 160
iris, 191
island, habitat, 27-8, 109, 219
island biogeography, equilibrium
    theory of, 224
isolation, of habitat patches, 219,
    226
isolates, 109-10, 115
Italians, 160
jack-in-the-pulpit, 3, 46, 59-64,
    191; emergence 197; fruit, 60
jay, blue, 115, 222
junco, 173, 176; northern,171,
    173, 175; yellow-eyed, 174
juniper, 29, 62
Kanawha Indians, 153
Kentucky, 155, 157
kingfisher, 82
kin recognition, 121-2
kin selection, 85, 172, 210

knobs, 41
kudzu, 236
labellum, of orchid, 52
Labrador retriever, 127
Lacey Act, 229
lady's slipper, 51-6; flower's aperture, 53; pink, 52; showy, 53; yellow, 52
landowners, absentee, 230
landfills, 229
landscape, 229
land-use planning, 226, 229-31, 240
larderhoarding, by squirrels, 147-8
larval parasites, 207
Laurasian faunal element, 12
laurel, 41, 237
Laurentia, 12
Laurentide ice sheet, 12-13
leaf damage, 191
leaf litter, 70, 119, 127, 128-9, 184
leaf-out, 38, 190-1
leaf vein, 143
learning, 54, 121, 201-2
leaves, 143, 165-8
Leopold, Aldo, 229
lichen, 46
light, 53, 63
light layer, horizontal, 20
limbs, as sites of heat loss, 181
limestone, 8, 233, 235
lion, mountain, 154
lioness, 171
lipids, 147
lizard, 101
locust: black, 17, 22, 237; clammy, 30; honey, 152; kelsey, 30
log cabin, 153

logging, 96, 154, 217
Lloyd, James, 74
magnolia, 34; Fraser, 30
Maine, 13, 25, 59, 96, 155, 181, 183
mammals, large-bodied, 152
map, 10, 151
maple, 13, 17, 19, 42, 45, 237; red, 34, 37; striped, 61, 206; sugar, 34. 167. 233
marcescent leaves, 168
Maryland, 222
Massachusetts, 63, 75, 236
mast-yearing, 144-6
mate choice, 104, 106, 122, 135
maternal factor, 121
mating season, 134-5
mating tactics, of gray tree frog, 197
mayapple, 46
Mesozoic, 12
metals, synergism with acid, 234
metabolic rate, 101, 103, 123, 180, 190; depressed during hibernation, 186
metabolites: primary, 208; secondary, 208
metamorphosis, 54, 120-2
mice, 147; deer, 36; jumping, 186
Michigan, 201, 237
microspermy, of orchids, 54
migrants, neotropical, 221
migration, 31, 47, 186, 221
milkweed, 211
mimicry: Batesian, 116; model, 116-7; Mullerian, 117
miner, locust leaf, 289
minerals, 3, 38
mineralized soil, 21

Mingo Indians, 153
mining: surface, 159
Minnesota, 98
minnow, 30, 81, 85; European, 84;
    fathead, 84
Miocene, 47
Mississippi River, 31, 205, 235
Mississippi Valley, 13
Missouri, 112, 140
mixed deciduous forest, 34, 37
mixed hunting strategy, 69
mixed mesophytic forest, 34
mixed-paternity clutch, 134
mobility, limited, 27
mole, 36
monogamy, 91, 174
moonshine, 157
morel, 51
mosaic management, 226
moss, 1, 20, 38, 43, 46
moth, autumnal, 208
moth, gypsy, 207, 36-9; balloon-
    ing, 238; cocoon, 238; egg
    masses, 238; food preferences,
    238; larvae, 207; overwinter-
    ing, 207
moth, winter, 183; Geometridae,
    188; thoracic muscles of, 183
mountain folk, 156
mountain lover, 151, 161
mountain talk, 156
"mountain whites," 155
mushroom, 60, 131
music, 157
mycorrhiza, 20-1, 55, 223
myth, 155
Nantahala National Forest, N.C.,
    115
Native Americans, 41, 151-3

neo-Darwinian evolution, 2, 160,
    167
neotropical migrants, 221
nested subset hypothesis, 223
neurogenesis, 202
neuron, 202
Nevada, 41
New England, 13, 28, 34-5, 38, 53,
    183, 233, 237
New Hampshire, 206, 225, 233,
    234, 236
New Jersey, 232
New River, 31
newt, 115
New York, 7, 61-2, 181, 186, 232
New York City, 36
New Zealand, 41
nitric acid, 232
nodding ladies tresses, 52
nonconformist plants, in emer-
    gence timing, 192
North Carolina, 8, 11, 29, 36, 41,
    109, 112, 121, 152-3, 187, 225,
    234
northern Appalachia, 7, 13, 26-7,
    102, 209, 225, 235
northern hardwood forest, 34,
    221, 233
Nova Scotia, 112, 205
nutcracker, 148
nuthatch, white-breasted, 171-2,
    176
nutrient cycling, 238
oak-chestnut forest, 34, 37, 238
oak-hickory forest, 37, 238
oak-pine forest, 34
oak, 13, 17, 19, 22, 31, 143-49,
    207, 238; black, 144, 147, 209;
    chestnut, 37, 146; fertilization,

144; germination, 144; mast failure, 146; post, 143; red, 34, 37, 42, 145-6; scarlet, 143; seed predators, 144; white, 34, 37, 143-5, 168
Oak Ridge, Tenn., 225
Ohio, 129, 176, 232, 237
oil, residual, 235
old-growth, 37
Ontario, 112
open-cup nest, 222
Orchidaceae, 51
Orchidoideae, 52
orchids, 46, 52-5, 63; showy orchis, 52
orchinol, 55
orgy, 120-2
Osage orange, 152
ovenbird, 199-201, 222, 225
overlearning song, 201
overwintering, 81, 119, 134, 149, 184, 187
ovulation, 134
Ozark Mountains, 41, 140
paddlefish, 46
Paleocene, 51
Paleozoic, 10
parabolic solar ovens, of early-blooming flowers, 190
parakeet, Carolina, 221
parasite, 106, 171, 207, 222, 238
parental care, 89
parsnip, 212
patchwork quilt, 37
pathogen, 59, 105, 145, 168, 236
patriarchal clan, 157
paw paw, 152
peck order, 173-4
pectoralis muscles, role in shivering, 180
peewee, 198
Pennsylvania, 7-8, 12, 28, 98, 143, 153-4, 195, 222
Pennsylvania long rifle, 154
perch, 26, 30, 81, 83, 122, 234
Percidae, 26
perennials, 18, 47
persimmon, 45, 237
petiole, 168, 210
pH, 99, 232-5
phenolics, 207-8
pheromone, 68, 206
phoebe, 189; eastern, 119
photosynthesis, 2, 55, 165-7, 191-2
physical barriers, 28
physiographic provinces, 7
Piedmont, 7, 10
pigeon, passenger, 154
pigs, 236
pike, 84
pine, 195, 229; jack, 13, 34; red, 34; Table Mountain, 30, 35; white, 34
Pine Cabin Run, 11, 51, 82, 86, 133, 143, 189, 237, 239
pinks, 191
pioneer species, 37
pit-and-mound relief, 36
pit viper, 136
plant community structure, 17-19
plant conditioning, 207
plantain, 52
plate tectonics, 10-12
Pleistocene, 12-13, 26-7, 29-30, 42, 47, 96, 111, 112, 152
Plethodontidae, 27, 101-3, 105, 109, 112

Poles, 160
pollen, 53, 60, 62
pollination, 60; chance, 54; mistaken, 54; pollinator-limited plants, 63; pollinators, 190; pollinators' learning ability, 54
pool and riffle, 81
poplar: balsam, 34; tulip, 19, 31, 34, 45, 46, 191, 237-8
population: crashes and explosions, 209; cycles, 28; definition of, 25; founding, 220; isolated, 28-30, 46, 95-6, 99, 101, 119, 156, 219, 226; minimum viable, 62-3; sources, 226
predation: and centripetal instincts, 171; in forest fragments, 222; on salamanders, 105-6
predator swamping, 121
preserves, nature, 224
prickle, 207
proximate cause, 121
Quebec, 7, 121
raccoons, 81, 131, 186
railroad, 96, 154, 224
rain forest, 223
red spruce, 42, 28, 233, 239
redbud, 167
redd, 97
redstart, 221
reference group, 158
refoliation, 237
refuge site, 196
refugia, 13, 26, 30
relict, 96, 109, 111-2
repertoire, 199-203
reproductive incompatibility, of divergent populations, 28
response, localized, 209; systemic, 209

rhododendron, 42-3; Catawba, 30
Ridge and Valley, 4, 7-8, 10
Rimsky-Korsakov, 196
riparian strip, 225
root exudate, 21, 82
rose, multiflora, 239
rue anemone, 190
Russia, 46-7, 152
sabotage of induced defense, 210
salamander, 26, 28-9, 101-17; Allegheny mountain, 105-6, 115-6; Cheat Mountain, 109, 111; distasteful, 115; fungal egg parasite, 106; Hoffman's, 112; Jordan's, 27-8, 115-17; Metcalf's, 27; Peaks of Otter, 112; poisonous, 115-16; ravine, 112; red-cheeked, 7, 115-16; red-legged, 27, 115-16; Shenandoah, 104, 110-12; Siberian, 184; slimy salamander, 109-10; spotted, 235; throat pulsations, 105; woodland, 115
salamander, lungless, 25, 27, 89; courtship, 103-5; eggs, 105; fecal pellet, 104; foraging, 103; gas exchange by diffusion, 184; spermatophore, 105
salamander, *Plethodon*, 105, 109, 112, 115; egg brooding, 117; egg laying, 117; metabolic rate, 101
salamander, plethodontid, 101-2; egg brooding, 105; egg rotating, 105
salamander, red-backed, 102-5; aggressive behavior, 103; congregation, 103; drought tolerance,

103; interference competition, 103; mimicry, 117; releasing and scenting airborne molecules, 103; sense of smell, 103; submissive displays, 104; territorial behavior, 104; use of protective cover, 103
salmon, 82
Salmonidae, 96
sandstone, 8, 11, 96, 153, 233
sassafras, 19, 38-9, 45, 237
sawfly, pine, 210
scale, ecological, 17, 26, 33
Scandinavia, 154
scatterhoarding, by squirrels, 148-9
Schwartz, Charles and Elizabeth, 127, 130
Scotch-Irish immigrants, 153
sculpin, mottled, 92
second-growth woodlots, 217
secondary compounds, 208
sense of place, 160
sequential hermaphroditism, 61
serotinous cones, 35
serum, 139
serviceberry, 191
sex, 197, 241
sex change, 60-4
sex ratio, 69
sexual parasitism, 2
sexy feces hypothesis, 105
shade tolerance, 18
Shavers Fork, W.Va., 31
Shawnee Indians, 153-5
sheep, 43
Shenandoah National Park, Va., 226
Shenandoah Valley, 8, 153

Shepherdstown, W.Va., 153
shipbuilding, 154
shivering, 180, 183
shrew, 239
Siberians, 152
silverbell, 45; Carolina, 34
silt, 83, 90, 96-8
size-advantage model, 62-3
skunk cabbage, 46, 190-1
slavery, 156
slick, 41
slime molds, 21
snake, garter, 119
snowbell, 45
snowbird, 173
softwater lakes, 233
soil types, 42
solitary bee, 53
songbirds, 37, 197-8, 201, 221, 223, 225; migrants, 221
sound: power, 197; shadow, 197; window, 197
South America, 51
South Branch, W.Va., 230
southern Appalachia, 12, 26-31, 35-6, 34
Southern Appalachian Biosphere Reserve, 225
Spain, 222
Spaniards, 151
sparrow: English, 222, 236; field, 196; song, 197; swamp 201; white-throated, 174, 176, 198, 200-1
spathe, 60
spatial memory, 202
spawning: explosive, 120-2, 125; rock, 89
speciation, 25

species-area relationship, 219
species: mixing, 29; number, 31, 218
sperm, 70, 71, 75, 105, 134-6
spider, 68-9; crab, 52
Spiranthoideae, 52
spring beauty, 190-1, 211
spring lizard, 101
spring peeper, 119, 122, 184
spruce, 13, 25, 27-31, 42, 109, 112, 237; black, 34; red, 28, 42, 221, 233, 239; white, 84
spruce-fir forest, 27
Spruce Knob, W.Va., 95
squirrel, 143-9; acorn preferences, 146; fox, 147-8; gray, 147-8; population fluctuations, 148; red, 147-8; sense of smell, 148
squirrel corn, 190-1
stand height, 34
starling, 171
Staten Island, N.Y., 11
stealing prey, 69
stem basal area, 34
stewartia, 45; mountain, 30
stickleback, 84
stigma, 55, 60
Stony Man Mountain, Va., 111
storage, underground organs of plants, 47
strata, 8
stream capture, 29
subcutaneous space, 185
submissive behavior, 104-5
subterranean life, of orchids, 55
succession, ecological, 17-22, 35-6, 39, 42, 229
sucker, 30, 81
sulphuric acid, 232

sumacs, 45
sunfishes, 30, 81
sunflecks, 19
sun-following flowers, 190
supercooling, 129, 182-3, 187
superterritories, 195
surface-to-volume ratio, 181
Swain, Roger, 239
sweetleaf, 45
sycamore, 237
synchronic flashing, 78
synchronized growth, 121
synchronized hatching, 122
synomone, 209-10
tadpole, 121-10
tail flagging, by deer, 85
talking tree hypothesis, 209
talus, 110-12
tanager, summer, 225
tannin, 147, 207
temperature cycle, annual, 190
temporary pond, 122
Tennessee, 8, 26, 31, 155, 157, 225, 232, 234
Tennessee River, 26
Tennessee Valley, 8
termite, 104-5
terranes, 10
territoriality: interspecific, 196; intraspecific, 196
territory, 97, 111, 195-6, 199, 201-2
tetrodotoxin, 117
The Pinnacle, Va., 111
thermal sum, 189, 191
thorn, 207
Thornhill, Randy, 68
throughfall, 233
thrasher, brown, 115

thrush, 207; wood, 115, 198
tit, great, 172-3, 197, 199
titmouse, tufted, 1, 171-6, 198, 222; breeding territory, 174; dominance hierarchies, 174; flocking, 174; interflock aggression, 174; song, 198
tobacco, as highlanders' crop, 156
topographic complexity, 82
tolerance limits, 42
tongue-flicking, 135
toothwort, cut-leaf, 190
topography, fragmented, 101, 218
towhee, 171
trade-off, in context of springtime emergence, 191
tree of heaven, 236
Triassic, 12
trilliums, 191
trout: brown, 96, 98; rainbow, 96, 98, 239; speckled, 95
trout, brook, 95-9, 234; fertilization, 97; fry, 97; incubation, 96-7; predation, 97; temperature sensitivity, 97; territorial behavior, 97; yolk sac, 97
Trouvelot, Leopold, 236
turtle: painted, 184; snapping, 128; wood, 128
turtle, eastern box, 127-31, 184; basking, 123; emergence, 129; foods, 131; form, 128; growth rings, 130; hibernation, 128-9; home range, 127-9; mating, 129; metabolism, 131; population size, 131; predators, 131; transients, 130; western box, 184
Ulstermen, 153

Unaka Mountains, Tenn., 155
understory, 19-20, 42, 206-7
veery, 221
venom, 137-9
Vermont, 183, 207, 209, 233, 236
violet, 191
vireo, 207, 221: Philadelphia, 196; red-eyed, 195-8, 203
virgin forest, 39, 154, 217
Virginia, 8, 11, 24, 33, 41, 99, 110, 140, 155, 157, 161, 226
volatile compounds, 209
Walker, Thomas, 135
walnut, 207; black, 19, 31, 237
warbler, 189, 207, 230; black-throated green, 239; worm-eating, 221
warning signal, 85
warning colors, 115-17; false, 116
water, in cells, 167
weather, 43, 102, 128, 145, 149, 179, 190-1, 197
webworm, parsnip, 212
West Gondwanaland, 51
West Virginia, 8, 11, 25, 28-9, 31, 36, 95, 109, 133, 140, 148, 152-3, 180, 187, 191, 217, 220-1, 231, 234, 236-8
whiskey, 157
White Mountains, N.H., 234
wildflowers, 1, 20, 22, 25, 38-9, 190
wild turkey, 36, 145
Wilderness Road, 135
Williams, George, 2
willow, 237
windstorm, 35-6
windthrow, 36-7, 18-19
winter-active animals, 189

Wisconsin, 12-13
witch hazel, 19, 45
wolf, 154
woodlots, 127, 217, 219-23
woodpecker, downy, 171-2, 176-7;
    ivory-billed, 221
wren, Carolina, 200
xanthophyll, 165
xanthotoxin, 212
yellowwood, 45
zebra, 171
zoning, 230

George Constantz and Nancy Ailes at home in West Virginia.

Author

Born in Washington, D.C. in 1947, George Constantz spent six years of his childhood in Barranquilla, Colombia, among the iguanas of the Magdalena River's floodplain, and in Chihuahua, Mexico, where he chased roadrunners through the desert. Since receiving a B.A. in biology from the University of Missouri-St. Louis and a Ph.D. in zoology from Arizona State University, George has worked as a park naturalist, a teacher of biology and environmental science, a fish ecologist, researcher, and writer. George founded Cacapon Institute, a nonprofit organization dedicated to conserving Appalachian rivers. At the West Virginia divisions of Natural Resources and Environmental Protection, George planned and implemented watershed management programs. Currently, he manages the Education Program at the Canaan Valley Institute. George lives with his wife, Nancy Ailes, in the Cacapon River watershed of West Virginia.